GUNNERY LEADER

First published in 2007 by

WOODFIELD PUBLISHING LTD
Bognor Regis ~ West Sussex ~ England ~ PO21 5EL
www.woodfieldpublishing.co.uk

© Tom Williams, 2007

All rights reserved.
No part of this publication may be reproduced
or transmitted in any form or by any means,
electronic or mechanical, nor may it be stored
in any information storage and retrieval system,
without prior permission from the publisher.

The right of Tom Williams
to be identified as Author of this work
has been asserted in accordance with
the Copyright, Designs and Patents Act 1988

ISBN 1-84683-040-0

GUNNERY LEADER

*The World War Two Chronicle of
Wing Commander Ken Bastin* DFC

TOM WILLIAMS

Woodfield

Woodfield Publishing Ltd
Woodfield House ~ Babsham Lane ~ Bognor Regis ~ West Sussex ~ PO21 5EL
telephone 01243 821234 ~ **e-mail** enquiries@woodfieldpublishing.co.uk

Interesting and informative books on a variety of subjects

For full details of all our published titles, visit our website at
www.woodfieldpublishing.co.uk

~ CONTENTS ~

Acknowledgements .... *ii*

Introduction .... *iii*

1. Formative Years and the Outbreak of War 1
2. First of the New Gunnery Leaders 9
3. On Operations – Disrupting the Blitzkrieg 26
4. The Summer of 1940 – Supporting the Battle of Britain 51
5. From Whitley to Halifax 77
6. Target Scharnhorst 98
7. The King, the USA and the 1,000 Bomber Raids 123
8. School & 'University' – Chief Instructor & Officer Commanding ... 148
9. Epilogue 182

    Bibliography *188*

    Index *189*

Acknowledgements

During my research for this book I have met and corresponded with very many people both here and abroad. Some were friends and colleagues of Ken Bastin, the subject of this book; others had records or specialist knowledge they were willing to share with me. I have been truly amazed at the generous help everyone has given me not only in the provision of advice and material but also in the wonderful support for my purpose. I thank them all warmly.

There are some who require special mention. Firstly, Phil Judkins, who inspired me to write the book. He voluntarily provided me with much key material and mentored me in the early stages. Also Alan Lacy, whose knowledge and expertise in air gunnery has been invaluable, as have his reviews of my drafts. I must mention too Eddie 'Taff' Gurmin, Ernie 'Conny' Constable and Rupert Astbury who have kindly shared their wartime experiences with me. Among those who have allowed me access to precious family archives are Dr Carol Downer, daughter of the late Sydney Bufton, Mrs Cherry Dawson, the widow of the late Monty Dawson, Dan and Hugh Russell, sons of the late John Russell, Robert Brochot of Aytré, La Rochelle, and Peter Cook who holds the late Harry Drummond's papers.

Here too I would like to say a particular thank you to my mother, Phyllis Williams. As Ken Bastin's sister, her recollections and the extracts from her wartime diaries have uniquely enhanced the personal aspect of her brother's story.

And lastly I must thank my wife Jenny for her diligence in correcting and improving my manuscript and for her unstinting support throughout, enabling me to achieve my aim.

Introduction

Understandably many airmen who saw action in World War II have been reluctant to talk about those days, their experiences often weighed down by painful memories buried deep by the passing years. But we are the poorer for their reserve because the fullness of their service to their country remains vague, neither properly understood nor rightfully acknowledged, although they sought no recognition.

This book reveals the story of one such airman, the author's late uncle Kenneth Montague Bastin. His story is unusual for he was a rarity in the RAF – an officer air gunner who rose to the rank of Wing Commander. The pages that follow set down his record and stand as a tribute both to him and to his fellow airmen.

Ken Bastin was educated at Gresham's School where his main interest was sports which he excelled at and where he also received basic military training with the School's Officer Training Corps. Tall, good looking and sociable he looked to the RAF for some excitement, joining the RAF Volunteer Reserve in early 1939. Like most young men he wanted to be a pilot; however, with the advent of war the RAF recognised they had an urgent need for Gunnery Leaders for their vitally important bomber squadrons and Ken was an ideal candidate. When called up he was granted an immediate commission. After his initial gunnery training, he attended the first Gunnery Leader course in November 1939. He went on to become the Gunnery Officer in two operational squadrons, 10 Squadron and 76 Squadron, surviving many bombing sorties over Germany and occupied territories.

In July 1941 he took part in the daring daylight raid on the German battleship Scharnhorst in the new four–engine heavy bomber, the Halifax. In a desperate effort to stop the Scharnhorst again causing havoc to our Atlantic convoys a hurriedly revised raid was mounted against her at the port of La Pallice on the west coast of France. The small formation of RAF bombers met fierce opposition and suffered heavy losses. For his part in the lead aircraft, Ken Bastin was awarded the Distinguished Flying Cross.

Just as the USA joined the war he was sent to America to test the armament for the new Liberator aircraft being supplied to the RAF. Later, he went on to specialise in training Air Gunners and Gunnery Leaders, qualifying many young men who would then go on to fly in all theatres. His final posting in January 1945 was Officer Commanding, Gunnery Leader Wing, at the prestigious Central Gunnery School, called by some the 'Air Gunnery University'.

What follows describes the essence of Ken's wartime experiences, including the many risks that came not only from Luftwaffe fighters and German ground defences but also from the intense cold at altitude, rudimentary navigation, adverse weather, mechanical failure, accidents and just about anything else that could and did go wrong.

Ken Bastin left the RAF at the end of the war. He died in 1987.

1. Formative Years and the Outbreak of War

According to family legend, the toss of a coin decided where Charles Montague Bastin and his family were to settle after leaving Calcutta, their home for the past six years. Charles and his wife Jessie had decided to leave India because they had concerns for the health of their infant children. But they could not make up their minds whether to return to London, where Charles and his wife were born and brought up, or to travel to a new life in New Zealand. Jessie's preference was London; Charles was swayed towards New Zealand. Which would it be?

The story tells they decided to settle it by the toss of a coin; 'Heads' would be England and 'Tails' would be New Zealand. The tossed coin came down 'Heads'; and Charles, Jessie and their two young daughters boarded the ship bound for London. The year was 1911.

Charles had come to love India and its people, and was very sad to leave. He had lived and worked there for over twenty years. In 1887 he was employed by a merchant bank in London when he was recruited by Messrs Coutts & Co to join the Bank of Bengal in India. His application was not immediately accepted as the Bank of Bengal's board of directors called for further information regarding his antecedents, 'as he did not appear to belong to the class from which candidates were usually selected'. Further particulars were submitted and the board resolved on 12 May 1887 that he be, 'considered an eligible candidate'. A wise decision indeed, as Charles was to give the Bank twenty-three years of loyal service, rising to become Chief Accountant and Deputy Secretary.

His father had been a businessman in London, owning a brush-making business and later a pottery. At the age of eighteen, Charles was a clerk in his father's brush-making factory, before he joined the respected banking partnership Fuller, Banbury Nix & Co.

Charles joined the Bank of Bengal's Rangoon office as a junior officer on 2 May 1888, his monthly salary paid in rupees. Thus commenced an illustrious career which took Charles to many parts of India – Benares, Serajgunge, Agra and finally in 1902 to the Bank's Head Office in Calcutta. He also travelled extensively, including Delhi and Lucknow in the north, Bombay on the west coast and Bangalore in the south. Every few years he was granted leave to return home, and on one such visit he met his future wife, Jessie. However, again according to family legend, they met on the last day of his leave and he had to return to India. But against all the odds the relationship continued through regular letters and postcards, despite their mail taking six weeks to be delivered. Somehow they managed to maintain this long distance correspondence for several years until Charles was next granted leave in the spring of 1905 when they married; Charles was then aged thirty-nine.

After their marriage they settled into colonial life in Calcutta. Jessie found the stifling summer heat too much and she would travel to Darjeeling in the cooler foothills of the Himalayas for the hottest months. Their first child Mary was born in March 1906.

Charles Bastin in Darjeeling
[Photo: Family Album]

Tragically though, a subsequent pregnancy in 1908 resulted in a daughter being stillborn, which greatly affected Jessie. Another daughter, Peggy, was born in 1910 in London during a spell of leave, but her children's health played on Jessie's mind and for their sake she wanted to leave the difficult climate of India. Although on the point of being promoted to Secretary of the Bank, Charles eventually agreed to apply for early retirement. His application to leave in the August of 1911 was put before the board on 4 May 1911 and was accepted. Generously he was granted twelve months leave on full pay and a handsome pension of 563 rupees per month. And so his long association with India came to an end with a wonderful send off from the executive and staff of the Bank.

Charles and Jessie set up home in a large house in Streatham Park, south London. They brought with them several of their servants from Calcutta – but the servants' loyalty lasted only one winter in England before they returned to the warmth of India! To supplement his Bank of Bengal pension, Charles became a consultant to the National Bank of New Zealand, commuting into the City of London. Thus the family settled to suburban life and two more children were born.

On 12 June 1913 Kenneth Montague Bastin was born, the only son of Charles and Jessie, and the subject of this book. He was generally called Ken.

The final member of the family was Phyllis, born towards the end of 1914.

When Ken was five years old his father made one more move, to the lovely village of Gerrards Cross, just to the west of London in Buckinghamshire. To Ken this was the family home. There he was sent to a local preparatory school, Gayhurst.

The Bastin Family in the garden at Gerrards Cross, c1917
(From left to right) Charles, Mary, Phyllis, Peggy, Jessie and Ken
[Photo: Family Album]

Not surprisingly given Charles's colonial background and his late marriage, the children were expected to be more in the background, being largely looked after by the nanny and the servants. Typically the household was run on very strict lines with the children required to behave accordingly. Nevertheless Charles and Jessie were very caring parents who allowed the children to develop their interests. Charles was a kindly and generous man who got on well with everyone. It was little known for a long time that he financially supported and educated the family of one of his brothers who had effectively abandoned his wife and children for a life abroad, and he also supported one of his sisters and her family in hard times. Jessie on the other hand was possibly more reserved although steely willed underneath; maybe because she herself had had a difficult childhood having been brought up by an elderly, childless aunt and uncle. Tragically her mother died when she was a baby, and her father was further devastated when the private school he ran had to close after two bouts of serious illness amongst the pupils, leaving him unable to care for Jessie and her older brothers and sisters. Remarkably Jessie became very astute financially, probably through a combination of the initial influence of her aunt and uncle who were business people and then of course from her banker husband Charles.

Needless to say, Ken and his sisters were given a good secondary education, as well as being supported and granted considerable freedom to build on their talents. The eldest two, Mary and Peggy, tended towards the arts, and all became very good at a variety of sports. All the girls went as termly boarders to Loughborough High School where Jessie's cousin was the art teacher.

As the only son, there was probably more expectation on Ken to achieve academically, but all the children were bright. After Gayhurst, Ken went to Gresham's School at Holt on the north coast of Norfolk. This was in 1924 when he was aged eleven. Ken's father had narrowed down his choice of school to Oundle or Gresham's. The selection of Gresham's was probably influenced by two factors. Firstly it was not then a large school, and because of this Headmaster J R Eccles was able to promote that he personally knew all the boys well; and secondly, the school was gaining a reputation amongst professional parents for its liberal, 'no caning' regime.

J R Eccles vehemently condemned the system of beatings by staff and older pupils operated at other schools. He practiced a different approach to discipline that was called the 'honour system', in which pupils were on their honour to behave and were encouraged to own up should they lapse. Headmaster Eccles would propound, "The more I see of 'no caning', the more I am convinced that the absence of caning has far-reaching results. It makes things possible that would not be possible otherwise. It makes for truth and frankness, for loyalty and fellowship. It destroys the sense of fear, for which as a master I have little or no use. It makes for happiness and freedom of development. It enables one to keep more in touch with whatever is going on. It prevents the formation of barriers and breaks down existing ones. We need never be foes to our boys."

In retrospect his father's choice of Gresham's and its liberal atmosphere probably suited Ken's nature very well. As did its excellent sports facilities, which Ken used at every opportunity, rather to the detriment of his academic studies. Indeed this imbalance characterised his whole time at Gresham's. As one contemporary put it, "Ken was more interested in sport than scholarship."

In his first year in Mr Gamble's form he gained only modest results and generally this set the pattern, although in the Upper Third with a very charismatic teacher Mr McEachran there was an improvement. Ken's underachievement was a continual source of exasperation to his father, but whatever parental and school pressure was applied to improve matters Ken did not join the usual crop of Gresham pupils going on to the major universities. In his final year he gained a moderate pass in the School Certificate – there were no 'GCSE', 'O' or 'A' Level examinations in those days and the School Certificate was designed to give pupils who did not intend to proceed to university a recognisable scholastic qualification.

If Gresham's did not inspire Ken academically, it provided every opportunity and wonderful facilities for him to develop his sporting abilities. He was in fact a very gifted sportsman. It was on the sports field that Ken excelled.

It really is quite difficult to see how Ken even managed to devote any of his time to take the School Certificate he was so busy with sport. The school magazine faithfully records all the sports activities at both school and house levels, and for the last two years at Gresham's Ken was in practically every team! He was in the first team for hockey, football, rugby and cricket. The school had an extensive programme of matches in these sports against local and more distant schools, universities, and sporting clubs. Add to that list, house matches, matches against the masters and teams of old boys. And then there were sports days. On one such day Ken was just pipped to first place in the 100 yards (winner's time 11.5 seconds) and was involved in a dead heat for first place in the 220 yards in a time of 25 seconds. There was even a special 'Throwing the Cricket Ball' contest, which Ken won in his final term in 1931 with a throw of 99 yards 2 feet, a yard better than his winning throw the previous year.

Representing the school with Ken at cricket, hockey and rugby was another very talented sportsman, the son of a Liberal MP. But this young man was also an outstanding scholar who after Gresham's went up to Cambridge and then into the Foreign Office. His name was Donald Maclean, the infamous Cold War spy who defected to the Soviet Union with Guy Burgess in May 1951.

Although Ken associated with Donald Maclean through various school teams there is no hint that they were in touch after they left Gresham's.

Boarding school life was much more enclosed in those days, albeit the liberal regime at Gresham's allowed the boys quite a bit of freedom locally. Contact with home was for most pupils by letter. Parents generally would only appear once a year on Speech Day. But Ken's father did visit more than that, and sometimes watched Ken play cricket, occasionally accompanied by Ken's youngest sister Phyllis. The family had a splendid car, which made such visits more possible. At least Charles could watch with pride his son's efforts on the cricket pitch, perhaps able to forget for a while his frustrations at Ken's lack of scholarly effort.

Curiously the final match of the 1931 hockey season was against opposition from a German school, Schule Schloss Salem. In the spring of that year pupils from the Salem school were on a visit to Gresham's and among the visiting group was their boy's hockey team. The score of 5-1 to Gresham's apparently flattered the home team. The Salem school was one of Germany's best-known boarding schools, situated near the northern shores of Lake Constance on the Swiss/German border. It was founded by a German Jew who fled to England in 1933 to become the Founder and Headmaster of the famous Gordonstoun School for boys in Scotland.

Gresham's School Cricket 1st XI 1930
[Photo: Courtesy Gresham's School]

One final aspect of Ken's time at Gresham's was to prove very telling later on. The school proudly maintained a very high standard at shooting, operated through a 'near-compulsive', as one pupil put it, Officers Training Corps. The OTC was taken very seriously, incorporating camps and manoeuvres. There was an annual inspection by a senior officer from a local regiment. When Ken was fourteen he was in the Recruits, and at fifteen was promoted to the Corps proper. In his final year Ken was promoted three times; to Lance Corporal on 19 September 1930; to Corporal on 16 January 1931 and to Sergeant, the highest rank apart from the Corps leader, on 4 June 1931. He became a good shot and obviously applied himself to the military training involved.

At that time Ken was very close to his youngest sister Phyllis. Both being at boarding schools meant they had few local friends and they spent a lot of time at home together blissfully enjoying the school holidays. But Ken was to start his final year at Gresham's desperately worried about Phyllis who in September 1930 suffered a dreadfully serious swimming accident in Torquay from which she nearly died. She was in hospital for months, but in time recovered.

Ken left Gresham's in July 1931 and was articled to a City of London firm of auctioneers and estate agents. By all accounts he was not too enthusiastic about this career, as it required more study including periods at home in preparation for examinations. And again his real energies were directed towards sport. He carried on with his cricket and hockey.

Tragedy struck the family in 1933 when Ken's father died at the age of seventy, a few weeks short of Ken's twentieth birthday. Not unnaturally Ken's mother was devastated, but his father's death only made for worsening relations with his mother. In the past his father was at his most severe if the children upset Jessie. But now their strong wills led to more and more clashes. Shortly after his father's death, his sister Peggy married and moved to Sheffield. And in 1936 his youngest sister Phyllis married and moved to Northampton. Not long after Ken's mother and oldest sister Mary too moved to Northampton.

Whilst enjoying himself socialising and playing sport, Ken still continued with his articles and managed to pass the Auctioneers' and Estate Agents' Institute intermediate examination at the March 1935 sitting. He was tall, good looking, well-spoken, athletic and very sociable. Not surprisingly he had plenty of girlfriends; the family had high hopes of one nice young lady called Mary he brought home at Easter 1939 – but their hopes were unrealised. He did particularly well at hockey. He had joined the prestigious Tulse Hill Hockey Club at Beckenham in Kent. This was a golden age for the club, which arguably became the best known in Europe. Ken was Vice-Captain from 1937 to 1939. In addition to playing for his club he represented his county, Buckinghamshire, and was selected for the International Trails in the 1937/8 season, playing for the South West Counties.

Each Easter the club went to a tournament in Germany, and Ken certainly went on one tour before the War. Possibly it was the last one at Easter 1938 to Hanover, described in the club's Centenary book as, 'A curious affair at which the team played badly. Hermann Goering presented the prizes in full Nazi regalia amid enormous pomp. The atmosphere was overpowering.'

All this time though the storm clouds of war were gathering. In the summer of 1938 the German military mobilised and Chamberlain appeased Hitler at Munich. The following March the Nazis took Czechoslovakia. Ken's youngest sister Phyllis, now a young mother, wrote in her diary:

Germans invaded Czechoslovakia. No resistance. So much for Munich last Sept!!

In April she wrote with obvious feelings of desperation after Roosevelt's message to Hitler:

Surely he can't ignore all these warnings and appeals and plunge everyone into war?

Ken, on the other hand, saw the worsening situation as an opportunity, an opportunity to leave his unenthralling career for some excitement, rather like a lot of young men at the time. He talked more and more of wanting to join the RAF. And so in April, consumed by the desire to fly, Ken joined the RAF Volunteer Reserve. He was nearly 26 years old.

At that time young men accepted for the RAF Volunteer Reserve remained civilians and received flying training in their spare time. They were paid and all training was carried out during evenings and weekends at local flying schools funded by the RAF where the fundamentals needed to become a pilot were taught.

In the next few months the whole country was increasingly being prepared for war. On 24 August Ken along with all Volunteer Reserve personnel were ordered to report to their mobilisation centres. A week later civilian evacuations began from London. To add to the concerns over the impending war, worries of another kind were troubling Ken's family. Mary, Ken's oldest sister, had to go into hospital on 31 August for a serious cancer operation. In the event the operation went well.

1 September saw the Nazis invade Poland, and complete mobilisation of the British Navy, Army and Air Force was ordered. Two days later War was declared and Phyllis wrote in her diary:

God, so it has come after all, how ghastly.

On 26 September, a Tuesday, Ken met his mother and Phyllis for a last lunch at Beaconsfield before he entered the RAF. They had travelled down to see him and some friends at Gerrards Cross, using the last of their petrol before rationing. Even if Ken was in buoyant mood, looking forward to getting into uniform and flying, it must have been an emotional time for his mother despite their differences. Back in Northampton the following day, a young evacuee arrived at Phyllis's house, a boy of eleven who went to Kilburn Grammar School. Her first evacuee had arrived on the day war was declared, but the lad had been able to go back a couple of weeks later. He had fitted in quite well, in contrast to the evacuees Jessie looked after who were a disaster. Friday's entry in Phyllis's diary read:

Last day of using the car. Ran out of petrol !!

The war had truly arrived for both Ken and his family.

2. First of the New Gunnery Leaders

During his part-time Volunteer Reserve training Ken had progressed to dual flying with an instructor but had just two hours in total by the time the war started and he was formally called up. He received notice to attend the Central Medical Establishment for his medical on 5 October 1939; passing meant he would enter an RAF at war. He must have been quietly confident of passing, knowing how fit he was with all his sporting activities. Predictably he was declared fit by the medics and moved on to the next stage, the selection board. Significantly, this board cast the dye for the whole of Ken's wartime service by making two almost unprecedented decisions.

It was more or less unheard of for a civilian to be granted an immediate commission on being called up, even for someone who had completed their Volunteer Reserve pilot training let alone someone still in the early stages. Yet this is what happened to Ken. He was granted an immediate commission with the caveat 'for the duration of hostilities on probation'. That meant with effect from 8 October he was Acting Pilot Officer K M Bastin. He was allocated a service number – 75168.

Despite his new title, however, his hope of continuing his pilot training was dashed by the board's second decision. Ken would fly as aircrew, but not as a pilot – the selection board decided he would be trained as an air gunner. Not an ordinary air gunner, but one of the first commissioned air gunners who would go on to become one of the new class of gunnery leaders who would hold senior positions in squadrons responsible for improving air gunnery. How these decisions were explained to Ken and what his reaction was to them are not known. After all he had set his heart on becoming a pilot, but he certainly could not have anticipated an immediate commission.

To understand the real significance of the board's decisions one needs to take a wider look at the emergence of the air gunner in the RAF. For Ken though his selection as a commissioned air gunner meant he was to be at the vanguard of what can be described as the RAF's new 'professional gunnery management', one of the most vital developments in the advance of air gunnery in the RAF since the early days of the First World War. In fact he was to remain one of the most senior officer air gunners of the RAFVR throughout much of the war.

Bearing in mind that Bleriot flew the English Channel in 1909, it is not surprising that planes were used in the early days of the First World War for simple observation to help direct ground offensives and defences. But inevitably as the war progressed, planes were rapidly developed for more active military roles, which in turn led to the development of planes to attack planes, which in turn led to armament to help planes defend themselves. In the early days, pilots and observers were armed with rifles, pistols and even shotguns! By the end of the war pilots could operate a fixed machine gun that fired straight ahead through the propellers by means of a synchronised gear, and the observer was able to defend his plane from attacks from various directions with a ring mounted Lewis .303 calibre machine gun. But these guns had not been specifically designed and commissioned for aerial combat; they were simply adaptations of guns used by the army and used army ammunition.

In the immediate years after the war there was little practical development in air gunnery, largely due to severely cut post-war budgets for running the RAF, and to some extent the need to use up the vast stocks of munitions left at the end of the war. But the lessons and experiences gained were taken forward and worked on in the background albeit under considerable constraints. In reality though, armament of the 1918 era was still in operation well into the late 1930s.

It was said that the conditions of firing from one aircraft at another are so complicated that even the best shot in the world would not have a sufficient chance of hitting if he were firing only single shots. The air gunner had fleeting opportunities only of firing at his attacker, so his chances were significantly improved if he had the means of firing the greatest number of shots in rapid succession. At that time an expert army rifleman in rapid-fire mode could let off one shot only every four seconds. Hence the use of machine guns, but the Lewis was capable of only 500 rounds a minute, although through adaptation and modification for use in the air this was increased to 800 rounds (about fifty times faster than the expert rifleman). It was still, however, a gun designed for use by ground forces.

There was another imperative, and this was determined by the increasing speeds of aircraft through continuous development. With the ring mounted Lewis the air gunner had to use his strength to swing the gun to aim and maintain that aim. As speeds increased he was less able to overcome the effect of the airflow on the heavy gun, tending to swing it to the rear, and so he needed some sort of mechanical help.

What was needed was a gun specifically designed for the job in the air. Some of the problems the armament developers were trying to solve were highly technical. Requirements included: the highest possible rate of fire; almost instantaneous achievement of the rate of fire, because there was simply no time for the rate to be built up; the greatest reliability so it could be placed in the best position to defend the aircraft, which may not be where the gunner can easily clear stoppages; being as light as possible without sacrificing strength to avoid breakages; capable of being belt fed continuously from either side; maintaining full rate of fire when being fired in all directions, not just level; operating at extreme temperatures and without lubrication; and the gun had to be short as space was at a premium. Add to all these the usual economic needs of mass production, ease of replacing broken or worn components, and still using army ammunition.

Inevitably there was no time for such a gun to be developed even if it were possible. So the solution was the best compromise, and this was the American designed Browning .300, adapted slightly to allow the use of our .303 ammunition. First testing of the Browning began in 1929 and the final version was introduced into service in 1936.

It is worth here just pondering the marvel of engineering in a rapid-fire machine gun. Firstly, consider the series of operations required to fire a bullet from a gun. The breech of the gun has to be opened; the cartridge placed inside; the breech has then to be locked to counter the huge forces generated; the trigger has to be pulled and the striker hit the cap on the cartridge; and once the bullet has left the barrel the breech has to be opened and the empty cartridge removed before the next cartridge can be inserted. The speed of the bullet leaving the barrel of a Browning .303 is about 2,400 feet (or nearly half a mile) per second and is spinning at 3,000 revolutions per second. To achieve this, the propulsive explosion in the breech creates some 20 tons of pressure to the square inch. A Browning machine gun fired 1,150 rounds a minute, nearly 20 shots a second, generating about 80 horse power, equivalent to the output of a small car engine. It was this generated force that was used by various means to power the mechanics of the gun enabling it to carry out the series of operations described above nearly 20 times every second the trigger was pulled. Imagine four of these guns going off all at the same time just inches away from you in the confined space of a gun turret!

The powered gun turret was a significant development. Early attempts to overcome the slipstream problem were not particularly satisfactory. Also there was a growing need to provide more protection for the gunner from the effects of higher wind speeds and greater altitudes. In the early 1930s development of a powered turret began and the first type was introduced into service in 1933. Much engineering development was subsequently needed to produce a turret that met very exacting requirements. Principally the turret had to give full and continuous rotation; movement of the gun had to be smooth at slow speeds when tracking and firing at a target and also at high speeds when swinging the gun to a new target; and with complete freedom of elevation of four belt-fed guns. Obviously weight was a consideration, but less so in the first of the heavy bombers coming through in the middle 1930s. These were twin-engine monoplanes of all metal construction, such as the Armstrong Whitworth Whitley that came into service in 1937. Of course the armament of fighter aircraft was also being improved and it was vital therefore that the defences of these new first-line bombers did not lag behind. The powered turret enabled the gunner to have a significantly beefed-up rate of fire at his trigger finger by mounting two or four Browning machine guns in the turret. A by-product of doubling or quadrupling the firepower was the need to carry much more ammunition. Initially the ammunition was carried in boxes in the turret, which limited the amount of ammunition available to the gunner. Later, storing the belted ammunition in the fuselage and feeding it to the guns along trays running aft to the turret solved this restriction. As war approached in 1939, the RAF had three types of heavy bomber equipped with power-operated turrets featuring single or multiple Browning guns. This made Britain the only major power with an operational force of bombers fitted with power-operated turrets.

Of course a military aircraft was of little use if there was no efficient means of aiming its armament. There were three main problems for the air gunner. The first was range estimation, a particular difficulty in the air as there is no fixed reference by which to estimate the range of the target. There was no point in firing when the target was beyond the range of the gun; a potentially dangerous waste as ammunition was limited. More difficult than range estimation was to determine where to aim one's fire – exactly where was that point in the sky where the opposition aircraft would arrive at the same time your bullets reached there? This point was somewhere ahead of the attacking fighter, so the gunner aimed not directly at the fighter, unless it was very close, but a distance in front of its path. This 'aiming off' or 'deflection shooting' was the art and skill of the gunner for most of the war. Lastly the gunner had to take into account the velocity given to his bullets by the forward speed of his own aircraft.

Fortunately considerable scientific effort had gone into the development of a new sighting system called the reflector gunsight. It was a very big improvement on the early sights that relied on lining up a close ring with a bead near the end of the gun barrel, or similar, which was very difficult when both target and gunner were moving around the sky. The reflector gunsight produced a circular image with a dot in the centre on a clear glass screen and this image appeared to be at infinity. The size of the circular image was such that it allowed the gunner to estimate range by gauging the ratio of the wingspan of the target to the diameter of the circle. For this, the gunner had to be on the ball with his aircraft recognition. The reflector gunsight was ideal for multiple gun turrets where sighting necessarily was remote from the guns. It enabled the gunner to be in the best position; in fact it forced him to be because if he moved out of position he lost the reflection and so had no sight at all. By a series of rods and levers the reflector gunsight moved in direct relation to the upward and downward movement of the guns. The intensity of the image could be adjusted for day or night flying and also the design allowed easy adjustment making harmonisation with the guns a fairly simple task. The model of reflector gunsight introduced just before the war proved to be so successful that it was standard on almost all RAF armament for most of the war. Towards the end of the war help was at hand to solve the problem of 'aiming off' through the development of a gyroscopic reflector gunsight, which dramatically improved the gunner's aim and success rate. And later still radar was introduced to take the estimation out of the range problem. The reflector gunsight was a piece of equipment Ken would have been very familiar with throughout his time in the RAF.

Despite all this advancement in the mid to late 1930s, it was not until January 1939 that the air gunner was officially recognised as a distinct aircrew category. In the early days he was usually a willing volunteer from the armourers or from ground maintenance crews; later on he was given formal training but was still part-time only with a few pence on his pay when he flew. As such the vast majority were from the lower ranks, mostly Leading Aircraftsmen. Under the Air Ministry Order on Aircrews dated January 1939 his position became full-time but only when trained in the wireless operator role also, with a few exceptions. Over time the majority of air gunners were trained as wireless operators, however at the beginning of the war there were still a few 'straight air gunners', that is gunners who were not trained as wireless operators, and they too were moved to full-time so that all aircrew were full time at the commencement of hostilities.

Because of this background to the body of pre-war air gunners, it had long been clear to Bomber Command that the standard of gunnery at squadron level left much to be desired. Supervision and leadership were weak and training had been somewhat informal under local arrangements and at short annual summer camps if spared. Even under the Air Ministry Order of January 1939 there was little prospect of promotion for air gunners. As late as May 1939, when urgent enquiries were being made by the government of the RAF about its preparedness for war, Sir Edgar Ludlow-Hewitt, Bomber Command's Air Officer Commanding-in-Chief, was writing:

> *There is little doubt that the weakest point of our bomber force at this moment lies in its gun defence. I fear that the standard of efficiency of air gunners and their ability to resist hostile attack remains extremely low.*
>
> *We have all this valuable equipment and highly trained personnel depending for its safety upon one inadequately trained and inexperienced individual, generally equipped with a single relatively inadequate gun in a very exposed position in the tail of the aircraft. Here he has to face the full blast of the eight-gun battery of the modern fighter. The demands which will be made on the coolness, presence of mind, skill and efficiency of this single individual are, in existing conditions, almost superhuman, and in his present state of knowledge and training it is utterly fantastic to expect the efficient defence of the aircraft.*
>
> *As things are at present, the gunners have no real confidence in their ability to use this equipment efficiently in war, and captains and crews have, I fear, little confidence in the ability of the gunners to defend them against destruction by enemy aircraft.*

And so it was in Bomber Command at the outset of the war, the most acute need perceived was for officer gunners to provide leadership for this essential but weak area. Sir Ludlow-Hewitt had been pressing for a suitable unit to devise and refine techniques and tactics, to train instructors and to produce specialist officers to fill staff appointments and to act as gunnery leaders. A new Central Gunnery School was to be established at RAF Warmwell on the south coast, with the first course due to commence in the middle of November. The immediate task was to find suitable candidates. They were looking for men who exhibited, 'quickness of mental reaction, dependability in an emergency and fighting spirit'.

At this moment of need, Ken appears at the selection board – the perfect candidate for a gunnery officer. He had been to public school (public schools were then still seen as the main source for the officer 'class'), he was more mature than most recruits at 26 years old, and had been a Sergeant in the Officer's Training Corps at his school plus a few months Volunteer Reserve training. With the focus on the need for officer gunner recruits rather than for pilots, Ken's fate was sealed. He was told he would be trained as an air gunner. Of course he wanted to be a pilot but apparently he was advised that he had 'flat feet' and was therefore unsuitable for pilot training. Was that just an excuse and a sop? Probably, but we will never know. What seems quite certain is that he was immediately earmarked for the new Central Gunnery School courses being planned for November because he was granted a commission even before the Treasury sanctioned the funds for such commissions on 19 October. Given that one Air Ministry document states that the grade of officer air gunner was introduced on 9 October 1939 and that Ken's commission is dated 8 October, he was undoubtedly one of the very first, if not the first such appointment in the RAF. Ken's commission of Acting Pilot Officer was announced in *The London Gazette* of 27 October 1939 quoting his service number – 75168. Commissions for three other Acting Pilot Officers were also announced in the same edition underneath Ken's name; they were Raymond Fletcher Lumb (service number 75169), Harold Francis Welte (75170) and Clair Neale Robinson (75171). In the event Ken together with these three newly commissioned officers attended the first Central Gunnery School course, as we shall see.

That was the background to Ken's appointment. Returning now to the selection board, the next decision was Ken's first posting which was to the No.1 Air Armament School, RAF Manby, south of Grimsby near the East Coast in Lincolnshire. Undoubtedly at that time Manby was the home of the RAF's armament training with nearly 1,000 officers and airmen, over fifty aircraft and half a dozen different armament and armourer courses running side by side.

Normally fresh recruits into the RAF would first be posted to an Initial Training Wing for six weeks' basic training. The Initial Training Wing syllabus covered RAF law, administration, lots of physical training, some basic armament, gunnery, aircraft recognition, Morse Code, some navigation and mathematics to a level most recruits had not reached in their schooling. But because Ken had been involved in the Officers Training Corps at Gresham's he was excused this initial training and this is why he was sent direct to the Armament School. And so were the three Acting Pilot Officers, Lumb, Welte and Robinson, mentioned above.

Ken's basic air gunner's course was four weeks' duration – not really long enough, and indeed later courses were extended to six weeks. The course was largely made up of lectures and practicals in about equal amounts, plus some signals practice. And at last Ken would have started flying; about twelve hours flying time was built into the course. The School's pilots were instructed not to throw their aircraft around too violently until the pupils had become used to flying, a sensation nearly all had not experienced before. The syllabus recognised that a gunner required 'marked powers of endurance' and time was made available for physical training and organised games. Also some drill and parachute landing drill was included. There was an awful lot to cover and Ken would have been hard pressed as he had to make up for some of the ground other pupils had already covered at their Initial Training Wings.

After an introduction and safety lectures, a great deal of time was spent on sighting – that is everything to do with the methods of aiming from a moving platform to hit a moving target. A very complicated subject, it included knowledge of the effects of gravity on bullets, how to harmonise the guns, that is to adjust them to give the correct pattern of hits at a given distance, and what allowances to make when the gun was not pointing straight along the line of flight. Then Ken would have learnt how to employ all that technical understanding to the tactics of an attacking enemy fighter.

A lot of time would also have been spent on a thorough understanding and familiarity with the tools of the gunner's trade, the Browning and Vickers machine guns, their ammunition plus the various types of gun turret. By the end of the course Ken would have been able to dismantle, clean and reassemble a Browning in his sleep. He would have been taught that once in the air the gunner could not rely on any help and in his confined space he had little chance to put right anything that went wrong. Therefore he had to be thoroughly conversant with his guns and totally 'at home' in his turret, to such a degree that he did not put anything out of action by his own mistakes or carelessness so endangering the aircraft and its crew. Then the practical exercises would commence with ground range firing using a variety of guns. Some of this would have been clay pigeon shooting. Air practices would have followed. This involved air to ground exercises at fixed targets as well as air to air exercises from various positions in the aircraft. Initial air to air firing was at a drogue, a sort of windsock, towed by another aircraft and firing would be practiced at different speeds, different angles and heights. During these training exercises the two aircraft would follow a defined set of patterns for safety reasons. The firing aircraft would have several gunners and an instructor on board. Each gunner had a different coloured powder or paint on his bullets, and when the firing was over the towing plane would release the drogue over the airfield and a WAAF would zoom out on her motorbike to retrieve it. The holes in the drogue where it had been hit would be tinged in a colour and so the scores of the different gunners could be counted. Later mock battles between a bomber and a fighter would be played out using a ciné gun on the bomber. The special ciné gun took a film when the trigger was pulled and this film was analysed by the instructor; then he and the gunner would use the film to discuss the gunner's performance. To simulate night firing some of these exercises were undertaken with special goggles. For many of the firing exercises Ken would have worn full flying kit.

In addition to all that, the course would have covered pyrotechnics, like the use of parachute flares for illuminating targets and Very pistols for distress signalling. There would have been time spent on the important topic of aircraft recognition – which included recognising the appearance of Allied and enemy aircraft in flight, learning the span-dimensions of enemy types, learning to classify aircraft in small, medium and large groups for range estimation, and remembering the armour, guns and arcs of fire of enemy types. And then there were drills on action stations for ditching in the sea, using life jackets and the dinghy, and of course parachute landing. But no jumps were made from aircraft – that was left till the real thing!

As an officer among the mostly non-officer pupils at RAF Manby Ken must have felt under pressure to achieve good results. Pass standards were high and were rigidly adhered to; sub standard gunners were an unacceptable risk to the aircraft and the rest of the crew. Fortunately Ken passed, as did his fellow officers Raymond Lumb, Harold Welte and Clair Robinson who no doubt got to know each other well during the four weeks. Raymond Lumb was at Rugby School and was a Rackets champion, so Ken had a fair bit in common with him. Harold Welte on the other hand came from a different background; he was a South African who had sailed to England at the outset of the war to join the RAF.

The starkness of the war was brought home to Ken during his first weeks in uniform. Aircrew losses were suffered right from the start, including air gunners. Although the first months of the war were called the 'Phoney War' because military activity on the ground was minimal, this was not the case for the RAF. From the day war was declared Bomber Command carried out sorties against the German Navy and regular patrols and reconnaissance sorties were sent out over the North Sea. Aircraft were also despatched over Germany itself to drop propaganda leaflets. Even closer to home for Ken was the fatal accident of one of the aircraft from RAF Manby at the nearby Theddlethorpe Range when the aircraft crashed killing the pilot and two air gunners. On the station there were numerous air raid warnings, station defence machine gun posts were manned and a platoon from the Lincolnshire Regiment provided anti-sabotage duties.

Having completed and passed his air gunner's course Ken was immediately despatched to the newly established Central Gunnery School at RAF Warmwell to attend the first Gunnery Leader course. Also, Ken was promoted to Pilot Officer with effect from 13 November. His three officer colleagues at Manby were also posted to Warmwell and they too were promoted to Pilot Officer. They probably travelled together down to the Dorset airfield. No respite then for this group of young officers; the new course started on 13 November with Ken's name first on the list of the fifteen attendees, then came his three officer friends and the remainder were sergeants from various squadrons.

Was the School ready for them? It had been formally established at Warmwell only seven days earlier; pilots and aircraft loaned by Bomber Command arrived only two days earlier and the Wing Commander who was to command the School arrived the day the course started. Fortunately there were some buildings available; 217 Squadron, which provided patrols over the English Channel out of Warmwell, had moved to St Eval in Cornwall in October. Also some instructors and equipment came across from the Bombing & Gunnery School that was also operating at Warmwell at the time.

But as late as 30 September 1939 the Officer Commanding-in-Chief Bomber Command was telling the Air Ministry, 'One of the main difficulties at present is the lack of air gunnery leaders and commanders in units. Now we are at war, the only possible way of dealing with that difficulty is the special enrolment of officers for air gunnery duty. Having obtained suitable men, the next thing is to provide a short and very intensive course for training them; and in order to provide training of the highest possible standard, it is necessary to establish a centre where the technique of air gunnery can be thoroughly thought out, evolved and developed.'

The following month, October, the Air Ministry decided to form a Central Gunnery School. But the Officer Commanding-in-Chief Bomber Command was not happy with the originally stated aims. On 17 October he told the Air Ministry the object of the School was not so much training of instructors as to be the real centre of gunnery technique. He further pointed out that the gunnery centre should incorporate a really virile and strong service element, which had hitherto been largely lacking in air gunnery training. Further, that it was absolutely essential to develop in air gunners, not only skill in the use of their arms, but also the characteristics which are required for a good fighter, such as high morale, fine physical condition, endurance of hardship, self control and discipline.

With the objectives of the Central Gunnery School still being debated in the middle of October, one can guess how prepared it was for Ken and his colleagues arriving on 13 November. Still the three-week course went ahead. Again there was a mixture of lectures and theory, practicals on the ground and in the air. Some of the air exercises would have been over Chesil Bank, one of the ranges used by Warmwell.

A special visitor arrived on 29 November, Air Chief Marshal Sir Edgar Ludlow-Hewitt, KCB, CMG, DSO, MC Air Officer Commanding-in-Chief Bomber Command, the architect of the new Central Gunnery School. The School itself was not under his command, it came under Training Command, but he was doubtless very interested to see and lend his encouragement to the new School and to meet its staff and first intake.

At the end of the course three of the four officers scored about the same results, Ken being one, but Pilot Officer Ray Lumb scored well above the others. Ken's scores were: Lectures and Theory 65, Practical Ground 75 and Practical Air 60.

No.1 Course Central Gunnery School, RAF Warmwell, November 1939
Ken Bastin front row 4th from the left. Pilot Officer Lumb on Ken's left,
Pilot Officers Robinson & Welte on his right
[Photo: Courtesy of The National Archives, Kew (AIR29/605)]

As we shall see later Pilot Officer Robinson was killed in a flying accident shortly after the above photograph was taken and Pilot Officer Lumb was killed in action; in all half those in the group were later killed or missing. Being an expert gunner did not guarantee survival.

The next process in training for newly qualified aircrew was to be posted to an operational training unit. And so it was for Ken; he was posted on 10 December to RAF Abingdon in Oxfordshire. Here was one of the RAF's training establishments devoted to bringing crews up to operational standard before they finally joined their operational squadrons. At RAF Abingdon it was called No.4 Group Pool, which consisted of a Station Headquarters and two squadrons of Whitley bombers, No.97 and No.166. Up to now Ken's training had been specific to his role as air gunner, but now the training was all about working with other newly trained pilots, navigators/bomb aimers, and wireless operators to produce a fully operational bomber crew capable of flying to targets well inside enemy territory.

It is clear from this posting that Ken was destined to fly in the Whitley bomber, the latest version of which would shortly come on stream. This carried the very latest in aircraft armament and was the most heavily armed of any bomber of its time.

Ken's gunnery training had been carried out under the watchful eye of experienced instructors, and when flying the pilots were very experienced. Now it was different. All the crew were inexperienced and although an instructor was aboard nevertheless the risk of accidents was increased. Accidents were bound to happen, and did – within five days of joining RAF Abingdon an accident landed Ken in hospital. A painful start to his operational training!

Entries on his service record under the heading of Medical Boards appears to read:

Disability and Date of Commencement	Date and Place of Board	Classification	Remarks
Injury to left arm Admitted Torquay Hosp 20.12.39			
Traumatic synovitis 14.12.39	19.1.40	A2BC (?)	
	Torquay 26.1.40	A1B on 26.1 40	Agreed 7 days S/L & RTU 26.1.40 ?? 7 days

Medical Section of Ken's RAF Service Record

It seems that on 14 December Ken suffered what must have been a severe strain or jar to his left arm resulting in synovitis, which is inflammation of the membrane surrounding a joint. The injury was obviously serious enough to require hospitalisation, and his fitness was downgraded to A2B.

Whilst the record would indicate quite a nasty injury needing over a month in hospital, his sister Phyllis's diary reveals he was able to travel home for a few days over Christmas. Her diary entry for Christmas Eve reads:

Ken arrived home very smart in his uniform – looking fine in spite of his bad arm – injured it in mechanism – & came from Torquay where Mol is.

By one of those wartime coincidences, the Mol referred to in Phyllis's diary was Molly Haig a very close friend of hers who had been sent to the RAF Hospital at Torquay as a trainee nurse under the Voluntary Aid Detachment scheme. When Ken arrived there on 20 December, someone mentioned to Molly there was a patient who said he knew her, and no doubt it boosted Ken's spirits no end to find a friendly face at his bedside. Molly later married a Dr Barber, who was also at the hospital. She and Phyllis remained lifelong friends.

On final discharge on 20 January 1940, Ken was granted a further 7 days leave, and he finally returned to his unit on 26 January after his fitness was re-graded to A1B.

But why did Ken go to Torquay for treatment? Earlier in 1939 it was decided to set up an RAF Officers' Hospital in a district with both reasonable rail access and good surroundings for convalescence. The Palace Hotel, Torquay was selected and converted to a hospital. The district was considered to be relatively safe from enemy air attack, an assumption that was, unfortunately, to prove far from correct. The first patients arrived in October, so Ken was one of the early arrivals.

Patients on the Terrace at RAF Officers' Hospital, Torquay, November 1940
[Photo: Courtesy of the Imperial War Museum, London (CH1695)]

Despite its supposedly relative safety from attack it did suffer a disastrous raid in October 1942 when twenty-one patients and staff were killed and forty others injured. The damage was so severe the hospital had to be evacuated, and before a decision on its future was made it was attacked again in January 1943. Although there were no casualties this time, considerable damage to the central block rendered the building useless and the hospital was closed down. The Palace was not repaired till after the war and finally reopened as a hotel again in 1948.

Because Ken had been at RAF Abingdon for a few days only before his accident, his operational training really started on his return towards the end of January 1940, having missed more than a month. But his colleagues had not been able to put in much practice during his absence since the weather had been pretty awful. It had been bitterly cold with snow and ice, and February was even worse with flying impossible for more than half the month. More depressing for the crews than the weather though had been the fatal crash on the Monday after Ken went into Hospital. Six miles to the west of the airfield at 11.00 a Whitley aircraft from the station lost height on completing an evasion exercise, struck a tree and ended upside down in a field. The pupil pilot, a gunnery leader and one other crew member were killed. The gunnery leader was Ken's close colleague Pilot Officer Clair Robinson with whom he had been since the beginning. Ken would have received the news at Torquay – a bitter blow so early on.

Elsewhere the news from two daylight shipping search operations in mid December off the German coast was ominous; half the thirty-four Wellington bombers had been shot down and the death toll was nearly ninety. The original strategy that formations of heavily armoured bombers could operate unescorted in daylight – the long held view that 'the bomber would always get through' – was heavily questioned as a consequence of these two raids. By the end of the year unescorted daylight bombing raids were virtually abandoned.

However, training for the crews of the new heavy bombers had not been geared to night flying even though the Whitley had been planned as a night bomber. Gunners had hardly done any, other than using special goggles to simulate darkness. As if to emphasise this point, at RAF Abingdon the proportion of night flying to daylight flying from December 1939 to March 1940 was very low. This lack of experience of night flying by crews took its toll on 10 February when at 21.45 Pilot Officer Bligh flew his aircraft, another Whitley, into trees on Boars Hill on the airfield circuit. The crash killed Pilot Officer Bligh and one of the other two crew members aboard. The third crew member escaped with injuries. Pilot Officer Bligh was buried with full military honours at Abingdon Cemetery on 16 February; Sergeant Dupe the other fatality was buried the following day.

Ken expected some night flying later in February, according to comments he made in a letter to Phyllis. In the letter he also mentions the possibility of going to the Isle of Man. In February 166 Squadron established a detachment from RAF Abingdon at RAF Jurby on the Isle of Man. So it seems probable Ken spent some of February and March there.

His sister recalls him saying he went on some leaflet raids, which must have been about this time and of course would have been night-time operations, although no formal records have been traced to confirm this. Leaflet raids over Germany and as far as Warsaw in Poland were a feature during the so-called 'Phoney War' period and it was normal for crews nearing completion of their final training to join these operations, which were usually at night. Indeed the experience gained by this type of night operation was to prove invaluable to Bomber Command with the emphasis now on night-time only operations for its heavy bombers. RAF Abingdon put on a special and rather sobering lecture towards the end of February. It was given to all flying personnel – the subject was, 'The Conduct of Prisoners of War'. No doubt this was organised because a number of crews were about to transfer to operational squadrons.

There was one further shocking incident as Ken neared the end of his operational training at RAF Abingdon. On the 12 March a Whitley aircraft, this time from 166 Squadron, stalled while turning at 200 feet over the airfield and crashed into the Officers' Mess killing all three on board. The upper storey of the Officer's Mess was completely ruined, and a civilian waiter in the Mess was so badly injured he later died.

There was something else in the air in March 1940. This time it was love, and marriage. Ken always had an eye for the ladies, and they had an eye for him. Just before the war he had brought one attractive young lady to meet his family and it was thought they made a very suitable couple. However, nothing came of it. But in the February of 1940 Ken became engaged to Leonore Howard-Strapp, affectionately know as 'Teddie'.

Teddie was the adopted daughter of Walter Strapp who came from a prominent family of civil engineers. Walter's father, John Strapp, was Chief Engineer of the Line of the Great Western Railway from 1856 to 1870. Walter himself became a leading engineer with the French railways in Paris and travelled widely in Europe. Teddie had become companion to Walter's wife, and in time they adopted her – they had no children of their own. Walter retired to London after the death of his wife in Paris in 1925. Later he gave away Teddie at her first marriage in 1929 to a Charles Clarke of Carlisle, but they divorced in 1934 and she went back to London to look after Walter. When Walter died in 1938 Teddie inherited a sizeable estate. All this meant Teddie was a very sophisticated young lady of independent means with a lovely cottage in Horsted Keynes in Sussex.

Ken certainly enjoyed the better things in life and was always keen to have a good time, but his affection for Teddie is very evident from a letter he sent to his sister Phyllis just prior to his engagement.

He writes in early February 1940 from RAF Abingdon:

My darling Phyl

Thank you for your note and all the wishes etc. It is rather amazing that a dream can come true after all these years. The only thing is that (it) didn't happen before this damnable (war) started because life at the moment is hectic flying or rather going in trains at all hours and nothing but farewells. I got back here at three o'clock in the morning on Monday from seeing Teddie – not that that mattered – I wouldn't have cared what time it was provided I was here in time for duty on Monday. Mother may have told you that I was going to Pawthcawl on Saturday – well I think it is going to be a place in the Isle of Man now, that is the latest at any rate – and is of course subject to weather and aerodromes not being U/S – stands for unserviceable. Teddie & I hope to come up on the 25th Feb – a Sunday but only for a few hours I fear. She is staying in Oxford on Saturday night – and I may be night flying – don't know yet of course & then we will set out on Sunday – early & come back here for Teddie to stay Sunday night. The announcement will appear on the next day – although I am afraid that we consider ourselves engaged now – Teddie is getting the ring on approval before 25th & Sunday is to me to approve – & pay for and then we can get officially engaged on the day before we see you all. The wedding will be very quiet – we hope.

Must go now – terrifically happy and longing for 25th March wedding day.

Love, and to Lionel

Ken

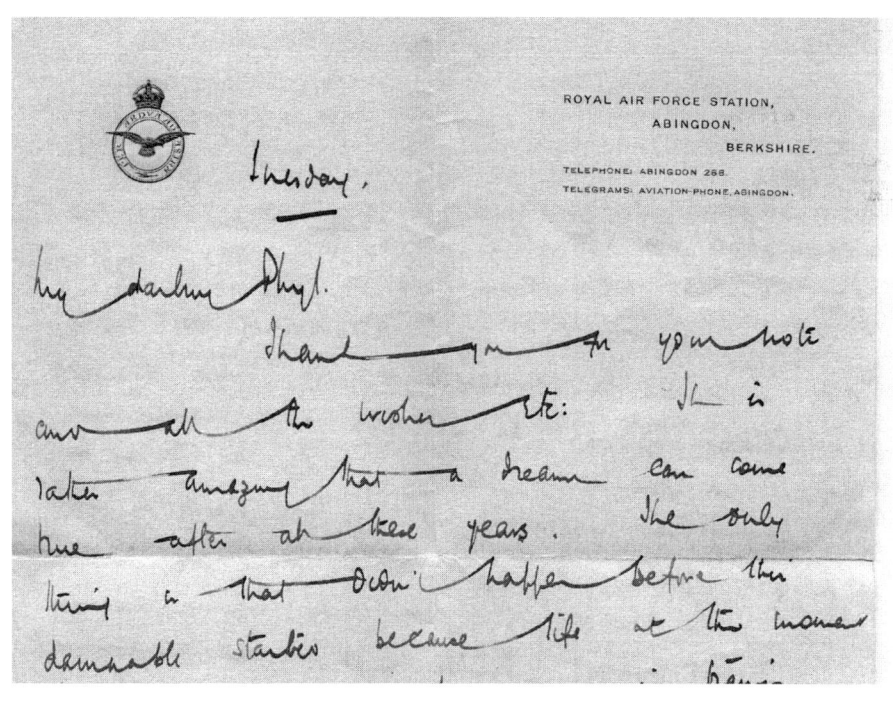

The beginning of Ken's letter to his sister Phyllis, in his distinctive handwriting.
February 1940

Ken's tone at the beginning of the letter was no doubt a reaction to the growing realities of the war. The farewells he mentions may well have referred to the loss of his friend Clair Robinson and the other RAF Abingdon aircrew killed in the last two months.

The wedding goes ahead as planned on 25 March 1940 at The Parish Church of All Saints, Lindfield, Sussex. Ken's best man was his RAF friend Pilot Officer Ray Lumb. Afterwards the couple had a short honeymoon in Bournemouth.

Ken and Teddie's Wedding
25 March 1940 Lindfield Church, Sussex
[Photo: Family Album]

In stark contrast to her previous way of life, Teddie became a service wife and moved with Ken, living on base when possible, as he was posted around the country. And like the wives of other operational aircrew, she 'counted the planes out and counted them back down again'.

By early April, Ken's training was virtually completed. The final stage was a short posting to 78 Squadron starting on 10 April. This posting followed the usual pattern. Crews trained on older aircraft at RAF Abingdon transferred to 78 Squadron at RAF Linton-on-Ouse in Yorkshire for conversion to the latest Whitley bombers used by operational squadrons. Just as Ken arrived at 78 Squadron, however, Bomber Command decided to change the current purpose of the Squadron from its training role to a proper reserve squadron. This meant that all the crews were rapidly moved out, and Ken stayed for two weeks only.

Other events were changing rapidly and very significantly. As Ken had travelled north to RAF Linton-on-Ouse, Germany's invasion of hitherto neutral Denmark and Norway began, signalling the end of the 'Phoney War'. The completion of Ken's air training came as these events unfolded. He received his posting to 10 Squadron at nearby RAF Dishforth, a fully operational squadron. In more sense than one, from now on it was the real thing.

3. On Operations – Disrupting the Blitzkrieg

Ken's experiences to date had probably not prepared him very well for the change he faced on joining 10 Squadron. Here was a squadron with as much history as was possible in the RAF, for its origins went back to the early days of the First World War. The Squadron motto was 'To Hit The Mark'.

Not only was it one of the oldest flying squadrons, it was also one of the most involved in the current conflict. As early as the night of 7 September 1939 the Squadron had eight aircraft over north-west Germany dropping propaganda leaflets. Regular shipping patrols, reconnaissance and leaflet missions had been carried out since, some leaflet raids as far as Berlin and even reaching Prague with a refuelling stopover in France.

It should be appreciated that in the first few days of the war President Roosevelt had called for restraint in bombing operations where civilians could be killed or injured. Britain and France, and Germany towards the end of the invasion of Poland, gave assurances. In practice this meant the RAF was restricted to leafleting and bombing shipping at sea or at anchor, but not at the dockside where civilian workers or nearby residential areas were at risk.

The middle of March had seen the Squadron involved in the first bombing of a German land target, the seaplane base at Hornum on the Friesian Islands. This raid was important for two reasons; it was the largest operation mounted so far and it was ordered in direct retaliation for a German raid on the Orkney Islands two nights earlier that resulted in civilian casualties.

Whilst these early operations were not what operational squadrons were really geared up for, they did provide very valuable experience with reduced risk, although no operation was risk free. 10 Squadron had suffered a number of crash landings, fortunately with few casualties, but one aircraft and crew were lost over the North Sea during a leaflet raid to Berlin.

So Ken was joining a very proficient squadron rapidly building a good deal of wartime operational experience. At that time nearly all the Squadron were regular RAF staff and a First World War fighter ace, Wing Commander W E Staton MC, DFC, led the Squadron. He was a giant of a man, both in stature and charisma. He led from the front, and gave every appearance that the war was put on for his personal entertainment. When his Squadron took off for its first operation of the war on 7 September, his was the first aircraft into the air.

Larry Donnelly was a wireless operator/air gunner on the Squadron and he remembered Ken arriving with three other Pilot Officers. He recalled Ken being appointed Squadron Gunnery Officer out of the four. Larry also remembered Ken was given the nickname 'Cliff' among the ranks, after the famous Arsenal footballer Cliff Bastin.

Ken may have been aware of some resentment from the older or senior non-commissioned officer regulars, some of whom may have been rather put out at these new and inexperienced Volunteer Reserves coming in at officer level. It was not Ken's nature to push his weight around, and he was probably not troubled by any antipathy. As well as settling into his new squadron and station, Ken's early days at RAF Dishforth would have been devoted to developing his role of Squadron Gunnery Officer and getting to know his air gunners. The arrival of a dedicated Squadron Gunnery Officer was a new departure for them and Ken would have explained he was there to support and represent them and to improve their efficiency and effectiveness through more organised training. Maybe there was a sergeant or two amongst them, but most were Leading Aircraftsmen at that stage despite being fully trained air gunners and wireless operators. That was to change shortly, but when Ken arrived most of his men would have had a great deal more experience and service than he, and he would have had to cope with that. He had two advantages; he was an officer and he had been trained at the new Central Gunnery School.

RAF Dishforth was one of the fairly new stations built to a standard design in the expansion period of the late 1930s. Sited next to the A1 Great North Road to the north west of York it covered some two hundred acres. It had modern accommodation in brick built, centrally heated barrack blocks on three sides of a large square parade ground. On the fourth side was the airmen's NAFFI. Not far away were the station headquarters, workshops and five large hangers. The runways were still the usual grass surface.

The Squadron was equipped with the two-engine Whitley bomber. At the beginning of the war the Squadron operated the Whitley IV version, but when Ken arrived conversion to the latest Whitley V was in process. Versions IV and V of the Whitley boasted the superb Rolls Royce Merlin engines giving a much needed improved performance compared to earlier versions. More importantly for Ken, they sported a power-operated rear turret with its four Browning .303 machine guns. When introduced the Mark IV was the first bomber in the world to be so powerfully armed against attack from the rear.

Ken would become very familiar with the rear turret of the Whitley V. Pressure for the hydraulic systems in the turret came from a pump driven by the port engine. In hindsight, having long pipelines of pressurised fluids to the rear turret was not ideal as any damage from flak or a fighter carried a high risk of fire. There was a handle that could operate the turret manually if pressure failed. Once in the aircraft the gunner made his way down the fuselage and clipped his parachute to the fuselage wall just outside the turret yet within his reach from inside the turret. He entered through small double doors, sat in a sling type seat, closing the doors behind him and plugged in his intercom jack. The guns were then loaded and checked – each gun had 1,000 rounds of ammunition stored in the turret. The reflector gunsight would be switched on and the illumination adjusted to suit the conditions. Apart from the intercom, the gunner and each of the rest of the crew had a system of coloured lights and buttons that could be used for signals if the intercom was out of action. The captain decided the signals and had priority on the system, which could prove a life-saver for the gunner in an abandon aircraft situation as he could not see what was happening up front. At the time, this turret was state of the art and the most heavily armed of any air force.

The Armstrong Whitworth Whitley V Bomber
[Photo: Courtesy of the RAF Museum, London (P009495)]

The Whitley was a robust if inelegant aircraft. It was quite cramped inside, particularly for the rear gunner who found it almost impossible to retreat out of his turret once the aircraft was airborne. There was no heating for the rear gunner and although versions VI onwards were less draughty for the rear gunner than the older versions he still had to struggle against the bitter cold. The aircraft was generally well liked by aircrews, although pilots needed to get used to some of its handling idiosyncrasies.

These aircraft carried a crew of five: two pilots (the senior pilot being the captain), a navigator/bomb aimer, the wireless operator/gunner and the rear gunner. Carrying nearly 850 gallons of fuel they had a range of some 1,500 miles and a top speed of about 230mph. A full bomb load was 7,000lb, or just over three tons. Carrying a full load in adverse weather conditions reduced range and speed and crews spoke of struggling to get up to140mph at times, but speed was not so critical for a night bomber.

Following the invasion of Norway, Bomber Command was quickly engaged in attacking the southern Norwegian ports and airfields. Reaching the south of Norway was hazardous enough given poor weather, 1,000 miles of featureless sea to navigate there and back and, because of the distances, no fighter cover. Northern Norway was beyond range.

The Four-Gun Rear Turret of the Whitley V
[Photo: Courtesy of the Imperial War Museum, London (C913)]

Despite the losses off the German coast in December, a large daylight raid on shipping at Stavanger was mounted on 12 April involving Wellington and Hampden bombers, but they too suffered heavy losses and this event directly led to the withdrawal of the RAF's heavy bombers from daylight operations for the next four years, with very occasional exceptions. 10 Squadron's first mission to Norway was on the night of 16 April but poor weather resulted in only one of the six aircraft despatched claiming to have found and bombed the target. 10 Squadron and its sister 51 Squadron at RAF Dishforth were involved in a number of raids to Norway in the following days with mixed results. The first night of operations since Ken arrived there was on 30 April and he would undoubtedly have watched with a strange sort of excitement as the twelve aircraft, six from each squadron, took off to attack Fornebu airfield. Two returned early because the bomb safety pins had not been removed, but during the early morning concern would have mounted for one of the 51 Squadron aircraft that was late returning. Eventually the news came through that it had crashed on the moors of West Yorkshire killing one of the crew and injuring the rest, one seriously. In all, seven aircraft were lost that night out of the fifty that were despatched, including three that crashed in poor weather on return to England.

Later the same day Ken would have seen his name on the crew list for operations that night. Only a week after joining 10 Squadron, he was on his first operation.

So this was it then. All the training, the practicing and preparations were now about to be tested in this his first attack against the enemy. How Ken must have been filled with a heady mixture of excitement and apprehension. This was to be his first taste of the reality of war in the air – how did his feelings now compare to those when he first joined the RAF Volunteer Reserve just a year ago?

The coming night posed many unknowns for Ken. Defending the aircraft and his fellow crewmembers was largely his responsibility – how would he stand up to the task? How would he perform under a fighter attack? He had had all the training he was going to get, but was he up to the real job? How would he cope with the fear of searchlights and ground defences or some dire emergency? There would be little hope of survival if anything went wrong during this trip, as the vast majority of the seven hours flying would be over the expanse of the North Sea.

Armourers install .303 Browning machine guns in the rear turret of a Whitley V
[Photo: Courtesy of the Imperial War Museum, London (CH246)]

Ken was allocated to Wing Commander Bill Staton's plane. It was probably a case of the Squadron Commander trying out the new boy, having a close look at this new rare breed of Officer Gunner. Being allocated to the

Commander's aircraft may have been both reassuring and nerve racking in equal amounts. For established aircrew, flying with the Squadron Commander would have been nerve racking enough, but Ken had only just arrived and Wing Commander Staton was this larger than life, fearless, bear of a man. But the man himself – a hugely experienced pilot with a massive reputation – may also have been a major comfort factor for Ken.

At the briefing in the afternoon, the six selected crews plus one reserve crew heard the target was Stavanger, Norway, and that take off was to be at seven minute intervals starting at 22.15. Ken would have listened intently to the details of the briefing.

The relevant entry in the Squadron Operations Record Book reads:

TARGET: Stavanger aerodrome. If target not bombed, ships in free bombing area may be attacked.

OBJECT/SPECIAL INSTRUCTIONS: To destroy enemy aircraft and aerodrome installations. Aircraft to be clear of Norwegian coast by 03.00 hours. Time over target for Dishforth aircraft 01.00 to 01.45. Dishforth aircraft which arrive late over target, may seize opportunity to bomb, i.e. may bomb a bit after 01.45 hours. Four flares to be carried and maximum use to be made of flares to blind defence and show up target. Machine guns to be used against searchlights. Suggest continual firing at searchlights during attack using guns singly. Anti Glare glasses and night binoculars to be carried and tested where possible. Target must be identified before attack and Captains to endeavour to plot fall of bombs. No bombs to be dropped on land other than aerodrome. Crews to confirm that Northern light aids location and attack of targets from 01.00 hours onwards. End of twilight Dishforth 21.14 hours; beginning of twilight Dishforth 04.43 hours.

ROUTE: Base to Target to Base.

METHOD OF ATTACK: Bombs to be dropped in two sticks if circumstances permit. Best height 4/6,000 feet. Minimum height 600 feet.

BOMB LOAD: First 3 aircraft are to carry two containers each, one of incendiaries and one of 40lb "F" bombs. Remainder of load 250lb General Purpose bombs fused NDT. Last 3 aircraft are to carry full load of 250lb General Purpose bombs fused NDT.

Wing Commander Staton, with Ken and the three other crew aboard, took off at 22.26. They were the fourth aircraft to take off and carried a full load of 250lb general purpose bombs.

The raid was largely successful with five out of the six planes bombing the target, setting fires in the hangar area and adjacent buildings. Good weather over the North Sea and the target helped, as did the Northern Lights, in identifying the Norwegian coast and getting a good navigational fix. All six returned safely despite the severe flak over the target and the worsening weather at home.

Doubtless Ken breathed a huge sigh of relief as his aircraft touched down after a flight of seven hours, exhausted from the mental strain of total vigilance for all that time and the sheer experience of the whole thing. He had survived his first offensive flight against the enemy. They had encountered two of the deadliest hazards – heavy anti-aircraft fire and poor weather – and come through. He was back safely. Debriefing over, he would have hurried to the mess and the grateful bliss of the traditional breakfast of eggs and bacon.

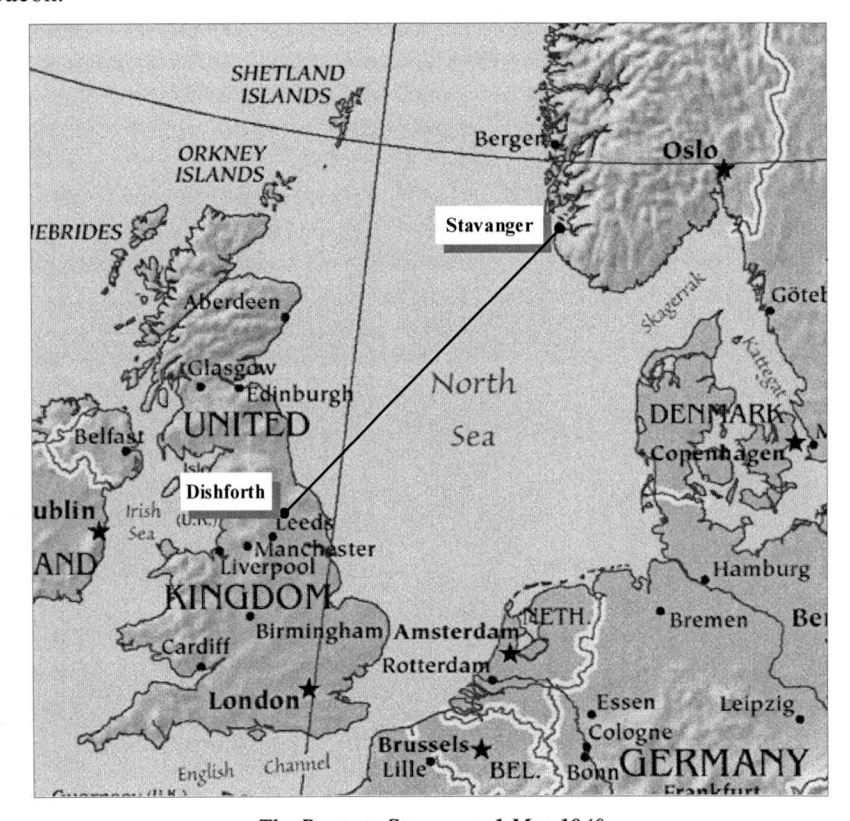

The Route to Stavanger, 1 May 1940

The captain of each aircraft made a brief report after an operation in the Squadron's Operations Record Book. This is the entry for Ken's first bombing operation, in all probability a huge over-simplification from Ken's point of view.

> The target was attacked successfully, one stick of bombs being put alongside front of hanger, and another along the side of a wood where enemy aircraft were dispersed. Great anti-aircraft activity was met with, being of both light and medium calibre. On the way out a convoy of 14 ships was seen and three flares dropped over it but owing to the possibility of it being a friendly convoy no reporting action was made until the aircraft was on its return journey. Difficulty was experienced in taking off and in landing because of bad visibility and low cloud base. Time down 05.30.

The detailed instructions for this raid illustrate the conditions and restrictions within which operations had to be conducted. Anything non-military was out of bounds. Testing and evaluation of equipment, bombing methods and navigation were all being carried out even as crews flew on operations. The reference to firing at searchlights may have followed the success of Aircraftsman George Chalmers who strafed and extinguished searchlights during a raid a week or so earlier on Kjeller airfield, Oslo. (George Chalmers later joined 617 Squadron and took part in the famous Dams Raid.)

Fulfilling his duty to improve the standard of gunnery at the Squadron, Ken organised a day's training on 8 May for his gunners over Filey Bay using RAF Driffield as a base. The day had been meticulously planned. Four aircraft were to ferry twenty-five gunners, an officer and two armourers leaving at 08.15 for the half-hour flight over to RAF Driffield. Two aircraft were to return leaving the other two to take it in turns to take up four/five gunners for air firing practice over the bay; each gunner having about twenty minutes each to fire off their 400 rounds from the rear turret. Range orders had to be read and signed and captains had to carry the correct letters and signals for the day. The firing times for each gunner were strictly laid down and anyone not finished in time had to unload his guns and ammunition. Even the times of lunch and tea breaks were all carefully programmed.

Ken must have cursed when he was called to a Gunnery Leader's Conference at Grantham to be held on the same day, and he left after lunch the day before using his own car. Nevertheless, the training went ahead as planned with Pilot Officer Fields, a gunnery officer like Ken, in charge. The four Squadron aircraft involved left for Driffield just after eight o'clock, but with twenty-one gunners only as four had been held back for flying purposes at base.

The first aircraft took off for Filey Bay at 09.00 and each of the four gunners had their practice after which the aircraft came back to exchange gunners. Meanwhile the second aircraft had already taken off, timed so the first gunner could start his practice just as the last gunner of the first aircraft finished. And so on the aircraft flew in rotation during the day until the programme was completed at about six o'clock. During the afternoon Wing Commander Staton flew over to see how the training was going. The orders laid down that, 'After firing, all gunners were to report to the Squadron Gunnery Officer (P/O Bastin)' but of course Ken was not there so the gunners would have reported to Pilot Officer Fields. The Squadron record of the training day is annotated 'Programme carried out successfully' – so Ken was no doubt pleased when he arrived back at base and learned everything had gone well.

The Grantham conference he was required to attend may have been to get comment from the operational squadrons prior to an Air Ministry conference on 21 May when gunnery was discussed. A decision was made at the conference to meet the need for increased facilities for gunners by giving them preference at the Bombing and Gunnery Schools.

Another entry in the Squadron records for the morning of Ken's training day reveals a somewhat laughable or even frightening example of equipment that was relied upon during operations still being tested. It reads:

> 8/5/40 11.30 W/Cdr Staton and F/Lt Bickford proceeded to the river at Boroughbridge to carry out further tests with an aircraft dinghy.

This after the Squadron had been forwards and backwards over the North Sea for a month now, flying thousands of miles!

Whilst the struggle for Norway continued, the focus rapidly switched nearer to home when the Germans invaded France, Belgium, Luxembourg and the Netherlands on 10 May, the same day Winston Churchill was appointed Prime Minister.

Hitler's decisive move into the Low Countries took the war onto another level altogether. Outflanking France's famous defensive Maginot Line, the German forces steamrollered their way into Holland and Belgium using overwhelming forces moving at speed; what became known as the Blitzkrieg. Holland surrendered in only five days.

Immediately Bomber Command's role was switched to supporting the Allied forces on the ground, the role the Command had always seen as its real purpose. The RAF's light bombers of the Advanced Air Striking Force, already stationed in France, attacked the German troop columns, suffering considerable losses. Following the German bombing of Rotterdam the bombing restrictions previously adhered to were lifted by Churchill. Bomber Command was now authorised to attack targets east of the Rhine, the emphasis being on oil, communications and industries and installations supporting the German air force. Bomber Command's heavier bombers commenced operations against bridges, road junctions and railway marshalling yards near the battlefront as well as factories and oil refineries further north and east in Germany itself.

On the night of 12 May Ken would have watched six of his squadron's aircraft take off for Mönchengladbach to bomb road and rail communications, and again on the 15 May when twelve aircraft set off for industrial targets in Germany. All returned safely and no doubt Ken was keen to hear the crews' experiences as surely it would not be long before he was scheduled to fly to Germany. He would have held formal debriefings for his air gunners to learn how they fared, building up a picture of what to expect.

In fact Ken was scheduled for the following night, 17 May 1940, for an operation to Bremen with, 'the object to bomb the oil plant, thereby destroying essential war material'. This was the first of many operations over Germany for Ken. Did he reflect for a moment that he may be about to aim his guns at the same young Germans he played hockey against not so long ago when at Gresham's School or with the Tulse Hill Hockey Club?

The Squadron was putting up fourteen aircraft of the twenty-four that were due to attack Bremen that night, but there was drama from the outset.

Ken was flying with Flying Officer Nelson, and was eighth in the order of taxiing for take off. For some unexplained reason there were only four in the crew on Ken's aircraft. The Air Observer, or navigator/bomb aimer, did not go and the second pilot probably doubled up as bomb aimer as well as navigator. Wing Commander Staton, the Station Commander, was first to take off at 20.05 as arranged. Squadron Leader Pat Hanafin piloted the next plane. He retracted its undercarriage just as he took off, but the aircraft suddenly dropped back on to the runway, skidding along until eventually it came to a halt. With a full load of fuel and bombs it was not surprising the crew evacuated in double quick time. As luck would have it, amazingly the plane did not explode or catch fire, and the other planes were able to take off, with Ken's plane only seven minutes behind schedule.

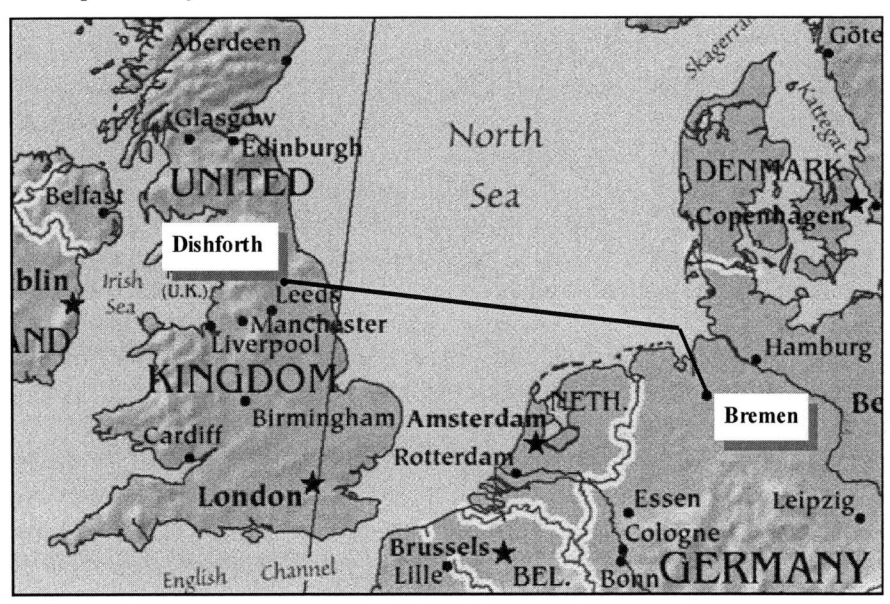

The Route to Bremen, 17 May 1940

Flying Officer Nelson's report in the Operations Record Book reads:

The route was the same as for detail A [i.e. to Wilhelmshaven and then to the target]. Identifying their target at Bremen with ease, this crew attacked by gliding down from 10,000' to 3,800', releasing their bombs at the bottom of the glide, but they were unable to observe the results of their bombing owing to the intense searchlight activity which was prevailing at the time. Intensive light and heavy flak fire was experienced with great supporting searchlight activity, especially in the Bremen area. Weather conditions on this flight were ideal. Observations made by the crew included the sighting and identifying of two aerodromes, both illuminated with full night flying lights. These aerodromes were Jeuer and Barge, which latter aerodrome beacon was continually flashing MX in white. A safe return journey to base was made and no enemy aircraft were seen throughout the flight. This aircraft dropped four 500lb. and six 250lb. bombs – all on Bremen oil plant.

The first aircraft on the scene had certainly stirred up the defences and most of the Squadron's planes were damaged by flak. Larry Donnelly, who was one of the rear gunners on the raid, described their approach in his book *The Whitley Boys* as running the gauntlet of a 'wall of flak'; and after the cry of "Bombs away!" with the pilot trying to evade persistent searchlights, the gunner was able to open up his four Browning machine guns on the defences. He wrote, 'At least I could retaliate, while the bods up front had to take it.'

The raid was deemed a success with six fires started, the largest being two warehouses at the docks. All the planes got back with no casualties among the crew, but some limped home after suffering severe damage, arriving much later than Ken whose aircraft touched down at 03.25.

Since nearly all the Whitleys required repairs, the Squadron was unable to operate the following night, drawing the comment from their sister squadron at Dishforth that, "They would do anything to get a night off!"

Ken's pilot, Flying Officer William H Nelson, was one of those amazingly young airmen, aged just twenty-three. He was in fact a Canadian, born and educated in Montreal where he became keenly interested in flying. He tried to join the Royal Canadian Air Force but was turned down – the intake of trainee pilots was very limited due to The Depression. So William Nelson travelled to Britain and was successful in joining the RAF in 1937. After training he was posted to 10 Squadron to fly Whitley bombers. He had been on the first 10 Squadron operation of the war on 8 September 1939 dropping leaflets over northwest Germany and many operations since. Wing Commander Staton had recommended him in April for the Distinguished Flying Cross for 'his determination, courage and above average success'. So although William Nelson was several years younger than Ken, he was, despite his young age, an experienced pilot.

On Sunday 19 May Ken's sister wrote in her diary echoing the concerns everyone felt at the time:

Germans now in Antwerp. RAF achieving wonderful things in raids on their communications. Winston Churchill broadcast a stirring speech at 9.00pm – we've just got to win & the danger of real raids on Britain draws nearer with every Belgium town taken.

Bomber Command's main effort now was to support the French defences and our troops in northern France in an attempt to delay the new German breakthrough.

Ninety-two aircraft were despatched on the night of 20 May to a variety of targets. 10 Squadron put up six aircraft and Ken was with Flying Officer Nelson again. The Squadron record details the objective for that night:

> Object:- To destroy road bridges over the River Oise and to disorganise and interfere with enemy movements in the area below.
>
> Targets:- Bridges at Catillon, Hannapes and Ribemont. Alternative target:- any large concentration of transport, A.F.V. or troops in the area given.
>
> Route:- Base – York – Corridor E and D to Crill and from thence to the target. Reciprocal route on return.

Flying Officer Nelson took off at 21.07, but then things started to go badly wrong. The navigator, Flying Officer Bagshaw, who had managed to get them all the way to Bremen and back on their previous trip, seemed to make some early and potentially extremely dangerous mistakes.

The Squadron's report against Ken's aircraft reads:

> This crew, on its way through Corridors D and E got lost through navigational errors and finding themselves adjacent to balloon barrages judged it expedient to land rather than proceed and cause damage and disorganisation to the Fighter Command. They landed at Ansty at 2220 stayed overnight and returned to base at 1200 hours the next morning.

RAF Ansty was an aerodrome just north of Coventry. The growing realisation that they were lost and in extreme danger from flying into balloon cables would have been a most unnerving experience for all on board. Landing at night on a strange airfield with a full bomb load and the fuel tanks nearly full was not an easy manoeuvre and all the crew doubtless sighed with relief when they came to a halt. What reception Flying Officer Bagshaw received when they returned to base the following morning is not known, but the Squadron Navigation Officer would have held a debriefing to understand what the problem was that led to a potentially dangerous situation a relatively short distance from base.

All the other 10 Squadron crews managed to reach the target area, picking up the River Oise as it meandered northwest from Paris towards the Belgian border and bombed from low level. They met little resistance, but one Whitley of 102 Squadron was lost near St Quentin. Another Whitley aircraft from 77 Squadron with the target of Catillon and Hannapes was badly damaged and crash-landed near Abbeville. Reports of the crash differ, but it seems all of the crew escaped unhurt and most reached Allied lines and eventually returned to their base at Driffield. Two other aircraft were also lost that night.

Every endeavour was being made by Bomber Command to help the French and British ground forces stem the German advance, and on 21 May the word was passed down the chain of command for 'Maximum Effort' that night, which meant every serviceable aircraft to be readied. Despite Ken and his crew landing back at base at midday after their wasted effort the previous night, they were scheduled to leave again that evening for Rheydt. Rheydt was an important railway junction just west of Dusseldorf, near to the southern end of the border with the Netherlands, and close to the battlefront. The total number of aircraft put up was 124, of which 10 Squadron's contribution was ten.

Diversion to Ansty on 20th May 1940.

However, there was one significant change to Ken's crew. Flying Officer Prior replaced Flying Officer Bagshaw, the navigator who managed to lose his way the night before. Flying Officer Bagshaw was instead allocated to 'Officer in charge of Night Flying from midnight onwards'. Was this a consequence of the events the previous evening? Very probably.

Details of the briefing for crews were:

Object:- To destroy railway junctions and to destroy and impede movement of enemy reinforcements and supplies.

Target:- Rheydt railway junction.

Alternative target:- Any marshalling yard or other railway junction in the area.

Route:- Base – East Retford – Waddington – Corridor G – and from Orfordness to target, returning from target to Orfordness, via corridor G to Base.

The raid was successful and all ten Squadron planes bombed from between 2,000 and 6,000 feet. All returned safely. The report for Ken's aircraft was:

Take off 2037. This crew located the railway junction at Rheydt and attacked this target from 0006 until 0011 from a height of 3,000'. Direct hits were claimed on the marshalling yard as a result of the attack. Weather conditions were fine and clear. A certain amount of light flak fire was encountered near the target, but it was not accurate. Not many searchlights were seen and those which were encountered failed to locate the machine. Time down 0259.

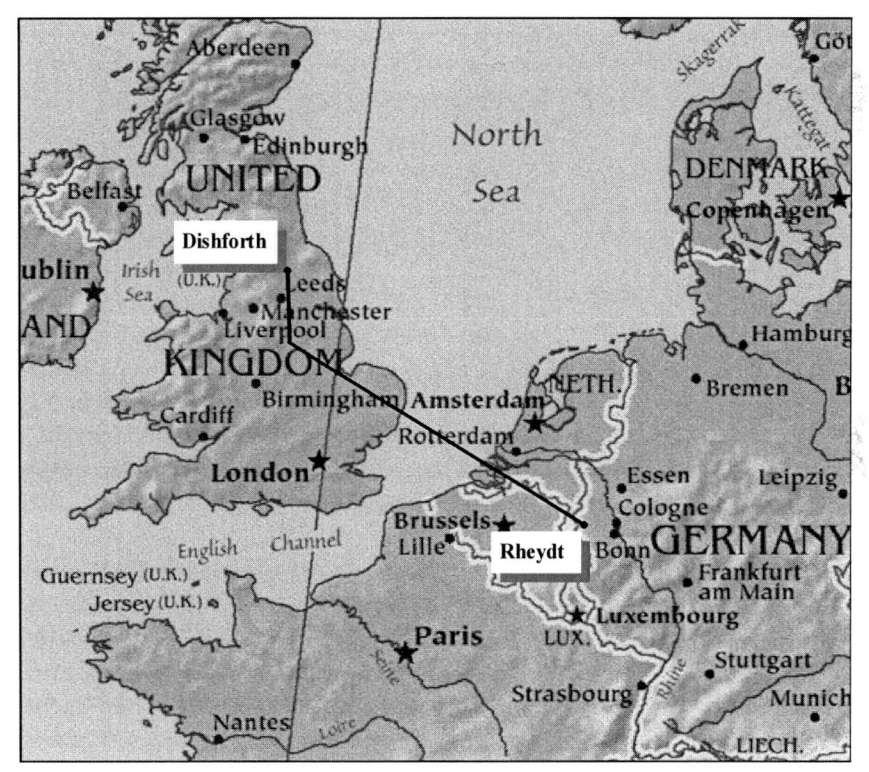

The Route to Rheydt, 21 May 1940

Not everyone escaped the flak however. One aircraft from 83 Squadron was hit over Germany and the pilot ordered the crew to bail out, which they did. Somehow the pilot managed to regain control and continued to fly homeward, only to be hit over the Essex coast by British anti-aircraft guns. The pilot bailed out safely and the aircraft crashed. Such were the hazards and sheer bad luck for some.

The Daily Telegraph of 22 May carried a map of the battlefront, showing just how far the Germans had advanced and just how desperate the situation was becoming.

Map Showing the German Advance, 22 May 1940
[Published with kind permission of *The Daily Telegraph*]

Late the previous evening Ken's sister wrote in her diary:

> 9.00pm news very grave – Germans have occupied Amiens & Arras so they're pretty near the coast. We all had to fill in our identity cards & have to carry them always. So the war is definitely nearer – but we'll drive them out & win in the end. We've got to – so a cheerful face will help.

There was no let up in Bomber Command's efforts in these desperate days. Although 10 Squadron crews landed back from Rheydt at three o'clock in the morning, they were told in the early afternoon that they were required again that night. And again the targets were on the border between France and Belgium.

Briefing for the Squadron's crews for that Wednesday, 22 May was:

> Object:- To destroy road and rail bridges and junctions and to impede the movements of the enemy re-inforcements and supplies.

Targets:- Hirson Railway and Road at Eastern exit from Givet. Alternative to both targets: Any concentration of troop or transport east of a line Mons – Mauberge – La Chapelle – le Cateau and forest of Mormel.

Route:- East Retford – Waddington – Corridor G – and from Orfordness to target, returning via corridor D and E to Base.

Ken's crew under Flying Officer Nelson again were detailed to Givet, an important junction that was seeing a lot of German frontline support passing through. In view of its importance it was heavily defended with 20mm and 37mm flak batteries.

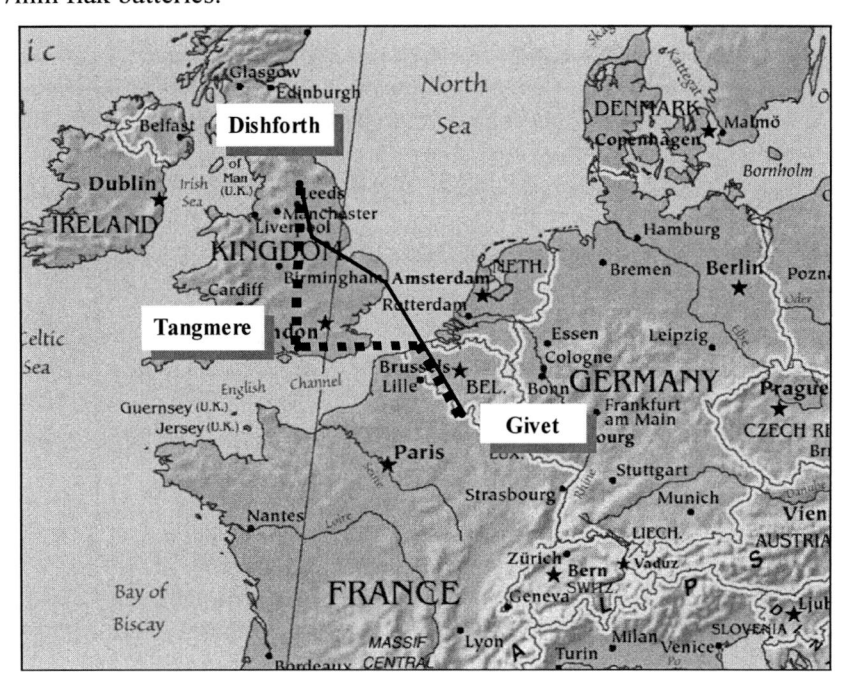

The Route to Givet and Return via Tangmere, 22 May 1940

In his book *The Whitley Boys*, Larry Donnelly whose aircraft took off four minutes after Ken remembered the outward flight was smooth and that after crossing the Belgium coast they headed for Givet, encountering little opposition. But it was a different story over the target, he recalled. Fires were seen in the town and the flak was coming up thick and fast. All ten aircraft bombed the target, and leaving the flak behind, the relieved and tired crews just looked forward to getting back to Dishforth and getting their heads down. But while crossing the coast a Morse Code message came over the radio that the weather was closing in at base and aircraft were to divert to aerodromes on the south coast and Oxfordshire. Flying Officer Nelson headed for RAF Tangmere, a fighter squadron base on the South Coast near Chichester where he landed just before two o'clock in the morning. Despite being denied the comfort of their own beds, the crew doubtless slept like logs. The weather in the north did not clear till after lunch the following day and in the end it was late afternoon before Ken and his crew finally touched down at Dishforth.

Flying Officer Nelson's report was:

> Take-off 2046. This crew attacked the road leading out of the East from Givet, from a height of 1,800' between 2345 and 2355 but no results of the bombing were observed. Weather was fine with patches of fog in the valleys. Intense flak fire was experienced over the target with at least twelve searchlights working in conjunction. Many searchlights were also observed in the St. Quentin area. This crew reported that at 2214 a large fire was seen burning on the sea 5 miles, 120° from Orfordness. This aircraft landed at Tangmere at 0150 and returned to Base at 17.20 on the same day.

Whilst none of the 47 aircraft sent out that night were missing over the battle area, the deteriorating weather in England claimed several planes, one crashing in Yorkshire killing all four crew.

Not long after Ken returned to base, back at home in Northampton his sister wrote in her diary:

> Germans officially in Abbeville on the French coast & heavy fighting in Boulogne. RAF at it still & doing magnificently against huge odds.

The following evening, Friday 24 May, as Ken was yet again heading out over the coast for Belgium, she wrote:

> Boulogne has fallen & is in German hands – so they really are getting close – but the RAF is superb – success after success. Thacky [a neighbour] came in to listen to the King's speech at 9.00pm. Very fine speech indeed.

Of course she was writing her diary each evening not knowing what her brother was doing or what danger he was facing.

There was little respite for the Squadron in the effort to stave off the advancing German Army that by 24 May was attacking the British garrison at Calais.

Whilst other RAF groups continued to attack the German land forces by day, the heavy bombers continued their night raids on communications targets now in the area between Brussels and the French border.

The orders for 10 Squadron for the night of Friday 24 May were:

> Object:- To destroy road junctions and traffic thereon, and to impede movements of enemy reinforcements and supplies.
>
> Targets:-   Avesnes road junction.
>
> Aulnoye road junction.
>
> Mons road junction.
>
> Binche road junction.
>
> Hal railway junction.

Alternative targets:- Any road junctions in the area specified.

Route:- East Retford, Waddington, Corridor G, Orfordness, Target. Target, Orfordness, Corridor G, Base.

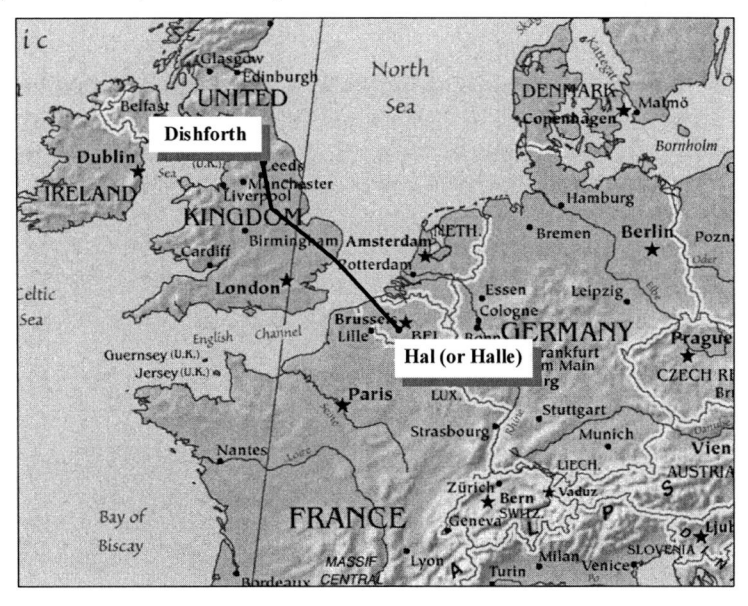

The Route to Hal, 24 May 1940

Ken was again with Flying Officer Nelson, same crew, same aircraft. The report of this operation is fairly brief:

> Time up 2158. The target at Hal was attacked by this aircraft from a height of 7,000' between 0030 and 0058 but no results of the bombing were observed. No flak fire was directed at the aircraft but some could be seen bursting near some other aircraft in the vicinity of Brussels. A few searchlights were encountered over Ghent and Brussels but they did not hold the aircraft. Brussels could be easily distinguished owing to the many scattered lights. Time down 0326.

The total effort that night was fifty-nine aircraft – twelve from 10 Squadron. The weather was fairly good, although some haze limited visibility. It was a pretty successful night as nearly all aircraft bombed their target and everyone returned safely.

One crew from 10 Squadron, however, had an apprehensive journey back to base as one 250lb bomb had 'hung-up', that is to say stuck on the rack in the bomb bay. Despite the crew's efforts to dislodge it, it refused to budge, and they were faced with the possibility of their landing causing it to drop and explode on the runway beneath them. Fortunately the bomb held, and it was left to the armourers to remove it safely.

Other Bomber Command squadrons had been attacking German positions in the northern corner of France in efforts to hinder and delay the Germans who were closing in on the main body of the British Expeditionary Force.

Now with its back to the sea, delaying the German advance was vital if any of the men were to be rescued off the beaches in the armada of small ships being organised.

Sunday 26 May was a National Day of Prayer, ordered by King George VI. In the evening the famous evacuation of the remaining troops from Dunkirk began, signalling the beginning of the end of the battle for France.

Day and night, Bomber Command sent sorties against the German positions and supply lines just to the rear of the front in last-ditch efforts to help the British Expeditionary Force and the retreating French army. Land forces commanders had been calling for 100% of Bomber Command's resources, but high-level directives meant that the strategic bombing of oil installations and infrastructure supporting the German military should also continue. And so it was on the night of 27 May seventy aircraft were launched against communications targets behind the battlefront in France and Belgium, while a further fifty headed for German oil refineries and railway yards in the Ruhr.

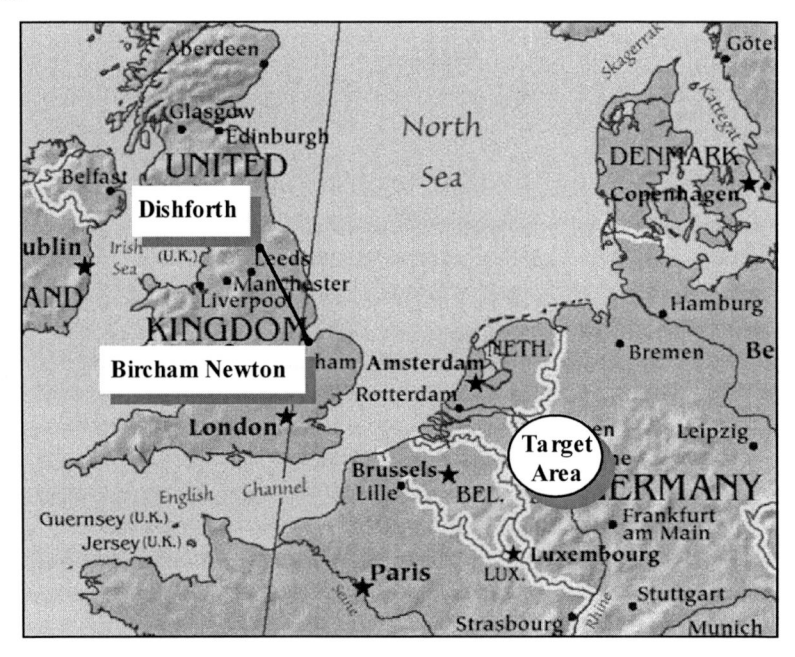

The Target Area, 27 May 1940
An Emergency Landing was made at Bircham Newton

The targets for the eleven strong 10 Squadron contingent were the marshalling yards at Neuss, Dortmund and Duisburg in the Essen area. The planned route out was via the coast at Great Yarmouth and back over Orfordness, Suffolk.

But three crews from the Squadron would have quite different and notable experiences before the night was out – Ken's crew amongst them.

Flying Officer Nelson was again Ken's pilot flying the same aircraft as the previous Hal operation. They took off at 20.19. On this occasion, however, the weather soon intervened, as the Squadron record shows:

> This crew had only reached the vicinity of Bircham Newton [near King's Lynn, Norfolk] before they encountered a severe electrical storm, which fused the W/T aerial and caused the pilot to suffer a severe shock through the inter-communication leads. The second pilot took over and decided to land the aircraft at Bircham Newton for inspection. The aircraft and crew landed safely at 21.50 hrs. No serious damage was sustained by the aircraft and only slight shock by the pilot.

During the storm the aircraft would have bucked about violently and, for a short while at least after the plane was hit, Ken ensconced in his turret must have wondered what on earth was going on, probably expecting the order to bail out was coming any second. Earlier each of the crew had psyched themselves up for the expected seven-hour trip over enemy territory. An hour and a half after take-off they were back on the ground somewhat shaken but fortunately unhurt.

Most of the other 10 Squadron planes reached their targets, dropped their bombs and returned safely. They met moderate to severe flak, but one of them, piloted by Squadron Leader Pat Hanafin, encountered a German fighter over Utrecht. This was fairly rare because at that time the Germans were in the early stages of developing their night fighter capability. The tail gunner, Aircraftman S R Oldridge, fired and shot down the fighter, believed to be the first German night fighter shot down in the war. Imagine the debriefing session between Ken and Stan Oldridge and the excitement of the other Squadron gunners as the news spread; especially when it was realised this was the first such claim of the war. Did Ken feel a little pride that it was a notable first for one of his gunners and for his Squadron? Stan Oldridge was one of the gunners on Ken's training day just a few weeks earlier – did that extra training make all the difference?

Another Squadron crew, though, failed to find their primary target and bombed what they thought to be an airfield in Holland. When the Dutch coast failed to show up on route for home they realised something was very amiss. A radio bearing check put them over England and with further radio assistance they made it back to base. Analysing their navigation data they came to the unfortunate and embarrassing conclusion that they had bombed an English airfield! They had in fact bombed RAF Bassingbourn near Cambridge. Fortunately, little damage was caused and no one was injured. Repercussions followed, however, and the pilot was demoted to second pilot, and he and his crew suffered much leg pulling. Subsequently it was discovered the plane's magnetic compass had been rendered unserviceable when the aircraft had flown through an electrical storm after crossing the English coast on its outbound flight; the same storm that hit Ken's plane. The Squadron certainly experienced the vagaries of war in the air that night.

The news on the ground took a grim turn when on 28 May King Leopold of Belgium surrendered his troops, much to the disgust of France who vowed to fight on.

'FIRST B.E.F. MEN HOME AFTER EVACUATION' was *The Daily Telegraph* main headline for Friday 31 May. The article started, 'Large numbers of men from the British Expeditionary Force in Flanders, who had been evacuated by the Royal Navy from Dunkirk, landed in England yesterday and were passing through London on their way to home stations last night. Weary, unshaven and bearing evidence of the heavy fighting in which they have taken part, they were yet in high spirits.' Some had obviously reached Northampton by the afternoon because Ken's sister wrote in her diary that evening:

> Had tea at Orange Café – 3 BEF came to the table & were talking of their operations in France – my God what they have been through! Yet they are so casual about it all.

She also recorded her mother had just returned from a visit to Ken:

> She was safely back & told me of Ken's exploits over Belgium, Norway & Holland etc – all very thrilling.

It is possible that Ken had had a few days leave after all the operations he had carried out during a hectic May and his mother was able to make a short visit to him.

Although still rostered with 'A' Flight as Flying Officer Nelson's rear gunner at the beginning of June, Ken did not fly again with him. In fact Ken did not fly on operations for a while although the Squadron was still heavily involved in the war effort. This was because the Squadron was increasing in strength with an influx of new Volunteer Reserve aircrew who had just completed their operational training at RAF Abingdon. Their arrival provided an opportunity to rearrange some of the established crews. As Gunnery Officer, Ken would have looked after the intake of his new gunners, a luxury he did not have when he joined the Squadron only a few of months before. The Squadron could now put up fourteen operational crews, divided into 'A' and 'B' Flights, as its strength was around 100 airmen, of which about 25 were detailed as tail gunners and a further 20 were Wireless Operators/Air Gunners. So Ken was directly responsible for two dozen or so airmen and was also in charge of the gunnery training generally.

The news of the fighting across the Channel continued to be grim, and over the next few weeks there was equally grim news for the Squadron. There had been no fatalities on the Squadron since October in spite of the frenetic activity, but June saw an end to that run of luck. On the night of 3 June Flight Lieutenant Phillips encountered thick fog on return to the UK coast and crash-landed near Needham Market in Suffolk. The rear gunner Pilot Officer Fields, a commissioned gunner like Ken, was killed and three others were admitted to Ipswich Hospital with quite serious injuries. In another incident Sergeant Keast and his crew were all killed on the night of 11 June when their Whitley crashed over the battle area near Abbeville in France. And pilot Flying Officer Smith died in the early hours of 20 June when he tried to land at RAF Honington in Suffolk after a raid on port facilities at Antwerp. While over the target an engine caught fire but he nursed the aircraft back over the North Sea losing height all the time. He had little alternative but to try landing at Honington, but Honington was under an air raid alert at the time and was in darkness. Tragically the aircraft crashed three miles short of the runway and burst into flames, killing Flying Officer Smith and injuring two others who suffered burns.

However, there were some better moments including Ken's promotion to Flying Officer, which came through effective from 23 May. In official terms he was promoted to Acting Flying Officer but the 'Acting' was purely academic officialdom and for all intents and purposes he was Flying Officer Bastin. Also, a welcome boost to Ken's gunners came when confirmation of an Air Ministry Order came through at the beginning of June announcing that all wireless operators and air gunners were to be immediately promoted to sergeant and in future the rank would be awarded on successful completion of training. At last there was proper recognition of their full-time aircrew role. This promotion meant a great deal to the men. It improved their status considerably, they could move into better quarters and they were paid more too – eight shillings and three-pence a day, equivalent to 41p in today's terms. They had been issued with an official Air Gunners chest badge last December and with the promotion to sergeant they were now at last on a par with other non-commissioned aircrew. No wonder, as one newly promoted aircrew remembered, they hurried to sew on their new stripes!

A further plus was confirmation that Ken's pilot Flying Officer William Henry Nelson was to receive the Distinguished Flying Cross. He was shortly to leave the Squadron as he had volunteered and had been accepted for training on Spitfires. Mid July saw him join 74 Squadron based in Essex where he excelled as a fighter pilot in The Battle of Britain. By the end of October he had been credited with shooting down five German fighter-bombers. But sadly on 1 November he was scrambled to meet a wave of German attackers over Dover and did not return.

Also receiving yet another decoration was the Squadron Commander. Wing Commander Staton was awarded a Bar to his Distinguished Service Order. His citation is interesting for two reasons. It is a testimony to the man and his leadership of the Squadron and also because the raid mentioned was one that involved Ken. The citation read:

> This officer has continued to display outstanding gallantry and leadership in recent air operations. One night in May 1940, he led an attack on the oil depot at Bremen. The target was very heavily defended and difficult to identify owing to the exceptional number of searchlights but, after worrying and misleading the defences for an hour, he dived

and attacked from 1,000 feet to ensure hitting the target. His aircraft was hit by six shells, the last one of which did considerable damage but he succeeded in reaching his home base. Wing Commander Staton organises and leads his squadron on all new tasks with constant courage and his work on his station is magnificent.

Without doubt he was a considerable example to his men and Ken could not fail to have been inspired or influenced in some way from being on his command. This larger-than-life figure led instinctively through the sheer power of a massive personality and an invincible spirit. Ken was doubtless still feeling his way as an officer; but any junior officer would surely have found it daunting to emulate even one aspect of such a character.

A Whitley V bomber being bombed up, June 1940
[Photo: Courtesy of the RAF Museum, London (P022093)]

Activity on the Squadron left little time for reading the newspapers or following the news bulletins on the BBC, but Ken would have been aware the situation was going from bad to worse. Norway had surrendered and Italy had declared war on Britain and France. Anticipating Italy's involvement the RAF had planned raids on industrial targets in northern Italy and 10 Squadron mounted an operation to Turin on the 11 June, the day following Italy's declaration. This was supposed to be launched from an airfield in southern France but this plan was abandoned when local French people, fearing reprisals, blocked the runway. The reserve plan was to use the Channel Islands, but there were concerns among the crews that the airfields there were too small for the big bombers. In his usual style Wing Commander Staton showed his crews that it could be done, by making a landing and a take-off fully loaded. He also took part in the raid – leading from the front yet again.

Ken's mother visited him and his wife Teddie for his birthday on 12 June. Ken was now twenty-seven. Even though there was his promotion to celebrate as well as his birthday, with all the dreadful news any celebrations were probably muted.

At this time Ken signed the Squadron Operations Crew List as Squadron Operations Controller, standing in for the usual Controller Pilot Officer Harcourt-Powell. The Controller's task was to sort out the crewing-up problems and to arrange the crews in order of priority for the night's operations. He kept a full record of operations carried out by each aircrew and sorted out problems with sickness, injury and leave, working closely with the Squadron Commander. His was a pivotal role in a squadron, knowing all the aircrew and looking after their concerns, at the same time as supporting his commander. Ken was obviously given the opportunity to look at this senior role while not flying.

All that was left of the British Expeditionary Force at Dunkirk was back home by 4 June and by the middle of the month the remaining Allied land forces had been evacuated from west coast ports. After covering the last evacuations the RAF's Advanced Air Striking Force finally flew back to UK bases having been forced to withdraw its HQ further and further west. A small RAF contingent in Norway had also flown home. The French had wanted the Advanced Air Striking Force to move to southern France and then to North Africa so they could continue the fight from there, but a high level decision was taken to withdraw to England. Britain no longer had land forces in France and because the situation was becoming very grave we were going to need all our aircraft to defend ourselves.

Winston Churchill's famous "We shall fight on the beaches …" speech to the House of Commons on 4 June emphasised the gravity of the situation. He concluded:

I have, myself, full confidence that if all do their duty, if nothing is neglected, and if the best arrangements are made, as they are being made, we shall prove ourselves once again able to defend our Island home, to ride out the storm of war, and to outlive the menace of tyranny, if necessary for years, if necessary alone. At any rate, that is what we are going to try to do. That is the resolve of His Majesty's Government - every man of them. That is the will of Parliament and the nation. The British Empire and the French Republic, linked together in their cause and in their need, will defend to the death their native soil, aiding each other like good comrades to the utmost of their strength. Even though large tracts of Europe and many old and famous States have fallen or may fall into the grip of the Gestapo and all the odious apparatus of Nazi rule, we shall not flag or fail. We shall go on to the end, we shall fight in France, we shall fight on the seas and oceans, we shall fight with growing confidence and growing strength in the air, we shall defend our Island, whatever the cost may be, we shall fight on the beaches, we shall fight on the landing grounds, we shall fight in the fields and in the streets, we shall fight in the hills; we shall never surrender, and even if, which I do not for a moment believe, this Island or a large part of it were subjugated and starving, then our Empire beyond the seas, armed and guarded by the British Fleet, would carry on the struggle, until, in God's good time, the New World, with all its power and might, steps forth to the rescue and the liberation of the old.

The inevitable happened; France fell on 22 June. The following day, Sunday, Ken's sister wrote in her diary:

> What a day. The French signed their armistice. The terms are total capitulation. Made one want to weep for the millions of Frenchmen who would rather die. Well we'll make the stand if they can't – & what a stand it will be.

As she was writing this, Hitler was touring Paris in triumph. And so at the end of just ten months of war the whole of the European coast from Norway to Spain was in enemy hands. German Generals stood on the cliffs at Calais looking through their binoculars at the English coast a mere 20 miles away plotting invasion.

And what a ten months it had been for Ken. He had been called up, been granted a commission and had since been promoted to Flying Officer. He had been denied his hopes of becoming a pilot but instead had been trained as an air gunner and as a gunnery leader. He had been further trained for an operational crew during which he had been injured and had a spell in hospital. After that he had flown on night bombing operations over Norway, Germany and France, while taking on the responsibility of Squadron Gunnery Officer. For much of this time Ken was at the forefront of developments in Bomber Command, both in the field of air gunnery and in operations against the enemy. He was one of the first Gunnery Officers in the RAF, was on the first Gunnery Leader Course and introduced the new role of Squadron Gunnery Officer to his squadron. He had been flying in one of the largest bombers of the time with the most advanced gunnery defence system of any air force. His bombing operations were at night, for which he and his crew had little training, and at a time when navigation was still somewhat crude. He had taken part in the early raids on Norway and in the earliest large-scale attacks on targets inside Germany itself. If this was not enough, Ken even found time to get married.

4. The Summer of 1940 – Supporting the Battle of Britain

Britain now stood alone in Europe facing the all conquering might of Germany's forces now controlling all the European coasts from the Arctic to the Iberian Peninsula. The Luftwaffe commenced sorties against southern RAF installations in their effort to gain air superiority prior to the invasion – the beginning of The Battle of Britain. Plans for the invasion of England were being drawn up by Hitler and his generals – dark days indeed.

We were not totally alone though, as we had support from our then Empire countries; aircrew joined the RAF from Australia, New Zealand, Canada, South Africa and the Caribbean in particular. Also many Polish and Czech airmen who escaped before their countries were over-run made their way to Britain to fly with the RAF. Much needed supplies of equipment and armaments were provided by Canada. America was still neutral at this stage of the war but Roosevelt tacitly supported democratic Britain's stand against Nazi Germany. Congress passed a Neutrality Act that enabled Britain to buy supplies from America on a 'cash and carry' basis, that is to say purchases had to be settled in gold, from currency reserves or from the sale of investments in the US. Britain was then responsible for transportation to the UK. But our Atlantic convoys were coming under increasing threats from the German Navy. In July German U-boats began operating from the French port of Lorient, a new forward base enabling them to patrol for longer and further into the Atlantic. In August Hitler proclaimed a total blockade of the British Isles, which meant that even ships of neutral countries heading for British ports would be attacked.

The RAF's main priority was of course the defence of the airspace over southern England, the responsibility of Fighter Command. Throughout the Battle of Britain Bomber Command was under pressure to support Fighter Command by attacking airfields used by the Luftwaffe and more distant German aircraft factories. These tasks were in addition to maintaining the strategic offensive against important industrial targets, particularly oil installations, and attacking German shipping. 10 Squadron continued to be heavily involved in all of these. However, arguably Bomber Command's most significant contribution at that time was the prolonged series of raids against the German build up of barges at Channel ports in preparation for the invasion.

To add to the gloom, Ken would have received the dreadful news that Ray Lumb, the best man at his wedding in March, had not returned from an operation over Germany. Ray who was then with 77 Squadron at Driffield was the rear gunner of a Whitley V crew that took off in the evening of 29 June to bomb an explosives factory at Frankfurt. Eventually all the crew were reported killed.

Life at the station was too hectic to dwell on events, even the momentous events being played out in the skies above the Home Counties. Although Ken was not on operations at the time there was a lot to do. The Squadron was on the move, but not very far. A new RAF station had just opened at Leeming a dozen or so miles further north along the A1 Great North Road and the Squadron was to move there on 8 July. An advance party left Dishforth for Leeming on 6 July and the remainder of the Squadron, with the exception of five crews, moved on 8 July as planned. The five remaining crews were required for operations that night. Ken would have been busy making sure the move went smoothly for his twenty or so air gunners.

The Operations Room at RAF Leeming, 1940
[Photo: Courtesy of Carol Downer, Bufton Papers, Churchill Archives Centre, (BUFT6/6)]

RAF Leeming was almost brand new; night fighters of 219 Squadron on detachment from nearby Catterick had been there for a couple of weeks only before 10 Squadron arrived. Despite having up to date facilities and accommodation, a central avenue plus four large hangers in an arc, the airfield was still grass. There would have been a great deal to do to maintain the Squadron's operational capability over the move. The five aircraft that remained at Dishforth took off for Kiel on the night of the 8 July, but only four returned to join their new station and it would have been a while before news came through that the missing crew had survived and been captured. Poor weather conditions prevented operations for a few days but the Squadron was flying on operations again from the night of 12 July onwards.

Not only was the Squadron on new premises but also it was to have a new Officer Commanding. Wing Commander Staton was promoted to Group Captain and to Commander of the whole station at RAF Leeming. Wing Commander S O Bufton was appointed his successor at 10 Squadron, assuming command on 19 July. Welsh-born Sydney Bufton was about four years older than Ken and had an engineering background. Essentially he was altogether quieter and more thoughtful than his predecessor. He had joined the RAF in 1928 and trained as a pilot in Egypt. In 1939 he was posted to the Advance Headquarters (North) of the Advanced Air Striking Force at Chauny, north-east of Paris. But as the situation in France worsened in May and June 1940 his headquarters was forced to move further and further west, until on 17 June Wing Commander Bufton, Air Marshal Barratt and the last two remaining officers left Nantes and flew back to England landing at RAF Gatwick. Wing Commander Bufton made his way to London and there persuaded his old colleagues at the Air Ministry to appoint him to a squadron. They had wanted him to take up an engineering post in view of his background but eventually he was granted his wish and appointed Officer Commanding 10 Squadron. However, before he could take up his new posting he was required to take a two-week familiarisation course on the Whitley bomber at RAF Abingdon. Although an extremely experienced pilot, his experience to date had been daytime flying on single engine-aircraft.

Wing Commander S.O. 'Buf' Bufton,
later Air Vice-Marshal Bufton CB, DFC
[Photo: Courtesy of Carol Downer]

Initially Wing Commander Bufton would have relied heavily on Ken and his other squadron officers to help him become familiar with an operational heavy bomber squadron of about eighty airman and eighteen Whitley aircraft. He had quickly formed an impressive opinion of his predecessor whom he described as an enthusiastic, buccaneering, press-on perfectionist type whose squadron had achieved high standards of efficiency and morale. A difficult act to follow, he thought, but Wing Commander Bufton was to make his own mark on the RAF, as we shall see.

Ken was back on operations on 18 August and he was flying with the new Officer Commanding. Ken would have been aware that Wing Commander Bufton had been on just five operational trips so far – two as second pilot and three as captain. Even so Ken would have formed an opinion on how the new Officer Commanding stacked up as a captain, in particular from his debriefings of Wing Commander Bufton's current rear gunner, Sergeant Elcoate, who had been on the trips to Wismar, Gelsenkirchen and Turin. It seemed clear the Wing Commander was pretty determined to get to the target and very keen to bomb accurately – as Ken was soon to confirm for himself. Wing Commander Bufton needed to form a new crew when he promoted his second pilot to captain and allowed him to retain the other crew members. For his new crew Wing Commander Bufton selected Ken as rear gunner, and Ken flew with him for seven operations in all.

Briefing on 18 August was at 17.00 when the crews learned the target for that night was an aluminium factory at Rheinfelden in the very southwestern corner of Germany on the Swiss border. Ken's aircraft was due to be the first to take off at 20.00. But a problem arose as they prepared for take off. The wireless was dead, apparently affected by the steady rain for the past couple of days. A reserve aircraft was available already fuelled and bombed up, so the crew switched to that and eventually took off twenty minutes late. No sooner were they in the air when the wireless operator reported to Wing Commander Bufton that the wireless set on this aircraft had just failed. Normally in such circumstances the captain would abort the operation, turn the aircraft around and land. However Wing Commander Bufton decided that whilst the poor weather conditions had been good enough to take off they were not good enough to land in the fading light without radio assistance. He decided that rather than circle locally for hours till a visual landing could be made in daylight they might just as well fill in the time by continuing with the mission in the hope that the radio would dry out on route, and so it turned out.

The Squadron record for this operation reads:

Object. To cause maximum damage to targets allocated.

Target. Aluminium factory at RHEINFELDEN.

Alternative Target. Aerodrome at FREIBURG.

Last Resort. A.D.I.E.U.

Route. Base - Orfordness - target. Target - Orfordness - Base.

Time up 2020. The primary target was attacked from a height of 5,000 feet in two runs. All bursts were on target, and one burst on a building was followed by explosions and white sheets of flame.

Weather was good in the area, and identification of the target was rendered very easy.

No damage or casualties were sustained.

Time down 0605.

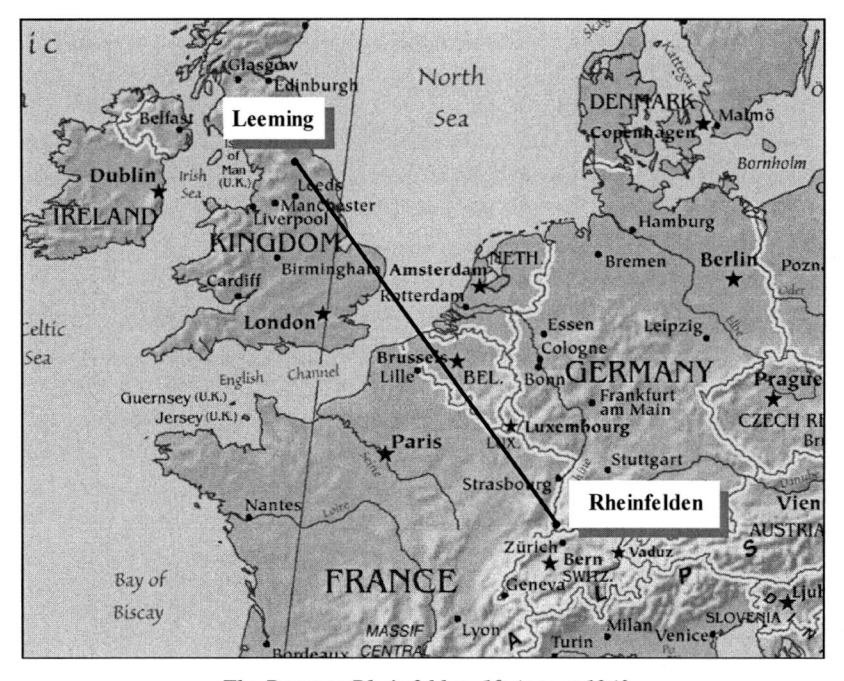

The Route to Rheinfelden, 18 August 1940

Ten aircraft from 10 Squadron attacked the same target that night and not everyone was so successful. One aircraft that left later experienced worsening weather and when they reached the target it was obscured by cloud. They spent as long as they could in the target area but with no luck, then headed for the alternative target. That too was under heavy cloud and in the end they headed for home, landing back at base with their bomb load intact after nine frustrating hours mostly over enemy territory.

A busy August saw the loss of four Squadron aircraft, the first on the night of 13 August that led to a remarkable rescue. Wing Commander Bufton had led a raid by ten Squadron aircraft to the Fiat works at Turin, during which one of the Whitleys was shot up badly by an Italian night fighter. Crippled with one engine put out of action and a damaged aileron the pilot struggled back over the Alps but could not maintain height across France. Over the English Channel the aircraft sank lower and lower until the pilot realised he could not reach the shore where he had hoped to be able to make a landing on a beach. About a mile off Hythe near Folkestone he was preparing to ditch when the weak aileron broke off and the aircraft crashed into the sea, killing the captain and second pilot.

The aircraft sank rapidly but the other three crew managed to escape – but without their dinghy. They inflated their Mae Wests and tried to make for the shore, but drifted apart. Luckily the crash was witnessed by two fishermen on shore, one of them a former lifeboatman. They set out in their boat and managed to rescue the observer and rear gunner. Another witness was a young physical training instructress at Dymchurch, who was also an Air Raid Precautions ambulance driver. Apparently still wearing pyjamas, Miss Peggy Prince pushed out her river canoe, helped by a soldier, and they began to search for the survivors, but returned without finding anyone. Not satisfied, Miss Prince set out again – on her own. This time she found Sergeant Marshall, the wireless operator, clinging to a buoy. Somehow, she managed to get the exhausted airman into her canoe and paddled back to shore, undoubtedly saving his life. For her courage and determination she was awarded the Order of the British Empire. Back at the Squadron, Sergeant Marshall was greeted by something like, "Trust you to be rescued by a young lady in her nightwear!"

Three more aircraft were lost before the month was out, two over Italy and one over Holland; in all six crew were killed, the remainder becoming POWs.

At a time when long distance navigation was still very rudimentary, August saw the introduction of an experimental navigation aid. A High Frequency Direction Finding radio beacon had been set up at Buster Hill, a high point on the South Downs, which aircraft could pick up from over 500 miles away – a much needed additional aid.

Ken's sister followed the news of the war even more closely than before. Day by day in late August the newspaper headlines were about air raids on London and air battles over the coast. On the evening of Monday 26 August she wrote in her diary:

> Mr Mayfield said the German planes were over Northampton for 2 hours last night and crossed over Duston [the village on the edge of Northampton where they lived]. As I'm writing 10.15pm 3 or 4 explosions have just shaken the windows and made rather a noise (Bombs?).

She learned the next day that bombs had destroyed a bungalow and damaged three others not far away and a local Air Raid Precautions warden had been electrocuted when he accidentally picked up a live electricity cable that had been brought down. With a friend she went along to see the damage. She wrote:

> By Jove they've made a mess of the bungalow and all the houses round had broken windows. Saw several bomb craters.

Just about a month into his new posting, Wing Commander Bufton wrote a letter to his father in which he set out his thoughts on his role and responsibilities. His words give a vivid insight into the mind of a bomber squadron commander at that critical period of the war. He wrote:

This week I am Station Commander, and am lord of some 1,800 souls. I'm off flying till the Station Commander comes back from leave next Sunday, so I do get a good night's sleep, and I'm seizing the opportunity of getting my correspondence licked into shape. Hence this letter.

The job – Squadron Commander – is really grand. It is the finest in the RAF and is <u>the</u> most important one. You are wrong when you say the Staff jobs I've held are more important.

We in the squadrons are the knife edge of the huge organisation behind us – in the Station, the Group, Bomber Command, the Air Ministry, the War Cabinet, the Govt., the whole aircraft industry with its sub-industries and thousands of workers. We are the knife edge, and mine is the responsibility of keeping it sharp and gleaming and directing its blow aright.

This is a fascinating and unending task. First the maintenance organisation must run like clockwork giving us our aircraft in a state of 100% efficiency, so that their engines do not falter in their 10 hour flights across the enemy territory, across 400 miles of sea each way in between, or across the gleaming peaks and yawning chasms of the Alps. Our guns and turrets must work with battleship precision; our radio must develop no fault for often with it we must feel our way home, and down through the clouds into the valleys where our bases lie. Each aircraft is as complicated as a submarine, and each must be perfect.

Then the operational Flights must be at all times trained to perfection. Each aircraft crew must be balanced and drilled like a hockey team.[1] The new arrivals must be fitted in and coached along under the care of the captain, older ones must be selected for captaincies when they become capable of bearing the responsibility. Characters must be weighed up; capabilities assessed. Defects or failures must be sifted in minute detail and explained to all crews so that they may avoid the same mistakes.

A squadron is not an organisation or a unit; it is a living writhing power which must be groomed, trained, and directed at its objective with everything done to make it effective, and with its mind filled only with a determination to find it and destroy it. For on these missions, when wireless fails, or motors falter; when ice gets you in its white clutching fingers, or black thunder clouds engulf you and there are still hundreds of miles of empty ocean, and the enemy's defences in front of you, it is determination which governs the captains' sole decision.

---

[1] W/Cdr Bufton played hockey for Wales, the combined services and the RAF.

The things that matter most in a squadron are a firm conviction that your squadron is the best there is, and a determination to do all you can to keep it that way.

For all this the squadron commander is responsible, and all this can only be fully achieved by leading, rather than by pointing the way.

So you see why this is the most important job in the RAF – and the most interesting job in the world.

A month later Wing Commander Bufton wrote another letter to his father in which he turned down a request for a contribution to a Spitfire fundraising scheme his father was involved with. Rather bluntly, he concluded:

If I did send anything it would naturally be a gift. However, I don't think we should be expected to fly the planes and buy the ruddy things too, so I'm not sending anything.

On the first anniversary of the outbreak of war, 3 September 1940, coincidentally Ken made his first visit to Berlin. He was again with Wing Commander Bufton in the same aircraft as the previous raid but with a different second pilot, observer and wireless operator. The primary target was an electricity transformer station in the Friedrichsfelde district of Berlin. This was one of the first operations by Bomber Command against the German capital; the War Cabinet had just authorised Berlin as a target in retaliation for the first German bombing of central London on 23/24 August.

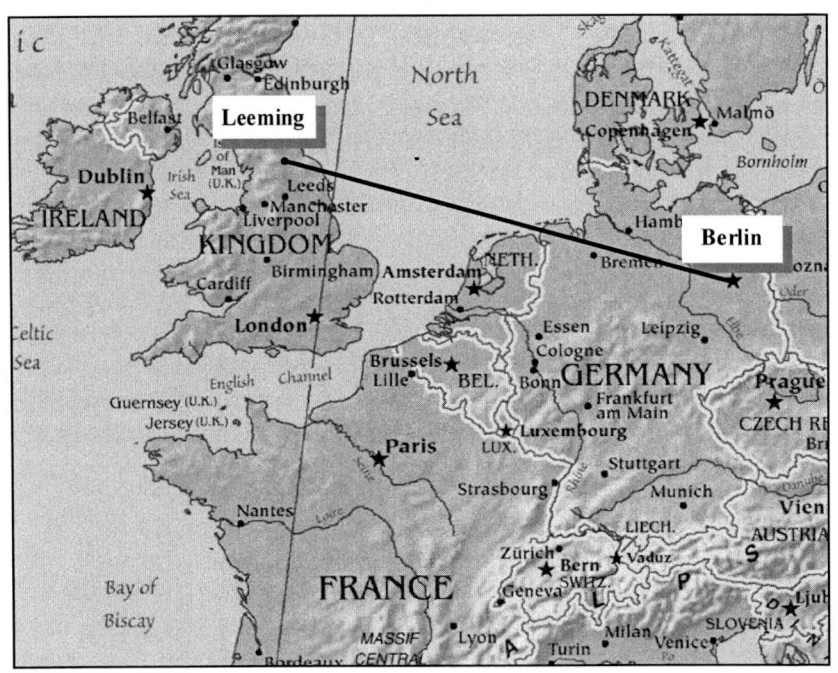

The Route to the 'Big City', Berlin, 3 September 1940

The squadron record for Ken's aircraft reads:

<u>Object.</u> To cause the maximum damage to targets allocated

<u>Target.</u> Power Transformer Station, Berlin

<u>Alternative Target.</u> Coal Gas Works, Berlin

<u>Last Resort.</u> S.I.M.O. or R.O.P.A.

<u>Route.</u> Base – Flamboro' Head – Target. Target – Flamboro' Head – Base.

Time up 2044. The primary target could not be located by this aircraft on account of the darkness, but an unsuccessful attack was made on a searchlight at Berlin with 1/250lb. bomb from 5,000 feet at 0205 hrs. An aerodrome was then attacked South of Berlin with 5/250lb. and 1/800lb. bombs at 0230 hours. Two bombs held up; no results were observed of this attack.

Weather conditions were 10/10ths. Cloud over Bremen and the target area at variable depths; also haze. Flak fire was intense, and a piece of shrapnel pierced the windscreen. Over Emden & Bremen, Oldenburg, Munster and Berlin Flak was also intense and fairly accurate. Time down 0605.

The casual mention of shrapnel piercing the windscreen in the above record and in Wing Commander Bufton's flying logbook below masks a very close shave. A near-miss flak explosion sent a piece of shrapnel the size of a walnut through the windscreen between Wing Commander Bufton and second pilot Squadron Leader McNair.

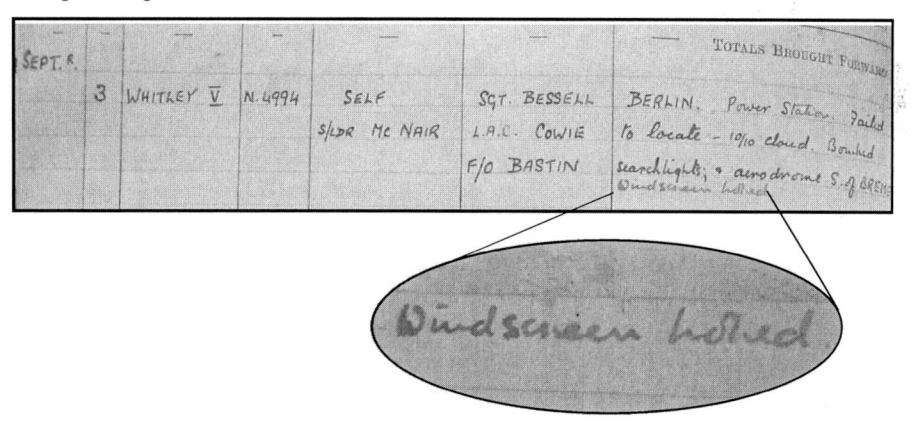

Wing Commander Bufton's Flying Logbook entry for 3 September 1940
[Image: Courtesy of Carol Downer, Bufton Papers, Churchill Archives Centre (BUFT2/4)]

Despite the weather one aircraft reported a direct hit and the gas works in Danzigerstrasse was also hit and a large fire started. But not everyone found the target because of the heavy cloud and haze and several chose targets of military importance around Berlin. Meanwhile weather conditions at home were closing in with mist reducing visibility considerably. One returning aircraft from the Squadron could not locate their base aerodrome and running out of fuel crash-landed at Nether Silton, near Northallerton. The aircraft was a total wreck, but fortunately there were no casualties.

The Daily Telegraph headlines of 3 September talked of more raids over London and a 'Day of Thrilling Air Battles'. Keen to portray positive statistics it mentions, 'Since mass air attacks on Britain began on 8 August 1,100 Nazi raiders have been destroyed. The Royal Air Force has lost 314 machines in these operations, but 158 pilots are safe.'

Phyllis wrote in her diary:

> Heard that bombs had fallen in Overstone Park and in a field near Weston Farell [where her mother lived]. Phoned to see if Mum was OK – she was. Tony [her husband] went to bed early as he had to go on [Home Guard] duty from 1am – 5am.

On the morning of the day after Ken got back from Berlin he was put in charge of that night's invasion stand-by party of three pilots and their aircraft. But within a few hours he was pulled off because Bomber Command wanted him to attend a conference on gunnery at Norwood, and by midday he had set off in his own car. At least a conference was one way of getting out of night duty and a welcome diversion from the relentless operational pressure on the Squadron.

Back from the gunnery conference, it was not long before Ken found he was on operations again. Wing Commander Bufton put himself down for the operation on the night of 11 September to Bremen. Bremen was very heavily defended, as the older crews knew only too well from their visit in May. This time the second pilot was Pilot Officer J A S Russell – Ken would subsequently fly with him on a number of sorties. Other Whitley squadrons were making the long trip to Berlin that night, which was a constant target at this stage together with the Channel ports.

During briefing at 14.00 hours crews were advised that all Squadron aircraft flying that night carried a new device called I.F.F. (Identification Friend Or Foe). When switched on this emitted a radio signal identifying the aircraft as friendly to UK defence tracking stations. To an extent it removed the concern of returning crews that they could be shot at by their own coastal defences, which occasionally happened. For the first time Ken's plane carried this new equipment; he must have hoped it worked properly.

The Operations Record Book for that night reads:

> Object. To cause maximum damage to shipyards and engineering buildings at the Dockyards and Petroleum Sheds.
>
> Target. Bremen
>
> Alternative Target. Wilhelmshaven
>
> Last Resort. Emden
>
> Route. Base – Flamboro' Head – Target – Flamboro' Head – Base.

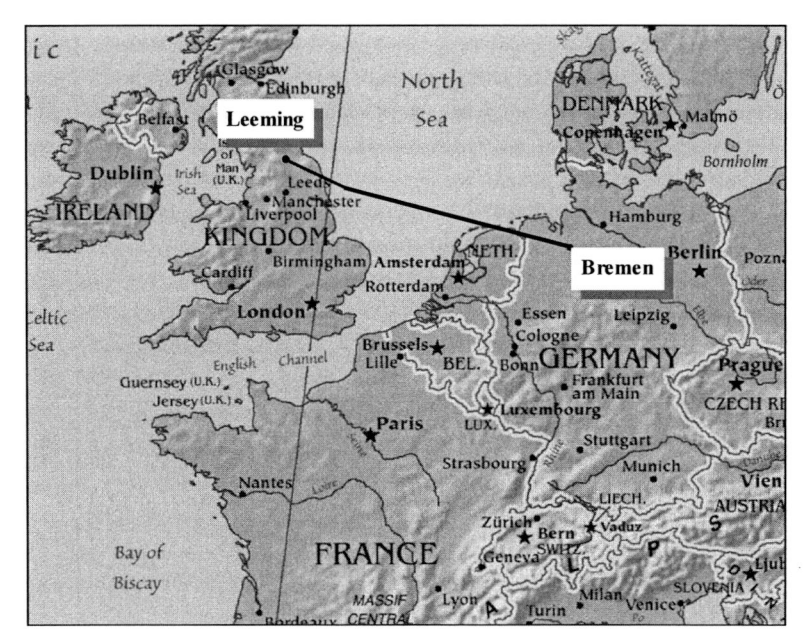

The Route to Bremen, 11 September 1940

Time up 1943. The primary target was successfully attacked by this aircraft between 2232 and 2259 hours from a height of 10,000 feet.

Weather conditions:- Broken cloud and ground haze. A red Very light – a signal by an earlier aircraft – was seen at back and E.T.A. over target area, also large fires were seen in the area; the aircraft was illuminated by these fires.

All bombs were dropped in one stick in direction N.N.E. to S.S.W. at 2253 hours, as it was apparent that it was clouding over.

Bursts were seen on the dockside parallel to some warehouses, which were on fire. On the North side immense fires broke out at once. This crew reported that the main fitting shops were adequately ablaze. All these fires were visible eighty miles away, but were obscured by clouds; in fact this aircraft made use of the fires by taking back bearings as an aid to navigation.

One compartment of incendiaries failed to drop.

AA fire was intense and accurate, but no damage was sustained.

The automatic pilot was very erratic, attempting to slow roll to port and when corrected dived the aircraft vertically.

It was reported that blast furnaces at Stockton on Tees were very badly blacked out.

Aerodromes were seen at 270º Bremen, forty miles away, probably Ipener and Huttesen.

Time down 0230.

From what was recorded this trip seems to have had its moments, with heavy ground fire as might have been expected over Bremen and with the autopilot playing havoc – both pretty disconcerting for Ken in the rear turret. Interestingly the record gives an insight into what Ken could see as they headed away from the target area. It also illustrates how Ken could occasionally help his navigator by giving regular bearings on a known point to the rear of the aircraft, this time the fires. Another aircraft too reported being able to see the fires from sixty miles away as it headed homeward. All planes returned safely and all the captains reported bombing the target.

Not all was well, however. Shortly after landing, Ken was to make a very disturbing discovery involving one of his squadron gunnery sergeants: a case of the Marie Celeste gun turret.

Ten minutes before Ken's aircraft landed, Flight Lieutenant Tomlinson had brought his aircraft down and reported Sergeant Angus McIntosh, his rear gunner, missing in most unusual circumstances. His report stated:

> This aircraft was "picked-up" by searchlights and evasive action was carried out to clear these; afterwards the Captain called up the Tail Gunner on the inter-communication, but received no reply. It was subsequently discovered that the Tail Gunner had abandoned the aircraft.

Further on the report reads:

> Damage was sustained to the elevator of this machine – apparently caused by the Tail Gunner when he abandoned the aircraft.

It was subsequently discovered that Sergeant McIntosh had been taken prisoner and had not been hurt when bailing out, but at the time his mysterious disappearance caused some unease. The truth of the matter is no doubt recorded in the Squadron's records.

> Searchlights were very active and held several aircraft; this caused one aircraft to carry out violent evasive action, after which it was discovered that the rear gunner had abandoned the aircraft – presumably believing that the aircraft had been shot down.

It seems clear from these records that Flight Lieutenant Tomlinson had not given the order to abandon the aircraft. Normally crew would hold station until the order was given. Thinking a crash was imminent, yet hearing no order, did Sergeant McIntosh call over the intercom only for his words to be drowned out by the noise of the screaming engines and general mayhem of the aircraft straining through a violent manoeuvre at nearly twice its normal speed? Flight Lieutenant Tomlinson doubtless needed all his strength and concentration to control the aircraft and bring it out of the manoeuvre. Did he not hear, or did he hear but delay responding? Whatever did or did not happen, Sergeant McIntosh made the decision to save his life and bailed out. Ken would have enquired into the circumstances surrounding the loss of one of his gunners; little knowing that he too would be faced with an almost similar set of circumstances before the month was out.

On the night of 17 September 10 Squadron scheduled ten aircraft to attack the German battleship Bismarck berthed at Hamburg. Ken was again with Wing Commander Bufton, the same crew and in the same aircraft as the previous raid.

This was a record night for Bomber Command – 194 aircraft were despatched, the greatest number of bombers since war began. Well over half were targeting the Channel ports and the assembled invasion barges; the remainder were sent to various targets in Germany.

The mighty Bismarck had been commissioned only a month earlier, and intelligence indicated she was setting off for sea trails in the Baltic.

Briefing was at 16.00 hours which no doubt described the heavy defences to be expected. This is what was recorded for this operation:

Object. To disable the Bismarck or Tirpitz: to prevent their moving from harbour.

Target. The Bismarck at Hamburg.

Alternative Target. The Tirpitz at Wilhelmshaven.

Last Resort. Petroleum Sheds at Emden

Route. Base – Flamboro' Head – Target – Flamboro' Head – Base.

Time up 2219. This aircraft attacked the primary target between 0044 and 0118 hours from heights of 12,000 and 10,500 feet. The first attack, at 0100 hours, consisted of 1/500 and 3/250lb. S.A.P. bombs, in direction 140°. The second, at 0117 hours, was made up of 1/500 and 3/250lb. S.A.P. bombs and twenty 4lb. incendiaries, and was carried out in direction 260°.

Bursts were observed on the docks, 4,000 yards East of the dock where the Bismarck is lying, but from the second attack bursts were not seen to fall on the ship, but across the dock in which the Bismarck is lying.

A.A. fire was intense and accurate and mainly of light calibre, but no damage was sustained.

Weather conditions were 9/10ths cloud over target area. This aircraft waited about twenty minutes so that a gap in the clouds would come over the target.

The Island of Norderney was well defended by flak fire, which was intense and accurate to 11,000 ft. Three green flares were shot up, accurate for height and direction, and burnt for 20 seconds; the aircraft was then at 12,000 feet. These were possibly indicatory points for fighter aircraft.

Shipping activity was noted 5 miles off Spurn Head.

Time down 0542.

Waiting around for twenty minutes for a decent sighting of the target and making two runs over a heavily defended area made for a rather tense trip for Ken and the rest of the crew, but again demonstrated Wing Commander Bufton's determination to be certain of his target.

The raid was considered successful with eight aircraft claiming to have bombed the target according to the de-briefings by returning crews. Of the ten aircraft from 10 Squadron, one aircraft failed to take off – wireless trouble delayed take off, by which time the engine plugs had oiled up and there was not enough power to attempt take off. The other one returned after about twenty minutes because the hydraulics to the tail turret failed.

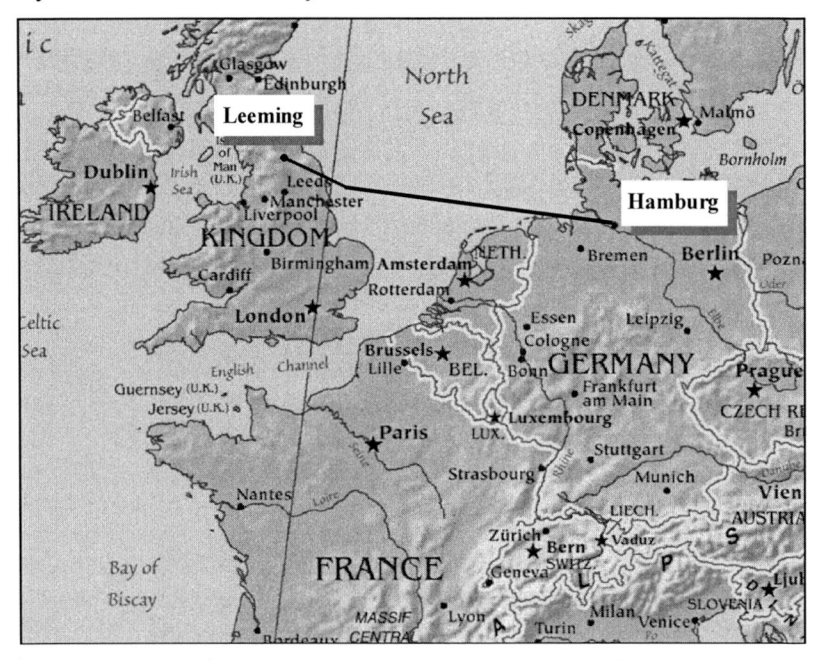

The Route to Hamburg, 17 September 1940

But what the crews did not know was that the real target was not there!

The Bismarck was not at Hamburg that night, having left two days earlier. In preparation for her acceptance trials, she had moved to Kiel via the Elbe and through the 60 odd miles of the Wilhelm Canal, which joins the North Sea with the Baltic. The Bismarck was actually at anchor at Scheerhafen, Kiel, on the night of 17 September. It is possible the Germans moved another ship into the berth vacated by the Bismarck and camouflaged it to look like the Bismarck. If agents had observed her movements, intelligence on her departure had obviously not filtered back quickly enough to cancel or amend the operation to bomb her at her berth in Hamburg docks.

Bismarck's career was short. Together with the heavy cruiser Prinz Eugen, she broke out into the North Sea on 20 May 1941. Shortly afterwards the two German ships were detected by British air reconnaissance and the British Navy set out to attack them. In the first skirmish the famous battle-cruiser HMS Hood, the pride of the Royal Navy between the two world wars, was disastrously sunk by gunfire from the Bismarck on 24 May. Eventually the

Bismarck was sunk on the morning of 27 May 1941 after a torpedo had jammed her steering the previous day. The Prinz Eugen escaped and headed for Brest, where she joined the German battleships Scharnhorst and Gneisenau.

Night after night Bomber Command continued with raids on key railways and canals in its efforts to disrupt Germany's build-up of invasion troops and supplies.

The Bismarck leaving Hamburg for the first time on 15 September 1940
[Photo: Courtesy of KBismarck.com]

Just three nights after the Hamburg raid, Ken was on operations again. 10 Squadron were to split their ten aircraft over three German railway targets, at Hamm, Soest and Ehrang. Ken was with the same team in the Wing Commander's aircraft, which had the Squadron identification letter 'U', for Uncle. Their allocated target was the important railway marshalling yards at Ehrang in the Saar district close to the Luxembourg border.

Ken's aircraft was to carry an experimental new secret weapon called 'Razzle'. Razzle was an incendiary device invented in America. It was a small sandwich of celluloid containing a piece of phosphorous. Whilst in water the pellets of phosphorous were inert, but when sufficiently dried out after contact with the air they ignited spontaneously. Scattered via a special chute in the aircraft, the idea was to set fire to crops and forests causing physical damage and affecting local morale.

This episode with Razzle was the only time Ken was involved with it. Early the previous month Wing Commander Bufton had given a demonstration on how to use Razzle and it had been dropped on a couple of occasions since. The devices were carried in the aircraft in watertight cans, about fifty of them, and at the right point these were unsealed and the contents, water and all, were emptied down the chute. A garden type spay pump was provided to wash away any that stuck in the chute!

Needless to say, aircrews were very sceptical at carrying such a dangerous cargo – a fire on board being one of the hazards most feared. And their fears were proved right, as on the first occasion Razzle was used by the Squadron six aircraft suffered damage by burning pieces. On one aircraft the pellets had been swept by the slipstream and lodged in the control hinges of the elevators. Although they dried out on the journey back to base, they did not immediately ignite due to the strong airflow. However once the aircraft slowed on landing they set fire to the fabric of the tailpiece. Fortunately it was only a small fire, noticed by the crew on taxiing to the dispersal area and ground staff quickly put it out.

Similar experiences elsewhere meant that Razzle was not popular. Fortunately for the crews they did not have to carry it for long as results were considered poor and the experiment abandoned after a few months.

The Squadron record outlined the night's work as follows. For the first time alternative targets included 'Self Evident Military Objective' (S.E.M.O.) and 'Military Objective Previously Attacked' (M.O.P.A.). As we shall see a military objective, Trier aerodrome, presented itself and was attacked.

> Object. To cause maximum damage and dislocation to marshalling yards allotted and storage sidings.
>
> Target. Hamm (4 aircraft), Soest (2 aircraft) and Ehrang (4 aircraft).
>
> Alternative Targets. For Hamm & Soest aircraft – Schwerte, and for Ehrang aircraft S.E.M.O., M.O.P.A.
>
> Last Resort Target. All aircraft S.E.M.O., M.O.P.A.
>
> Route. Base – Hornsea – Target – Hornsea – Base.

The official report below masks the drama that unfolded over the target.

> Time up 2114. This aircraft was in the target area between 0115 and 0120 hours at varying heights of 6,000 to 10,000 feet, but could not locate the target because of 10/10ths cloud down to 2,000 feet. An attack was then made on the aerodrome at Trier as a last resort. This aerodrome was fully illuminated with a flare path in use. Four hangers with white lights were seen.
>
> One attack was carried out consisting of 3/250lb and 1/500lb. bombs at 0036 hours from 5,000 feet. A.A. fire of light and heavy calibre was intense and accurate. The aircraft descended to 2,000 feet and the front and rear gunners put out several searchlights, which were of great intensity.
>
> This aircraft then carried out an attack on a factory 1 mile east of Maastricht, where 3/250lb & 1/500lb bombs were dropped at 0145 hours from 8,000 feet; the attack was made on the glide.

Razzle was carried out between the two attacks at 0120 hours.

The aircraft was hit several times in the action at Trier, where A.A. fire and searchlights had proved extremely trying. As a result of the first attack one hanger was seen to be hit and the tarmac was struck. The remainder of the bombs fell on the aerodrome.

At Maastricht a large fire was started which could be seen for 50 miles after leaving the target. Some of the damage to the aircraft was caused by machine gun fire.

An aerodrome was also seen 5,000 yards North West of the aerodrome at Trier which was attacked.

At 80 miles North West of Maastricht a lighthouse flashing every 4 seconds and a beacon flashing YD were seen; both were white.

A.A. fire at Maastricht was moderate and of heavy calibre.

At 2234 hours two ships were seen heading 270° with guns firing just prior to aircraft arriving over them.

Large fires were seen at Ostend and Flushing.

No casualties were sustained.

Time down 0434.

Many years later Wing Commander Bufton wrote an account of the events that night, and what follows is based on his detailed writings, which include exchanges between the crew over the intercom system.

When the crew arrived in the Saar area about 00.15 the cloud over the target was difficult and they could not locate Ehrang. They dropped flares and searched for three quarters of an hour without any success, quite enough time in a potentially hostile area, and Wing Commander Bufton decided to abandon the primary target. In Wing Commander Bufton's words, 'At that point a very fruity looking airfield presented itself.' They could see the tarmac and the outline of the hangers. Identifying it as Trier Airfield he decided to attack it. He announced his intentions over the intercom saying the first run in would be a glide at 5,000 feet when he wanted half the bomb load dropped, followed by a low level run for the remaining bombs. Ken would have been listening to the exchanges on the intercom, anticipating some German reaction to their airfield being attacked.

Wing Commander Bufton brought the Whitley round to port and Sergeant Bessell, the navigator, moved to the bomb aiming position and took over guiding the aircraft to the bombing point. Wing Commander Bufton eased back the throttles and the roar of the engines died away as he put the aircraft into a glide towards the target. Little could be heard now other than the whistle of the slipstream, then there was a momentary rumble as the bomb doors opened. Sergeant Bessell could see dead ahead the dim image of the airfield. He confirmed one 500lb bomb and three 250lb bombs had been selected. "Steady. As she is. Left a little," he guided the captain in. "Bombs gone," he soon announced. Ken would have been on the alert for action and to see what they had achieved.

Almost immediately after the bombs had been released, all hell let loose. A blue searchlight caught their aircraft in its brilliant beam, followed immediately by at least a dozen others catching the aircraft in a cone of light in the night sky. Because the plane was much lower than the usual bombing height the intensity of the light was blinding and it was almost impossible to see; even Wing Commander Bufton had to duck below the cockpit combing in order to see his instruments. Moments later the flak began to burst all around them; not very accurate immediately, as the gunners below needed a few shots to get their range.

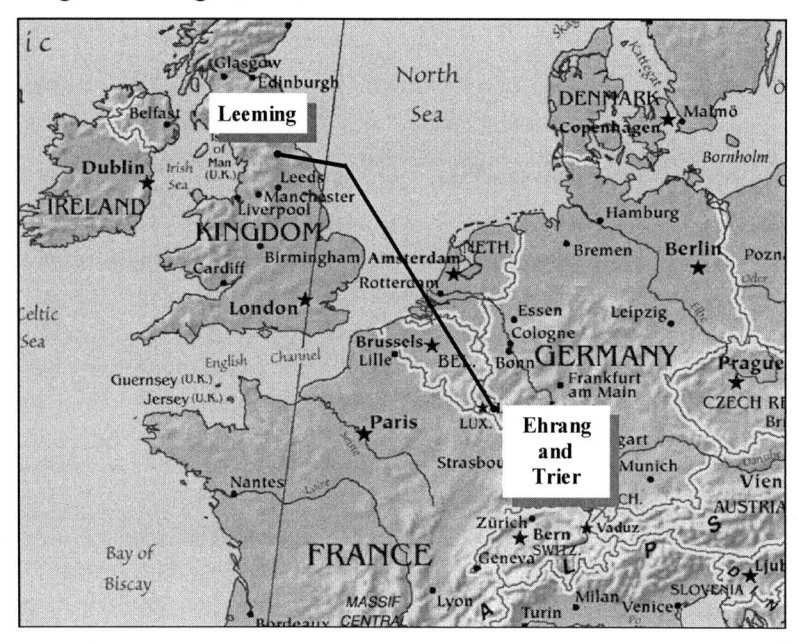

The Route to Ehrang, 20 September 1940

Wing Commander Bufton put into action his plan for such a deadly situation. Opening the throttles right up he announced to the crew that he was diving down wind and ordered the bomb doors shut at once. Then he pushed the nose of the aircraft steeply down and swung hard to eastward heading down wind. The theory was to gain as much speed as quickly as possible hoping to take the aircraft away from the area and out of the searchlight cone, at the same time rapidly changing altitude making it difficult for the flak gunners to range their ammunition.

Ken in the rear turret was probably blinded but could feel the aircraft accelerating earthward, knowing they had been at a relatively low altitude when all this started. The air speed kept building and building until Ken must have sensed they were hurtling at nearly twice normal speed, close to the aircraft's terminal speed of 280mph, beyond which it was not built to go.

Heavy and light flak was bursting all around and a near miss rocked the plane. Ken concluded they were about to crash and prepared to bail out. Taking off his intercom earphones, he pushed open the doors of his turret and reached back inside the fuselage for his parachute, clipping it on as quickly as possible. He swung the turret sideways ready to fall out backwards into the blackness.

Whilst Ken was deciding he had only moments to get out Wing Commander Bufton realised he could get no more speed and with the altimeter showing below 4,000 feet, eased the nose up, aiming for the darkness beyond the cone of light. But more searchlights opened up ahead of them. He ordered Pilot Officer Russell, the second pilot, to the front guns to try and put out as many lights as possible and called to Ken to do the same as they passed over the lights. When no response came from Ken, he ordered Sergeant Cowie the wireless operator back to investigate.

But then Ken sensed the aircraft coming under control and suddenly the face of Sergeant Cowie appeared out of the end of the fuselage. Seeing him made Ken realise all was not lost and he swung his turret back in line – relief must have flooded over him. The Sergeant told him to reconnect his intercom and report in to the captain, which Ken did hurriedly saying, "Tail Gunner to Skipper; sorry, thought we had had it."

The Wing Commander's voice came through to Ken, "Roger, Tail Gunner. We're heading away. I'm going to level out in a moment at 1,000 feet; daren't go any lower on the altimeter. Try and put the lights out with your guns, and clobber any flak batteries you can see." Ken acknowledged the order, stowed his parachute and opened up his guns with relish. With all guns blazing away the aircraft shuddered from nose to tail. Yet still more searchlights appeared in front of them and light flak was hosing up at them from all directions. Over the intercom came the Wing Commander, "Tail Gunner from Skipper. Can't you put those ruddy lights out. We must be just over their heads now." Ken responded, "I'm trying hard Skipper. Have put about four out, but my barrels are overheating now." "Never mind the barrels; just keep firing till they jam," was the reply. "Roger, Skip."

Suddenly, U for Uncle sprung out of the cone of lights and into the welcoming darkness, somewhere east of Trier, still with half its bomb load on board. With huge relief all round the crew heard the captain tell Sergeant Bessell he would climb to 8,00 feet on the current heading to take them well clear of Trier, then ask for a heading for base. But in true commander style he added they would attack any likely looking target on the way. After a few minutes Sergeant Bessell advised the Wing Commander to climb for ten minutes then steer 325°. Once matters had settled down, Sergeant Cowie made his way back down the fuselage, this time to pour the contents of the Razzle cans down the special chute. By about 01.30 they were approaching the area near Aachen when Sergeant Bessell reported seeing what seemed to be an industrial plant with a furnace flaring occasionally. Perhaps a steel plant at Maastricht, he thought, and suggested dropping the remaining bombs on that. Wing Commander Bufton agreed and again he set up the aircraft for a glide attack. Again Ken must have braced himself for action. But this time there was far less drama, the attack went smoothly and the remaining bombs were dropped in one stick. Ken could see the bombs straddle the target and start large fires as the captain put on full power to climb away back on heading 325°. There was some flak but that died away and as U for Uncle sped for the coast Ken could see the fires for quite a while. At 02.16 Sergeant Bessell wrote in his navigation log about the lighthouse and Ken too would have seen its sweeping beam gradually disappear behind them as they headed out over the North Sea. At 02.40 Sergeant Bessell recorded they were flying at 12,000 feet in 9/10th cloud and that his estimated time of arrival at Hornsea, the planned crossing point on the Yorkshire coast, was 04.40, underlined twice. U for Uncle made better than expected progress as Flamborough Head, just north of Hornsea, was sighted at 04.06, and Sergeant Bessell wrote in his log, '04.07 Set course Base 292°M ETA 04.30'. Then at 04.30 he wrote 'Base' and finally in large writing, '04.41 Landed – Thank God'. The operation had lasted just under seven and a half hours.

The Final Entries in Sergeant Bessell's Navigation Log for the Operation to Ehrang
[Image: Courtesy of Carol Downer, Bufton Papers, Churchill Archives Centre (BUFT3/3)]

When the ground crew got to look at the aircraft they counted thirty-six holes in the skin.

The heavy raids on London and other major cities led to children being evacuated again. On Sunday 22 September Ken's sister wrote:

Nice morning – but no invasion – air raids not so severe last night. Evacuees arrived. I took in two sisters aged 14 & 6.

These two sisters May and Daphne, came from a poor home in the East End of London and were rather slow and naive. Phyllis thought May, the older of the two, should help around the house but was somewhat taken aback when, having asked her to lay the table, found she had used newspaper for a tablecloth. Although needing help and encouragement, the sisters were nevertheless essentially kind and good. The following Thursday Phyllis recorded in her diary:

Heard that the bombs that rattled our windows fell near Towcester!! Most people heard them. May and Daphne brought me some lovely blackberries.

That same afternoon, 27 September, Ken attended the 15.30 crew briefing – the target that night was the port of Lorient, on the southern coast of the Brittany peninsula. The aim was the destruction and dislocation of invasion preparations, a recurring theme at this time.

The route to the south coast was down an allocated corridor, crossing the coast at Bognor Regis and across the Channel to the target via occupied Cherbourg, which was the alternative target. This was seen as a pleasant change from having to cross the North Sea and then spend nail-biting hours over the heavily defended German mainland to targets well over six hundred miles from base. On the face of it this trip carried less risk but through the summer the Germans had strengthened their air defences and had extended them into the occupied territories so attacking Lorient was by no means risk free.

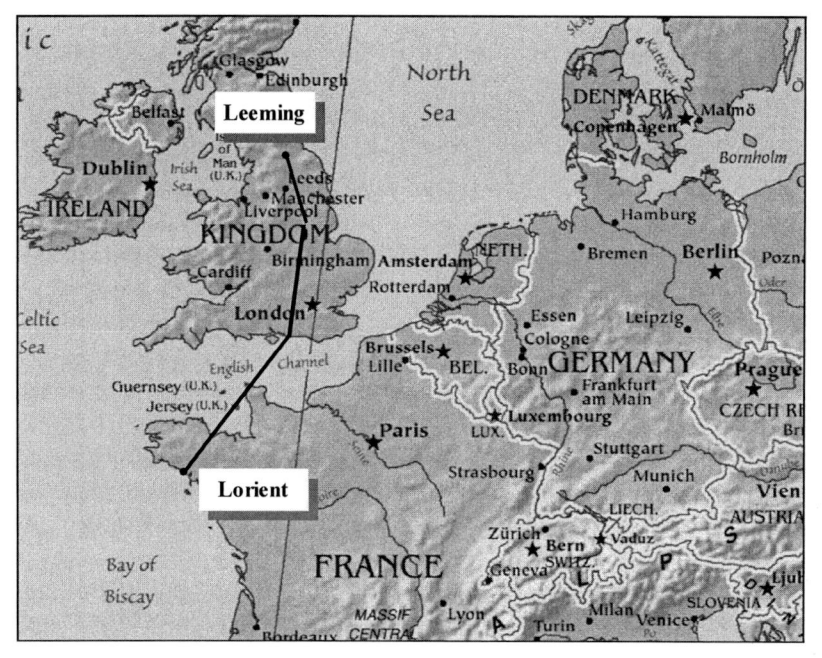

The Route to Lorient, 27 September 1940

Ken was with Wing Commander Bufton and the usual crew, Pilot Officer Russell, Sergeant Bessell and Sergeant Cowie. Take off was at 19.39, and for once the weather was good.

The Squadron record reads:

Object. To destroy and dislocate Invasion Preparations.

Target. LORIENT.

Alternative Target. Any Invasion Port, S.E.M.O. or M.O.P.A.

Route:- Base – Finningley – Harwell – Bognor Regis – Cherbourg – Target – Cherbourg – Bognor Regis – Harwell – Finningley – Base.

The primary target was attacked by this aircraft between 23.00 and 23.10 hours from 9,000 feet. The weather was good, but there was slight haze. The target was identified by a green signal over a flare dropped by another aircraft.

The first attack was made at 23.00 hours from North to South and consisted of 3/250 and 1/500lb. bombs. The second was from South to North nine minutes later and was made up of the same number and weight of bombs. Bombs from the first attack fell along wharves on the Eastern side, north of the Pont du Caudan.

Bombs from the second fell across the area North and South of the bridge.

Fires were started and green explosions noted in rapid succession.

A.A. fire was fairly intense as regards light calibre; heavy calibre was moderate. Neither was very accurate.

Searchlights were moderate and fairly well handled. No signal was received from this aircraft owing to a W/T failure (Transmitter).

A Beacon was seen at Cap Frehel, west of St Malo, flashing every 5 seconds at 22.25 hours.

East of Cherbourg a white beacon was seen flashing every four seconds.

The black-out at Rugby, Leicester and Nottingham was very bad, especially marshalling yards. At Oxford streets were clearly lit up.

Two lights were seen 10 miles East of Mansfield in a wood illuminating the leaves, as though two car headlights had been turned upwards.

All twelve planes bombed the target and all returned safely. Ken's plane touched down at 04.23 – after very nearly nine hours.

This operation and the earlier one to Bremen on 11 September were the beginnings of a very significant development in the history of Bomber Command, although this could not have been known at the time. The clue lies in the sentence contained in the Squadron record above: *The target was identified by a green signal over a flare dropped by another aircraft*. The Bremen report contained similar words: *A red Very light – a signal by an earlier aircraft – was seen at back and E.T.A. over target area*. The key development behind these reports was the identification of the target by coloured lights dropped by an earlier aircraft.

Wing Commander Bufton had been musing on how to improve the effectiveness of his bombers in locating and identifying the target. At that time squadrons were left to devise their own tactics to achieve the estimated time over the specified target required by their orders. Pilots then were seeking individual targets such as military installations, industrial plants or railway marshalling yards; area bombing came later. When an aircraft reached the target area, flares were dropped to help visual identification of the target. These powerful flares lasted about 3½ minutes as they floated down on parachutes. Wing Commander Bufton had already identified one problem with these flares. The point at which they ignited was decided by a timer, which meant the control was how far below the aircraft the flare ignited not how high above the ground. Maximum timing gave ignition about 3,500 feet below the aircraft that might be flying at 10,000 feet. If there was lower cloud or haze, as was very often the case over the Ruhr area, the glare was reflected back from the cloud or haze obscuring any features of the ground below. What Wing Commander Bufton recognised was that a barometric fuse was needed so that the flare ignited at a predetermined height above the ground, say 1,000 or 2,000 feet. He put this forward as a requirement.

That was one issue. The other was the problem faced by a pilot as he approached the target area. A number of aircraft may have already arrived and dropped their identification flares, which may be spread over a wide area like so many candelabra hanging in the sky. But which one was over the target? On a 'big' raid involving a number of squadrons, requiring central organisation and coordination, there could be a confusing number of flares for a period of time as waves of squadrons arrived over the area. Wing Commander Bufton reasoned that the more experienced pilots were those most likely to find and correctly identify the target. The idea came to him that if these pilots went in first and one of them was absolutely certain his flare was over the target he could mark it using a pre-agreed coloured Very light. Each aircraft carried a set of coloured Very flares that would be fired off out of the aircraft under certain circumstances, for example to signify distress or to identify the aircraft as friendly to home defences. With the target positively identified, other crews, particularly those less experienced, would be guided on to the mark and so the whole operation would become much more effective.

Wing Commander Bufton talked through his ideas with his two Flight Commanders and other experienced captains and officers. The scheme was tried out on the raids on Bremen and Lorient, when the weather was good, and it worked like a charm. Subsequently it became standard practice in 10 Squadron with aircraft carrying extra flares for this purpose. Later, as we shall see, from these beginnings and the continued development and promotion of his ideas, the famous Pathfinder Force was formed in August 1942.

Continuing a busy month, the target for the night of 30 September was an extremely ambitious one, a single but significant building – the German Air Ministry in the Leipzigstrasse, Berlin. The alternative target was the West Power Station, Berlin; and last resort targets were the BMW factory at Spandau, Berlin, SEMO (Self Evident Military Objective) or MOPA (Military Objective Previously Attacked). The squadron put up ten aircraft, but not all would return.

Yet again Ken was flying with Wing Commander Bufton, Pilot Officer Russell (Second Pilot), Sergeant Bessell (Observer) and Sergeant Cowie (Wireless Operator) in 'U' for Uncle. Briefing was at 13.50 and take off was to be at one-minute intervals starting earlier than usual at 18.00 for the long trip.

'U' for Uncle took off at 18.06 and followed the designated route out via Flamborough Head to the target. The flight report reads:

> 10/10ths cloud obscured the primary target, so this crew attacked a factory with blast furnace at Verden in one stick, all bombs being dropped at 0015 hours from 10,000 feet. As a result of this attack fire broke out; as the aircraft left the area the entire factory was seen to be in flames. A.A. fire over Berlin at 10,000 feet was of heavy calibre of moderate intensity. At Verden, at 12,000 feet, light calibre was accurate. 20 miles NW of Hanover a very intense flak barrage was put up of red-coloured burst, but no gun flashes were seen. 10 miles N. of Deepholz also, a very intense flak barrage was put up. Searchlights at Berlin were moderate, but at Verden they were intense and working in groups forming a cone. Ten miles west of Bremen many red lights close together, forming an arrow pointing west, surrounded by an oval of brilliant white lights were seen. No damage or casualties were sustained.

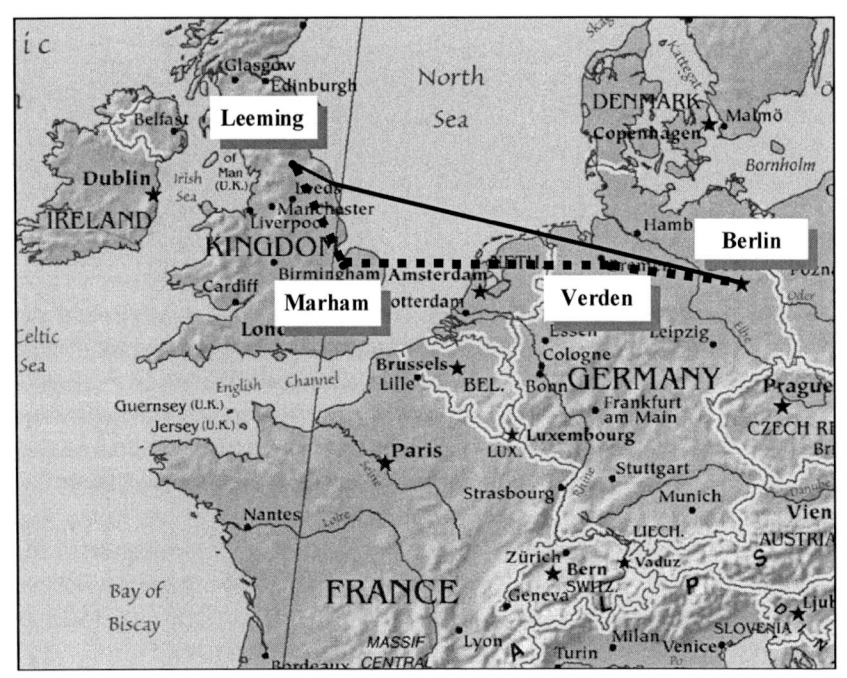

The Route to Berlin and back via Marham, 30 September 1940

After another nine hours plus in the air with almost total cloud cover, Wing Commander Bufton brought the aircraft down at RAF Marham, near King's Lynn, at 03.20. At the briefing crews were advised the intended route home was via Great Yarmouth landing at Bodney, Norfolk, for refuelling and interrogation before returning to base. In the event Wing Commander Bufton landed 'U' for Uncle at RAF Marham, about 15 miles north west of Bodney and flew back later in the day from there to RAF Leeming.

Other planes reported heavy flack over Berlin and elsewhere, with one report of a plane going down in flames on the way out over Wilhelmshaven. Heavy cloud conditions over the target area meant that bombing was haphazard. Although many crews, including those from other squadrons, claimed to have found the target and aimed bombs at it, only a few bombs fell in Berlin mostly in the western suburbs. The German Air Ministry was not hit that night; indeed it took until 1944 before it sustained any damage, courtesy of the Americans!

At about 23.00 a 'bombs away' signal was picked up from 10 Squadron Whitley 'B' for Baker by another Squadron plane, but about twenty minutes later the aircraft was shot down by a German night fighter over Badbergen. The pilot, Sergeant Snell and his second pilot Sergeant Ismay were killed, the other three crew members survived to become POWs. In the early months of the war the Luftwaffe fighters were not geared up for night attacks but gradually, using improved techniques supported by ground control, they became an ever greater threat, evidenced by the above incident and a comment in Wing Commander Bufton's Flying Logbook entry for that night. He wrote within the brief notes of the operation, 'Fighter trap', but what had happened that led him to make that comment is not recorded.

Also that night the experience of another crew from the Squadron vividly illustrated one of the many hazards of flying to distant targets. Flying Officer Wood must have had severe navigation problems as his wireless operator called for a fix at 04.43 when well overdue. The fix placed his aircraft miles out over the Irish Sea having overshot England. An SOS was picked up an hour later, which meant they were about to ditch in the sea. Fortunately for them, however, a trawler had been fairly near and the whole crew were picked up unhurt and landed at Holyhead.

Just over one hundred planes flew on raids that night – three others were missing over enemy territory, another crashed on take off and another crash-landed in Norfolk.

For the past few months Wing Commander Bufton had been suffering from progressive back pain and had only been able to keep flying with the aid of an air cushion. A particularly severe attack of pain early in October saw him referred to the Army hospital at Catterick, which meant Ken was spare again. Wing Commander Bufton's problem was diagnosed as sciatica and he was moved to the Royal Bath Hospital, Harrogate where a couple of weeks of hydro waters, massages and radiant heat therapy completely cured him.

Gradually during the month, with the truly superb pilots of Fighter Command winning the Battle of Britain and Hitler postponing his invasion plans (Operation 'Sealion') until the next spring, the threat of invasion receded.

Despite all the activity during September the Squadron did manage to assemble for some group photographs in front of one of their Whitley V aircraft.

No.10 Squadron Officers, September 1940
(Back row from left to right) P/O Dickinson, W/O Steel, F/O Landale, P/O Boxwell, P/O Humby, P/O Andrew, F/O Bastin, P/O Brant, P/O Jones, P/O Bridson, P/O Russell, P/O Cooney, P/O Peers, P/O Beeston
(Front row from left to right) F/Lt Cohen, F/O Wood, F/Lt Tomlinson, S/Ldr Sawyer, S/Ldr Hanafin, W/Cdr Bufton, S/Ldr Ferguson, F/Lt Raphael, F/Lt Phillips, F/O Prior, F/O Wakefield, F/O Warren, F/O Bagshaw
[Photo: Courtesy of Carol Downer]

No.10 Squadron Operational Crews, September 1940 – Ken Bastin circled
[Photo: Courtesy of Carol Downer]

5. From Whitley to Halifax

With the Wing Commander in hospital, October brought Ken some respite. This meant initially that he was placed on the spare list and he also took the opportunity for some well-earned leave. His sister mentioned in her diary that he and his wife Teddie visited her briefly on 9 October and also on 19 October when they met up for supper. A well-earned break indeed as it had been a tough few months, particularly the last four weeks with six operations.

Phyllis and her mother would have told Ken and Teddie how they had been faring during the constant bombing raids coming over night after night. Some nights Phyllis herded the children under the stairs when the bomb blasts rattled the windows – too close for comfort. Northampton, where they lived, was under the flight path the German bombers took on their raids to Coventry, and they suffered their fair share of inaccurate and stray bombing. On a number of occasions Phyllis could see in the night sky the pounding that Coventry was taking. Her diary entry for Wednesday 30 October describes the events of the previous night:

> Well what an evening yesterday. 10.30pm I was smoking in the playroom when 6 bombs fell one after another somewhere. Debated about getting the kids up when we heard the plane & a few more fell – so got them up. 3 huge ones when they [the children] were down – we could hear the guns. Finally got them to bed around 11.45. We watched the barrage at Coventry from our window – the guns sounded like thunder & the flashes lit up the sky like lightening.

There was a curious juxtaposition between Ken and his family. Night after night Ken's family sheltered under their stairs from the German bombers as they flew overhead, whilst at the same time Ken flew over German towns and cities where, similarly, families took whatever cover they could. Phyllis wrote about her great sympathy and empathy for Londoners and others who suffered heavy German raids, but in retrospect she could not recall having any thoughts at all for German families caught up in RAF raids. Not that the plight of German civilians was dismissed because they were the enemy, rather trying to cope with their own situation and worries over the threat of invasion simply left no room for such thoughts.

The Squadron's losses continued to mount during October. As soon as Ken returned to RAF Leeming he would have learned of the night of 14 October when three of their aircraft were lost, not over Germany but in England. One returning from an attack on Le Havre ran into a barrage balloon cable in Surrey and all five crew were killed. The other two ran into poor weather when returning from Germany, and because they were unable to land, the crews abandoned their aircraft, but two crew members were killed. That particular night Bomber Command lost more aircraft over England to bad weather than were brought down over Germany. A week later another crew failed to return from a sortie to Stuttgart; there were no survivors. Fortunately no one was hurt when one of the Squadron's Whitley aircraft burnt out on the ground at the station on 27 October following an electrical short circuit. And remarkably two days later the whole crew survived when the aircraft Pilot Officer Peers was flying crashed into a hillside in Northumberland during an operation to Wilhelmshaven.

November saw three further Squadron losses. Two crews were missing returning from raids on Milan and Merseburg, believed lost over the North Sea. Another aircraft crashed in South Wales on route to Lorient, but this time only one of the crew was killed although the other four were all injured.

Ken's official confirmation and appointment to Flying Officer became effective from 13 November 1940, one year after being appointed Pilot Officer. This was really a non-event for Ken as he had in every respect been a Flying Officer since May. The official announcement appeared in *The London Gazette* on 31 December.

During this time Ken attached himself to a number of training crews, carrying out his training duties as replacement crews came onto the Squadron. The Squadron not only needed new crews to replace the losses being suffered but by now quite a number of aircrew had been on operations from the beginning of the war and were due to be screened. Being screened meant an airman came off operations and was transferred to an Operational Training Unit or other training establishment where he would use his experience to help train others. It was seen as a deserved rest, away from the strain of operations. Although in the early part of the war there was no set point at which an airman would be screened, about this time an airman was screened after thirty operations, known as a 'tour'. Many airmen returned to operations after a spell in a training role to complete a second, or even a third, tour. All this meant a constant stream of new gunners for Ken to install, assess and bring up to the Squadron's standards.

The recent heavy bombing of English cities, in particular Coventry and Southampton, prompted the War Cabinet to authorise Bomber Command to make retaliatory strikes against the centre of a German city. This was a significant decision in terms of the conduct of the war, and marked the departure from the hitherto restraint of attacking only military or industrial targets.

Mannheim was the city chosen and on 13 December authorisation was given for an attack to be made on 16 December, code-name Operation Abigail Rachel.

Originally it was planned to put up 200 aircraft but the weather was forecast to deteriorate over the target area and the force was reduced to 134. Even so, this was the largest force of the war so far despatched by Bomber Command for a single target. The plan called for six very experienced Wellington crews to go in first with incendiary bombs to set fires as markers for the following bombers.

At briefings the significance of the mission would not have been lost on the crews as they gathered round. Not only was it the first 'area' bombing of the war, it was also the first time Bomber Command had tried to put a large and concentrated force over a single target. All aircraft were given the same route but time over the target was spread over two hours.

10 Squadron were tasked to put up seven aircraft, taking off at one-minute intervals commencing 22.30 hours. The briefing would have emphasised the critical importance of timing, as the plan was considered highly dangerous – the possibility of mid-air collisions being far higher than ever before. At that time, two hours was thought to be the minimum time in the target's airspace to allow the phasing of so many aircraft while maintaining an acceptably low risk of collision.

Ken was in Whitley 'S' for Sugar with a new crew piloted by Pilot Officer J A S Russell. In the event the weather was clear, but bitterly cold.

Pilot Officer J A S Russell – a man of many talents.
He was a Squadron Leader with the Distinguished Flying Cross
before he was shot down on 30 May 1942 and made a POW.
[Photo: Courtesy of Dan & Hugh Russell]

The briefing detailed the night's objective:

Object. To cause maximum damage to targets allocated.

Target. Mannheim

Route. Outwards:- Base – Finningley – Yarmouth – Haamstede – Target: Return:- Wiesbaden – Dutch Coast- Flamboro' Head – Base.

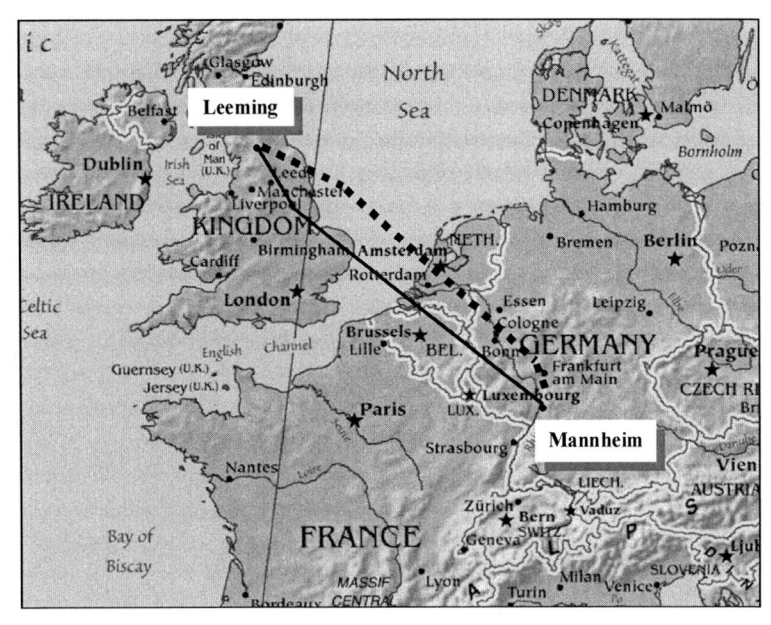

The Route to Mannheim and the northerly Return Route, 16 December 1940

The report for S for Sugar reads:

> Time up 2235. This aircraft obtained a fix over Moselle with the target to the East and this could be seen at a great distance owing to the flak and fierce fires. Weather was very clear over the target which was ringed with fires. Bombs were dropped in two sticks in the centre of the fires from 10,000 feet. Roads, buildings etc., were seen clearly in the bright moonlight. The run up was made parallel with Auto-Bahn to the target. First stick was at 0220hrs. of 1/500, 2/250 and one container of incendiaries track 300°.
>
> Second stick of same load and track at 0237hrs. Fresh fires were seen to start as a result of this attack. Flak seemed to wait until the aircraft was actually bombing and it was then intense for a short time, few searchlights were seen. The aircraft was caught and held by searchlights for a few moments at Frankenthal on the return journey. The Rhine appeared to be frozen, the surrounding country being flooded.
>
> A camera was carried on this aircraft but the mechanism seized with the cold. No enemy aircraft were seen and the aircraft landed safely at base at 0702 hours.

This must have been one of the most chronically uncomfortable operations Ken experienced. No heating was available to the rear gunner in a Whitley, and even in moderate weather, the height the aircraft flew at meant he normally had to cope with very cold conditions. Plenty of layers were the best counter to the arctic temperatures, plus a flask of tea or coffee. But even well wrapped up the job was very uncomfortable and called for immense powers of endurance. Any sort of exercise to help circulation was virtually impossible in the cramped turret.

On this night Ken suffered eight and a half hours of exceptionally bitter conditions; conditions so intensely cold that equipment on the aircraft was rendered unserviceable. He must have been so relieved to arrive back at base and begin the long thaw out.

The outcome of the raid was not as successful as had been anticipated and was examined in some depth by the authorities. It became clear from reconnaissance that not as many aircraft actually bombed the centre of Mannheim as claimed, and this was put down to the lightweight incendiaries carried by the first six aircraft being scattered in their slipstream. Consequently the bombing of following aircraft was even more scattered.

The raid was reported in the press over the next few days; not unnaturally the reporting did not specifically mention the revised tactics. On 18th December, *The Times* reported:

> *The Air Ministry news service, describing the RAF attack on Mannheim, a city which occupies a key position in Germany's economic system says:-*
>
> *A heavy attack was made on the main railway station, goods yards, and industrial buildings on the right bank of the Rhine. Successive waves of bombers were over these objectives from just before 8 o'clock in the evening until the early hours of the morning, and the attacks continued without respite. Thousands of incendiaries fell on this single area, as well as an exceptionally large number of heavy high explosive bombs. The fires and consequent explosions were of unusual intensity. Pilot after pilot saw a cluster of fires as he reached the objectives and a greater number when he left. This was only one target out of many. Ludwigshafen and the Neckarstadt district burned almost as brightly as Mannheim itself. One pilot said that anti aircraft fire seemed to be coming up "like a continuous golden fountain," but the very weight of the attack seems to have harassed and bewildered the ground defences so that some aircraft had to run the gauntlet of intense aircraft fire while others were left almost entirely alone.*

The following day *The Times* carried a large, but rather indistinct, photograph taken by one of the bombers during the raid, with arrows pointing to various features, and again the text highlighted the industrial targets hit.

Also reported in *The Times* was a short piece headed 'German Version Of Mannheim Raid'. It read:

> *Yesterday's communiqué of the German High Command stated:-*
>
> *Attacks by British aeroplanes in German territory were restricted during Monday night to Western and South-Western Germany. In Mannheim, damage and fire were caused by high-explosive and incendiary bombs on buildings, among them the castle and a hospital. In*

another town another hospital was hit. The decrease in production caused in two factories is insignificant. Losses among the civilian population amounted to 1 dead and 50 injured.

An official report concluded that the Mannheim raid was not a success despite the claims of three quarters of crews to have bombed the target. The first aircraft inaccurately dropped their incendiaries, which resulted in the main force bombing being scattered. This area raid on Mannheim, together with follow-up raids on the next two evenings, was the only such event that winter, but it was definitely a forerunner of the methods employed throughout the strategic bomber offensive later in the war.

In his report of the Mannheim raid Pilot Officer Russell mentioned there was a camera on board his aircraft. Around this time cameras began to be installed in some aircraft, usually those with experienced crews. A powerful flash was timed to go off as the bombs hit the ground and an image taken which was later examined to determine the extent of the damage caused. Initially crews were definitely not keen on these new cameras because the pilot had to maintain his straight and level course for the time it took the bombs to reach the ground, an extra period of maybe 30 seconds when they remained particularly vulnerable. Gradually all aircraft were fitted with cameras and resistance to them waned. However one serious consequence of the introduction of cameras was that skilled interpretation of the images led to growing concerns that the accuracy of bombing was far less than previously believed.

Ken had only a few hours rest before preparing for Mannheim again. Despite having landed from last night's operation at 07.02, his well-earned rest was short-lived because he was called to an unusually early briefing at 14.00 only to learn he was to go all the way back to Mannheim again that afternoon. Again he was in 'S' for Sugar with the same crew as the previous night. Take-off was planned for about 16.40 whereas the previous night the first aircraft was off at 22.30. Of course the previous night's take-off time was determined by the Group planners aiming to phase the large number of aircraft safely through the target area. There were no such constraints this night as only nine aircraft were to take part. The very early start was probably more to do with the time of year and possibly the hope of catching the Mannheim defences off guard.

But despite all the planning, the anticipation and preparations, soggy turf on the way from the dispersal point was to bring proceedings to a complete halt for Ken and his crew.

The Operational Record Book reads:

Object:- To cause maximum damage to targets allocated.

Target:- Mannheim

Route:- Base – Flamboro' Head – Dutch Coast – Target: Target: – Dutch Coast – Flamboro' Head – Base.

Bomb Load:- 2/500, 4/250 N.D.T. and two containers of incendiaries.

This aircraft became bogged on the aerodrome whilst taxiing to take off position and this aircraft's operation was cancelled.

Emotions amongst the crew were no doubt a mixture of frustration and relief. Having been through the briefing and all the planning, there was the usual quiet period before the crews moved to the hangers to kit themselves up and make those last minute preparations before the truck would ferry them out to their aircraft. There each of the crew would have their own routine checks to make before the engines were started up. This time between the end of the briefing and before the wheels of the aircraft began to turn was one of considerable tension, made worse if the weather forecast was poor. That tension was relieved when the wheels started turning and everyone concentrated on the business of flying and the mood turned to suppressed excitement. Imagine the frustration when only a few minutes later their whole operation came to a somewhat ignominious halt. Add to that the thought that having gone through all the briefing and preparations this cancelled operation would not now count towards their tour of operations, and all this after a meagre rest from the difficulties of the previous night. On the other hand the frustration may well have been tinged with some relief that they had at least for that night cheated one of their biggest enemies – the weather.

Although all the aircraft that did get away that night returned safely they encountered heavy flak and had to be diverted to land at another airfield due to poor weather, and one even turned back after encountering 'very bad weather'. So those crews who were able to notch up another operation on their tally had a fairly rough trip.

Just a week after getting stuck in the mud, Mannheim raised its head yet again and once more take-off was timed for just after 16.00. The Squadron put up six aircraft, three of which were described as 'Nursery's' (at that time 'B' Flight consisted of three sections: Fully Operational Crews, Nursery Crews and Training Crews).

Ken was, naturally, with one of the three experienced crews, but in a crew he had not flown with before, the captain and pilot being Pilot Officer G S Williams in aircraft 'Z' for Zebra.

The Squadron record for that night, 23 December, reads:

Object:- To cause maximum damage to targets allotted.

Target:- Mannheim (Navel Armaments)

Secondary and Last Resort:- S.E.M.O. and M.O.P.A.

Route:- Base – Flamboro' Head – Maemstede [sic] – Target : Target – Haemstede [sic] – Flamboro' Head – Base.

Bomb Load: - 2/500, 2/250 G.P. and 4 containers of incendiaries.

Time up 1617. Owing to the heavy cloud over the target area no attack was made and all bombs were brought back. Clouds were 10/10th at 3,000 ft. the base being undiscovered. At position D.R. 51° 35' North 03° 58' East white lights forming a square were seen to the starboard six miles away – green signal lights were flashed at the aircraft from this area. At position D.R. 50° 07' North – 07° 08' East numerous small lights were switched on and a small fire started, this is presumed to be a dummy town. Very little anti-aircraft fire was encountered and none of this was accurate. Time down 0100.

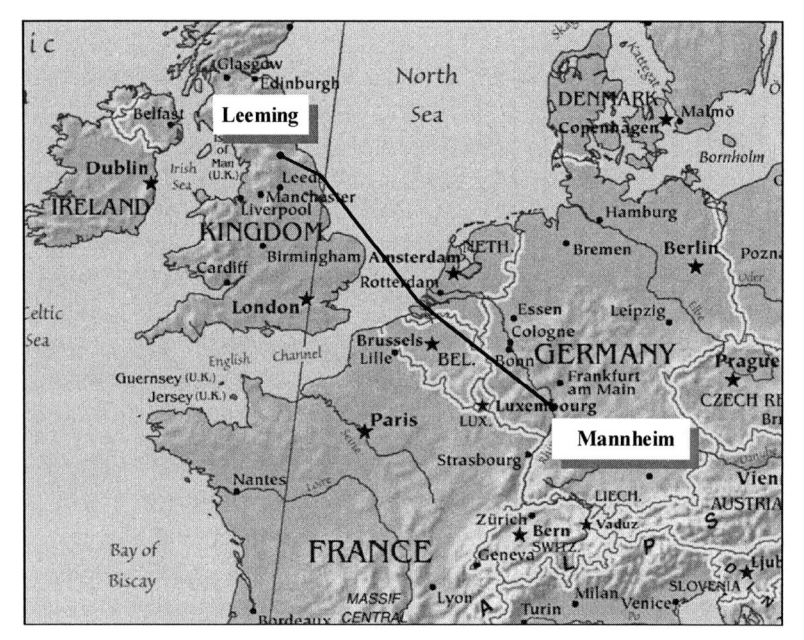

The Route to Mannheim, 23 December 1940

Again, nearly nine hours at risk with precious little to report other than blanket cloud and bombs brought back. The reference to the signalling green light appears to have been near the Dutch coast crossing point, at what is now known as Burgh-Haamstede on Zeeland (mistyped 'Maemstede' and 'Haemstede' in the Squadron's record of the route out and back). The reference to the dummy town was close to Mannheim itself.

Still they were back safely for Christmas, unlike most of the crew on a training flight the previous day. A Whitley V from the Squadron piloted by Pilot Officer Gough crashed on taking off after clipping the roof of a farmhouse just beyond the runway. The aircraft burst into flames and Pilot Officer Flewelling, one of the newer pilots, was killed and three others of the crew were injured. Two days earlier another squadron crew had a lucky escape when on their way home from a raid on Berlin engine failure over Suffolk led them to abandon their aircraft. Fortunately, this crew were all safe.

Back at Northampton, after the young children had gone to bed on Christmas Eve, Ken's sister and May, the elder of the two evacuee children, laid the table and decorated the Christmas tree. Phyllis thought how lovely it all looked, although she thought it a strange Christmas. On Christmas Day everyone had their presents and Phyllis's mother and sister, Mary, came round in time for 'a grand Christmas lunch'. Up to Christmas the evening air raid warnings had been pretty constant and just before Christmas Phyllis had heard that her other sister Peggy was safe after terrible air raids on Sheffield where she and her husband lived. But now there was some respite, although the news was full of warnings of a major German offensive in the spring. The respite was not universal though; London had a massive raid on the night of 29 December, the worst so far. Phyllis's diary entry for Tuesday 31 December 1940 sums up her feelings on the year. It read:

> It's now 10.10pm – Tony not yet in from the office – the 3 children are asleep upstairs. One noteworthy feature is no sirens so far! ... That 1941 will be grim goes without saying – but that we shall win through whatever happens, I have no doubt. What a year it has been with its tremendous disasters and amazing recoveries & about it all stands the unshakeable spirit of the ordinary men, women & children of these islands under the greatest aerial bombardment in history.

Bremen was the focus of attention for Bomber Command during the first days of the New Year. A large attack on the town on the night of 1 January started many fires and damaged an aircraft factory. A small raid the following night added to the fires. The local fire units struggled in the snow and ice to cope with the situation and had to call in reinforcements from as far away as Hanover and Hamburg.

Ken and his wife were expecting to make a quick visit to his family on 2 January but they did not go; maybe it was the snow that fell over night that prevented them travelling or more probably it was because Ken was on standby for operations as he flew the following night. He wrote to his sister a few days later no doubt explaining, as far as he could, why they had not been able to make the visit.

Although Ken was not to know it, the night of 3 January 1941 was to be his last operation with 10 Squadron and also his third and last visit to Bremen. As usual Bremen was no easy ride.

The entry for in the Squadron record reads:

Object:- To cause maximum damage to targets allotted.

Target:- Bremen

Route:- Base – Flamboro' Head – German Coast – Target; Target – German Coast – Flamboro' Head – Base.

Bomb Load:- 2/500lbs., 2/250lbs. N.D.T. No.36. Detonators. And 4 containers of incendiaries.

Ken was in the same aircraft as his last operation 'Z' for Zebra, and the crew was the same save for a new wireless operator.

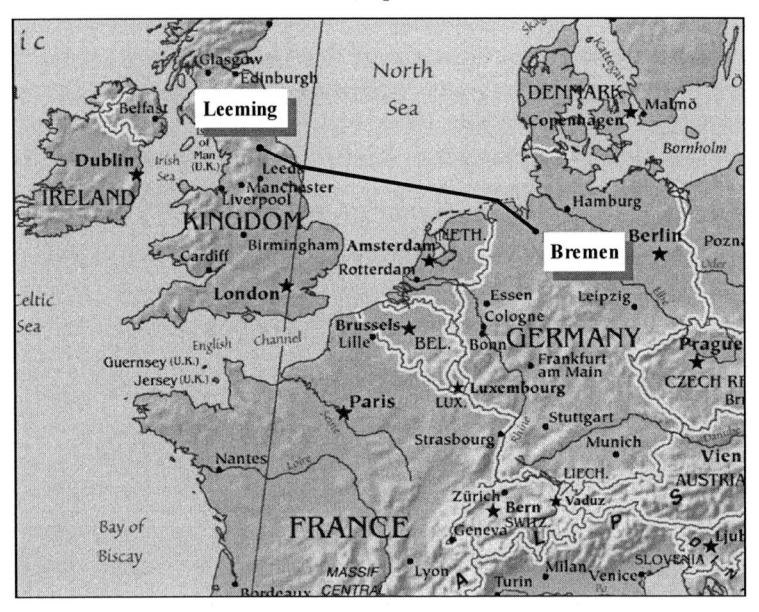

The Route to Bremen, 3 January 1941

Time up 1710. A successful attack was made on the primary target in excellent weather conditions, although between Base and target clouds were 10/10ths most of the way. Two sticks were dropped as follows:- 1st at 2122hrs. from 12,000ft. track 320° of 1/250 and one container of Incendiaries. 2nd stick at 2132hrs. also from 12,000ft. track 005°, comprising the remainder of the bomb load. Bomb bursts could not be located owing to the large number of fires already burning but an extra fire was seen burning on the target after the bombs had fallen. Fires were visible for 90 miles at least. Anti-aircraft fire was intense but inaccurate, only a few searchlights were seen. At 2135 hrs. I.F.F. was switched on as a result a searchlight which was holding this aircraft was extinguished. On the way out at 1752hrs. at 8,000ft. a multi red Verey cartridge light was observed ahead – followed by a burst of tracer bullets, this coincides with the position of an enemy aircraft reported by Catterick. A flare path and obstruction lights were seen at position 53° 14' North, 07° 48' East; all lights were extinguished as the aircraft approached. Path and lights were separated by 2-3 miles and it was thought to be a barge. No damage or casualties were sustained. Time down 0017.

Of the four Squadron planes scheduled to take part in this raid, one aircraft was unserviceable and withdrawn, one returned owing to an unserviceable air speed indicator and so only two successfully attacked the target. Although the two aircraft took off at the same time, Ken's aircraft arrived over the target twenty minutes later than the other one for no apparent reason and returned to base nearly forty minutes later.

The report tells that a searchlight held the aircraft just as the second stick of bombs had been dropped; a potentially very dangerous situation that needed immediate action. Some pilots told of a trick that might work in such circumstances and that was to switch on the I.F.F. (Indicator Friend or Foe) system that emitted a blip recognised by the British radar defences. On occasions this somehow seemed to jam the German searchlight control system and the searchlight would go out. The trick worked for Ken's aircraft that night and the immediate danger passed. Many pilots believed for some time the I.F.F. system could help them and left it on all the time despite scientists warning that German radar could pick it up. It was not until 1944 that Bomber Command was finally convinced of the dangers – it had taken deciphered Luftwaffe Enigma codes from Bletchley Park to persuade it to issue orders to pilots to switch the system off in range of German radar.

Two Whitley aircraft from other squadrons were lost on this raid. One from 51 Squadron at Dishforth was lost without trace, and the other from 78 Squadron, also at Dishforth, was abandoned over Devon due to wireless failure. The crew of the latter aircraft survived, but how they came to be over Devon is a mystery! At least Ken's navigator got Z for Zebra and its crew back to base, albeit rather later than their squadron colleagues.

Poor weather during the winter months meant a significant reduction in night bombing operations, although the pattern of small numbers of aircraft being despatched to many targets continued. Losses too continued and the Squadron lost one aircraft and crew on 16 January on an attack against Wilhelmshaven.

That night Ken's brother-in-law Tony (Phyllis's husband) went after work to be kitted out with his Home Guard uniform. Later on he was to have machine gun lessons – lessons Ken could easily have given him being rather more familiar with them than the local Home Guard! *The Daily Telegraph* of 23 January carried a statement by the chairman of the National Provincial Bank Limited, where Tony worked, that explained 28% of their pre-war male staff was in the armed forces but that the bank despite all the difficulties were maintaining services to their customers. No wonder Tony was always so late home from his branch office. Needless to say the bank's chairman went on to praise his staff in glowing terms.

Ken spent the next couple of months in his usual Gunnery Officer role, attaching himself to several operational crews. But he did manage a spot of leave in February. Phyllis wrote on Wednesday 5 February:

> Went over to Mum's for tea. Ken & Teddie arrived soon after I got there – on leave or rather having had leave & on their way back. Ken had lots of thrilling stories to tell.

On the following Sunday she recorded listening to Winston Churchill on the radio:

9pm Mr Churchill spoke – till nearly 9.40 & surely the grandest speech he's made – he's super. I've never enjoyed anything so much. ... Tony & I were going to have a drink of sherry to toast old Winston & victory & then found we couldn't as the sherry had gone bad!!

The Squadron was involved in a raid on 1 March against Cologne when over 130 aircraft attacked two targets there, and sadly losses were heavy with thirteen aircraft lost and over forty airman killed or injured. Among the losses was the 10 Squadron Whitley piloted by Sergeant Hoare which went missing over the North Sea after calling for help on the radio just before 01.00; there were no survivors. March saw two more Squadron losses. Returning from Kiel in the early hours of 19 March the port engine of Sergeant Watson's Whitley seized and caught fire, which spread to the fuselage. As they were over Yorkshire he ordered the crew to bail out which they did, but sadly he was overcome by the fumes and his body was found in the wreckage. Another Squadron aircraft was abandoned returning from Dusseldorf on the night of 27 March, this time over Rutland and with a happier outcome – just one injury.

Significant events for Britain were also happening on the other side of the Atlantic. By the end of 1940 we were increasingly unable to afford war materials manufactured in the neutral United Sates and President Roosevelt was sympathetic to our plight. At a press conference in December 1940 he said:

In the present world situation of course there is absolutely no doubt in the mind of a very overwhelming number of Americans that the best immediate defence of the United States is the success of Great Britain in defending itself; and that, therefore, quite aside from our historic and current interest in the survival of democracy, in the world as a whole, it is equally important from a selfish point of view of American defence, that we should do everything to help the British Empire to defend itself.

It was at this press conference he gave his famous illustration of why the USA should respond to Churchill's appeal for help.

Suppose my neighbour's home catches fire, and I have a length of garden hose four or five hundred feet away. If he can take my garden hose and connect it up with his hydrant, I may help him to put out his fire. ... I don't say to him before that operation, 'Neighbour, my garden hose cost me $15; you have to pay me $15 for it.' ... I don't want $15 – I want my garden hose back after the fire is over.

After much debate Congress passed the 'Lend-Lease' Bill on 11 March 1941 under which materials could be supplied without immediate payment. We shall see later how these important events across the Atlantic impacted on Ken.

Back in Europe, a series of events in March would ultimately lead to Ken's most significant moment of the war. The Battle of the Atlantic was going badly; if the Germans succeeded in cutting off supplies from across the Atlantic the consequences could be catastrophic for Britain. Churchill ordered Bomber Command's main effort be directed at the threats to our shipping – the U-boats and the long-range bombers, wherever and whenever they could be found. The German battleships Scharnhorst and Gneisenau were added to the list when they docked at Brest for repairs towards the end of March. They had been particularly devastating on their Atlantic patrols, so there started a long and arduous bombing campaign against these mighty warships at Brest, which of course was heavily defended. In a few months time Ken was to become directly involved in that campaign.

Before that, however, much was to change for Ken. Wing Commander Bufton was directed to re-form 76 Squadron at RAF Linton-on-Ouse and he was to take a number of experienced operational crews from 10 Squadron with him. 76 Squadron went back to the First World War but had been absorbed into a training unit. The Squadron motto was 'Resolute'. This revived unit was to be the second RAF squadron to fly the new four-engine Halifax heavy bomber, the other was 35 Squadron who were already at RAF Linton-on-Ouse and had been flying Halifaxes since the end of 1940. Ken was chosen by Wing Commander Bufton to go with him as the Gunnery Officer for the new Squadron. Being involved with the newest and biggest of Bomber Command's fleet of aircraft carried quite a degree of kudos in the Command and no doubt Ken was rather keen on the move.

Wing Commander Bufton had more good news for Ken. He was to be promoted to Flight Lieutenant, officially Acting Flight Lieutenant but effectively Flight Lieutenant for everyday purposes, with effect from 12 April. After eighteen months in the RAF he was just one rank below Squadron Leader – such rapid progress was possible only in times of war.

Just as the new commander of 10 Squadron arrived at RAF Leeming for a hand-over from Wing Commander Bufton a lone German bomber swooped out of the clouds and launched a strike at the airfield. This was not the first occasion the station had been attacked; the first time the bombs had dropped harmlessly in some nearby fields. This time the attack hit home. No sooner had the alarm sounded than a Heinkel 111 appeared just under the low cloud base heading towards the line of hangers. It dropped a stick of sixteen bombs right on the centre of the station resulting in tremendous explosions. Soon after the sound of the intruder had faded, airmen appeared from all sorts of shelter to inspect the damage, when all of a sudden the Heinkel was back low overhead blazing away with its guns pursued by two Spitfires. In no time the Heinkel pulled up into the cloud and was gone. Local radar defences tracked it until they lost it off their screens way out over the sea. Surprisingly little damage was done and luckily no one was hurt, this time. Most of the bombs had fortuitously landed in open spaces leaving craters.

The Motor Transport depot was worst affected and other buildings suffered superficial damage. Such raids were not unusual. Back in August nine Whitley aircraft were destroyed in a single raid on RAF Driffield.

Damage to the Motor Transport depot at RAF Leeming, early April 1941
[Photo: Courtesy of Carol Downer, Bufton Papers, Churchill Archives Centre (BUFT6/3)]

General view of bomb damage at RAF Leeming, early April 1941
[Photo: Courtesy of Carol Downer, Bufton Papers, Churchill Archives Centre (BUFT6/3)]

On 12 April the order to establish 76 Squadron forthwith was received and the detachment of aircrew and ground staff began at once. Their new home, RAF Linton-on-Ouse, was situated about eight miles northwest of York and was a fairly new station completed in 1937. It had three concrete runways and five large hangers to accommodate the new heavy bombers.

Ken's mother visited him and his wife shortly after the move. His sister wrote in her diary on 18 April:

Mum back from visiting Ken & Teddie. Ken got moved to Linton & is now learning to pilot these new American 4 engined bombers.

Their mother seemed to have come away from the visit with altogether the wrong impression. Ken was not about to become a pilot, nor were the planes American. Ken may have called them American of course to conceal their true identity – the existence of the Halifax had not been made known to the public at that point.

Here it is worth briefly recording the story of the Halifax so far. Instigated as a replacement for the Whitley, early designs had two engines but with the expansion of the RAF the concept was developed into a four-engine aircraft. This would allow a larger bomb load and therefore a greater tonnage delivered to the target per sortie. The first prototype flew in October 1939 and the test programme began a year later. 35 Squadron was reformed to convert to the new aircraft and training began in November 1940. The first operation involving the Halifax was in March 1941, but it was not until July that its existence became known to the public.

76 Squadron Halifax I aircraft MP-L flown by Flight Lieutenant Christopher Cheshire shortly before it was shot down over Germany on the night of 12/13 August 1941
[Photo: Courtesy of the Imperial War Museum, London (CH3378)]

The statistics of the aircraft were impressive. It had a wingspan of 98 feet 8 inches (just allowing it into the standard 100 feet wide RAF hanger) and four Rolls Royce Merlin engines. It could carry a bomb load of 13,000 lbs (over five and half tons), 2,243 gallons of fuel giving it a range of 1,860 miles and carried a crew of seven. Maximum speed was 255 mph and cruising speed 195 mph. It was heavily armed with four Browning machine guns in the rear turret, two in the front turret and, in the first version, two Vickers machine guns could be fired from positions each side of the main fuselage – called waist or beam guns.

The same Halifax I aircraft being prepared by ground crews at RAF Middleton St. George, early August 1941
[Photo: Courtesy of the Imperial War Museum, London (CH3393)]

The introduction of the Halifax was not without its problems. In January 1941 during an air test a crew from 35 Squadron were killed when their aircraft crashed. The cause was thought to have been a leak of a fine spray of hydraulic fluid from the undercarriage system that caught fire. Flying was put on hold shortly after Ken arrived while modifications were made. There were also difficulties with the twin rudders, which were not very effective during take-off. More seriously, under certain extreme flying conditions the rudders could lock if taken beyond a critical point causing the aircraft to go into an uncontrollable spin. It took a while and a number of crashes before this condition was finally recognised and the shape of the rudders modified in later versions.

The Halifax made its first operational appearance on the night of 10 March 1941, but the event was marred by tragedy. Six Halifaxes of 35 Squadron took off from RAF Linton-on-Ouse for an attack on Le Havre. On the way back an RAF fighter accidentally shot down one aircraft on the Hampshire/Surrey border believing it to be an enemy bomber. Only two of the crew survived.

For Ken his immediate tasks at RAF Linton-on-Ouse were to get his gunners installed, make himself known to the station staff, particularly the all important armourers who would be looking after the guns and ammunition, and then to make plans to bring his gunners and himself up to operational standard on the new aircraft as soon as possible. The other squadron officers were doing the same with their groups, pilots, and navigators, etc., including the new position of flight engineer. A flight engineer was needed on the Halifax to help the captain manage the four engines, the fuel load and all the other electrical and hydraulic systems on the aircraft. He sat behind the pilot with his bank of switches, gauges and dials, which, as one ex-flight engineer said he, "Used to watch like a hawk!"

Ken's plans to convert his team from the Whitley set-up would have centred on the turrets and the new beam position. The machine guns on board were the familiar Browning and Vickers makes and the reflector gunsights were the ones they were used to. But the aircraft designers had decided on Boulton Paul turrets, a different make of turret to the Whitley. The main difference for the gunner was the means of operation. Instead of the 'racing motorbike handles' type of controls in the Whitley rear turret, a 'joystick' control lever with the firing button on the top operated the Boulton Paul. Other significant differences were the amount and storage of ammunition and the power provided to the turret. By storing the ammunition in the fuselage and feeding the guns along tracks running back and into the turret the gunner had 2,500 rounds per gun available to him, two and a half times as much as in the Whitley. Power to the Whitley turret was brought via hydraulic pipes direct from one of the aircraft's engines – a system that was vulnerable to damage in attack, resulting not only in power being lost in the turret but posing a fire hazard from the spilled hot flammable fluid. Boulton Paul turrets were still powered by hydraulics, but an electric pump housed in the turret itself provided the pressure to the hydraulic system, the electricity coming via wiring from a generator linked to one of the aircraft's engines. There were a number of other features that made the Boulton Paul turrets popular with gunners.

This was the procedure the rear gunner followed after he climbed aboard the aircraft. He made his way back along the fuselage, clipped his parachute to the rack just outside the turret and entered through the double doors. He would take his seat, fasten the wide safety strap across his lap, lower the two armrests into position, close the doors and plug in his oxygen and intercommunication jacks. He needed to check the drive motor lever was in the 'Engaged' position before then cocking his guns and setting the 'fire and safe' control to 'fire'. Next he turned on the gun-firing master switch and the switch for the reflector gunsight. He was then able to adjust the dimmer control on the gunsight to achieve the right image intensity for the conditions. He was then ready to switch on the turret's main motor and a red indicator light would show the turret was now operational. The gunner would then test the turret. The control lever incorporated a switch to the drive motor so that gripping the lever turned on the power and moving the lever like a joystick operated the turret and guns. The gunner would test rotating the turret, fast and slow, and elevating the guns, plus, if allowed, firing a test burst of the guns into the ground by pressing the button on top of the control lever.

Ken's gunners needed to become thoroughly conversant and be 'at home' in the new turrets and also would require instruction and practice at the new, unfamiliar beam position. The field of operation of the beam gun was quite limited and the gunner would have the briefest view only of an attacking aircraft. As such this position would not be particularly effective against a skilled attack; rather it was probably more of a deterrent to a less determined fighter pilot.

During this period of conversion to the Halifax, 76 Squadron was non-operational and crews could concentrate on their training. However they were not free from danger, as on the night of 10 May the airfield was subject to a sustained attack by three or four German bombers. A serious fire was started in the centre of the camp by the first stick of bombs, and using this as their aiming point, more attacks followed in which incendiary and fragmentation bombs were dropped. The airfield defences made some effort but as they had no searchlights it was pretty hopeless. The station commander, Group Captain Garraway, was directing the fire fighting when he was struck by shrapnel from a fragmentation bomb and killed – he had joined RAF Linton-on-Ouse only the day before. Several other airmen were killed in the attack and more were injured. None of the Halifax aircraft was damaged as they were well dispersed and apart from the paint store, which was gutted, generally there was just superficial damage to some buildings. In the event the station and squadrons were able to carry on.

By the end of May 76 Squadron with its six Halifaxes and crews was just about ready for operations. At this point the RAF decided to promote Wing Commander Bufton to Group Captain and post him to establish a new airfield and station not far away. On 28 May Wing Commander G T Jarman arrived to take command of the Squadron. Almost his first task was to move the Squadron on 4 June to its operational home, RAF Middleton St George, only thirty-odd miles away. The last seven weeks had been all change for Ken; new aircraft, a new squadron, a new commander and yet another RAF station.

Ken's new Officer Commanding, Wing Commander Geoffrey Twyford Jarman, was a thirty-five year old New Zealander who joined the RAF in 1930. Previously he had been Officer Commanding of 77 Squadron, a nearby operational squadron flying Whitleys, like Ken's previous squadron.

RAF Middleton St George was fives miles east of Darlington. Now it is Teeside International Airport; but then it was a very modern RAF station, opened for just over a year. Even the H-block accommodation had the luxury of central heating. It had concrete runways and five hangers, hanger No.1 being allocated to 76 Squadron. Yet another operational squadron flying Whitleys, 78 Squadron, shared the station. Of course Ken had briefly been with 78 Squadron just over a year ago when it was a training unit, just before it transferred to operations.

Wing Commander Geoffrey Twyford Jarman

It was not long before 76 Squadron became operational and back in the mix. Three Squadron crews were included in significant raids on the Ruhr, but two returned with engine trouble and the third could not find its main target and dropped its bombs on Essen with uncertain results. Not a particularly auspicious start. Five more operations were joined in June with one loss, the first for the newly re-formed Squadron. That loss was on the night of 23 June when Pilot Officer Stobbs's aircraft was shot down by a German night-fighter near Hamburg with only one survivor. Before that two of the Squadron's Halifaxes were severely damaged in landing accidents on 15 June. The first was caught by a cross wind when about to touch down and the aircraft veered off the concrete runway. As soon as the wheels hit the soft grass the undercarriage collapsed and the plane slewed back across the runway, coming to a halt where it completely blocked the main landing strip. Because the main runway was blocked the pilot of a second Halifax attempted a cross-wind landing on one of the other runways. He too caught a gust that sent him onto the grass with the same result. No one was hurt, but the second aircraft was deemed so badly damaged that it could be used only for ground training. Wing Commander Jarman himself led his Squadron on 2 July to Bremen, having completed his conversion to the Halifax.

Having seen his gunners work up to operational standard on the Halifax and having watched them in action over the past few weeks, it was time for Ken himself to test his own latest training. On the night of 8 July he was on the crew list for the operation to the IG Farben Leuna synthetic oil plant at Merseburg in north-eastern Germany. Altogether that night 13 Halifaxes attacked the target. All six planes from 76 Squadron returned, not without incident, but one 35 Squadron Halifax crashed in Holland; three of the crew were killed and the others were captured.

Ken flew with Flight Lieutenant W S Hillary who had been with 35 Squadron before moving over to the Squadron in May, so he had a little more experience of the Halifax.

The records for 76 Squadron are very brief. For Ken's aircraft L.9516, the entry for the raid on the Leuna plant reads:

Time Up 22.21.

This aircraft attacked the primary target at 11,000 feet. Bombs dropped North of target. No results seen. Hazy. No Cloud. Aircraft returned safely to base.

Time Down 05.37.

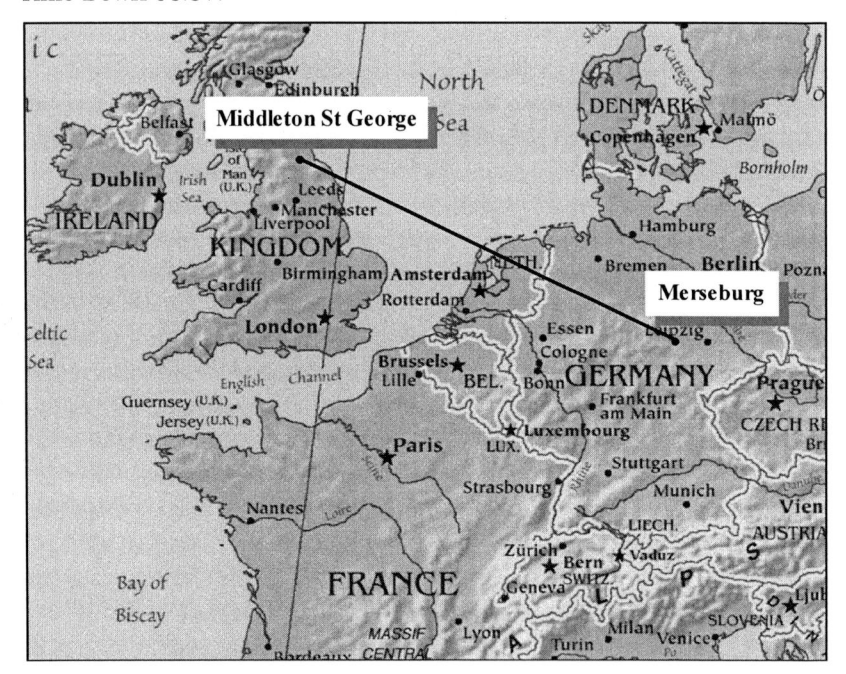

The Route to Merseburg, 8 July 1941

That night Squadron Leader Bickford led the Squadron. Over the target his plane was caught in a concentration of searchlights and was damaged by flak. Only swift and drastic evasive action secured their escape. Very shortly after that however, an enemy fighter attacked the plane and a cannon shell exploded in the nose causing further considerable damage. Both Squadron Leader Bickford and his flight engineer, Sergeant Kenworthy, were wounded but fortunately the night fighter did not press home its advantage. Part of the windscreen was shattered and many of the instruments were put out of action. The compass was shot from its mountings but was picked up and put on the injured Squadron Leader Bickford's lap; and by the light of a torch he set a course for home. Eventually, overcoming many difficulties, by sheer skill and determination Squadron Leader Bickford and his crew made it back to base where medical assistance awaited the two wounded crew. Squadron Leader Bickford's injuries from shell splinters were unfortunately serious enough to require hospital treatment.

Two other squadron aircraft were hit by flak over the target and on their way home. But Ken was in the lucky half of the Squadron, returning without damage or injury from a flight of nearly seven and a half hours for little tangible result.

Over the last few weeks the war had taken a significant change of direction. Hitler had launched his assault on the Soviet Union on 22 June, which meant his resources were now stretched across eastern and western Europe as well as North Africa. It also meant the threat of invasion receded further. A strategic review of Bomber Command's operations led to a change of emphasis away from the maritime effort to the German transportation system and industry. The revised strategy was partly aimed at denting the morale of both civilians and industrial workers. As the danger at sea had reduced somewhat and the Luftwaffe was heavily engaged supporting the Soviet front the prospects were better for resuming the offensive against Germany itself. But there was still a requirement on Bomber Command to harass the U-boat bases in France and to contain the important German battleships in the port of Brest, as we shall see in the next chapter. There was of course the expected better weather over the summer months, and the new heavy bombers coming on stream, although they continued to be dogged by technical problems. But these positives were countered by the Luftwaffe improving its night fighter capabilities and effectiveness and RAF losses mounted. So neither was there any let up in the pressure on Bomber Command nor was there any reduction in the appalling risks taken by the airman as they set off night after night.

6. Target Scharnhorst

For Ken, Thursday 24 July 1941 was the most significant day of his time in the RAF – and the most perilous. Indeed it was to prove one of the key moments in his life, for in recognition of his actions that day he was presented with the Distinguished Flying Cross by King George VI himself. Yet in all the years that followed he spoke virtually nothing of it to his family or to his friends.

On a classically beautiful English summer's day he took part in a raid that disabled the mighty German battleship Scharnhorst. In the early months of 1941 she and her sister battleship the Gneisenau had been playing havoc with our Atlantic convoys, sinking or capturing 22 ships bringing essential supplies from America. Following the 24 July operation, not only would the Scharnhorst be out of commission for the rest of the year, but as events played out, she remained only a threat until her sinking at the end of 1943.

But the cost of that success was very high, and Ken was fortunate to survive. Undeniably, the hurriedly rearranged plan for the raid considerably reduced the survival odds for the force sent against the Scharnhorst: even so losses turned out to be much higher than anyone anticipated. Of all the operations Ken took part in, of everything else he did in the war, this was the most dangerous.

The Scharnhorst

The Scharnhorst was one of Germany's major capital ships with a fearsome armoury and phenomenal speed. At nearly 32,000 tons she carried a crew of almost 2,000 men. Along with her sister ship the Gneisenau she was the pride of the German navy where she was known as 'Lucky Scharnhorst', and was a focus of national pride in Germany.

After months at sea, however, both the Scharnhorst and the Gneisenau were in need of repairs and the Scharnhorst particularly needed improvements to her turbines. They docked at Brest on 22 March 1941. Brest afforded the necessary facilities for the work and, crucially, there they could be well protected. Brest was also convenient because once the refit and repairs were complete the ships could quickly resume their operations in the Atlantic. A third German warship joined them on 1 June. This was the heavy cruiser Prinz Eugen, in need of urgent maintenance on her engines. She had been an escort to the battleship Bismarck which had only been in active service for a short while before being sunk off the coast of Brittany on 27 May in one of the legendary naval engagements of the war.

In early 1941, vital supplies from America were being devastated by Germany's U-boat fleet and also by raiding surface warships including the Scharnhorst and the Gneisenau; and so in March 1941 Churchill directed the RAF to target the facilities Germany used to support its naval operations in the Atlantic. The Scharnhorst and Gneisenau were specifically added to that directive when it was known they had entered Brest for repairs.

During the months that followed Bomber Command organised many bombing raids against these ships at Brest which were very heavily defended, and although damage was caused to both Gneisenau and Prinz Eugen requiring further repairs, 'lucky' Scharnhorst miraculously escaped any damage. Despite the successes against two of the three capital ships, experience was showing that the results of raids by night were quite disproportionate to the effort involved.

So, in early July Bomber Command began working on a new tactic and devised a major daytime attack with the object of hitting the Scharnhorst and Gneisenau by precise bombing. Considerable preparation had gone into this plan involving all five of Bomber Command's Groups and two Groups from Fighter Command which would provide fighter assistance. The broad outline was for the first phase to be a light attack at very high altitude, causing the enemy's fighters on immediate readiness to be sent up. The second wave was to follow immediately and was to be of sufficient strength that the enemy would commit all his remaining fighters to intercept. This phase was to be heavily protected by Spitfire escorts to 'dispose of' the enemy fighters. The main attack would then follow when the enemy fighters were either destroyed or were forced to withdraw to rearm and refuel. This main attack would be over 100 strong and would include 15 of the new Halifax heavy bombers. As a diversion and to draw away some enemy fighters from the area, a secondary raid was to take place on Cherbourg. The night before, a normal attack on Brest was to be made by Whitley aircraft 'with the object of using up the enemy's night fighters and preventing them being available to intervene against the daylight attack'. The plan was circulated to appropriate commanders in early July. It stressed that the success of the plan would be seriously prejudiced if the enemy reinforced his fighter defences in the

Brest area to any considerable extent, and that the strictest secrecy should be observed and the plan divulged only to the fewest possible number of people. The code name given to the plan was 'Sunrise'.

At the same time as the RAF was planning 'Sunrise', the German High Command was preparing exercises for the Scharnhorst prior to her resuming operations in the Atlantic. With the refit complete and in view of the RAF's constant attacks on Brest the German High Command decided that essential sea trials and crew training exercises should be carried out from a more southerly port in the Bay of Biscay. The decision was made to base these trials at La Pallice, the deepwater port of La Rochelle, some 250 miles south of Brest. The port had been chosen for the shoals offshore, which provided a measure of protection against Royal Navy submarines and reduced the number of escorts needed to keep watch. Compared to Brest, however, it was not as well protected and some extra anti-aircraft units and fighter aircraft would need to be moved down there. Preparations were put in hand for the Scharnhorst to sail south on the night of 21/22 July. These preparations included a flotilla of five escort destroyers sailing up from La Pallice overnight on 20/21 July; the main channel south would be swept for mines during 21 July; on the passage south, more than a dozen fighters would provide air cover from dawn; and two further aircraft would mount anti-submarine patrols. Also, a large order for provisions was put in hand with the strict instruction that it should be delivered by 20 July. As it happened, a dockyard worker, who was an agent for the French Resistance, learned of the provisioning order from a catering clerk and, knowing the Scharnhorst's refit was nearing completion, passed on the information for transmission to England. Meanwhile, the RAF continued to carry out reconnaissance patrols over Brest.

Then on 20 July Bomber Command issued further detailed instructions stating the 'Sunrise' operation would take place on the first suitable day after 23 July. Paragraph 13 of these instructions read, 'In order to obtain the required concentration over the target and to provide a degree of mutual protection, Halifaxes and Wellingtons are to fly in sections of three at open formation distance. Section leaders are to be selected from the most experienced Officers available.' This need for formation flying had been heralded in an earlier 'Sunrise' communication which, because the two Halifax squadrons in particular had done little if any such flying, prompted some practice exercises although crews were not told why.

The log of the Scharnhorst reveals she left Brest at 22.00 hours on 21 July. The Germans moved a large tanker into the berth vacated by the Scharnhorst in an effort to mask her departure, but before the tanker was covered with camouflage netting a reconnaissance Spitfire flew over at 05.20 hours and spotted what was going on. The Scharnhorst, however, proceeded otherwise undetected to an area off the Isle de Ré where she carried out torpedo practices the following morning with fighters providing air cover. She behaved perfectly during her trials, worked up to 30 knots with no difficulties and the crew carried out gunnery trials. On completion of these she proceeded to La Pallice, entering the harbour at 16.00 hours.

With the discovery early on 22 July of the Scharnhorst's departure, the race was on to find her and to stop her. But where had she gone? It was vitally important to attack her immediately in case she was about to resume her Atlantic forays. Air reconnaissance sorties over likely ports were mounted but failed to locate her. That was until 09.15 hours on 23 July when she was discovered alongside a jetty at La Pallice.

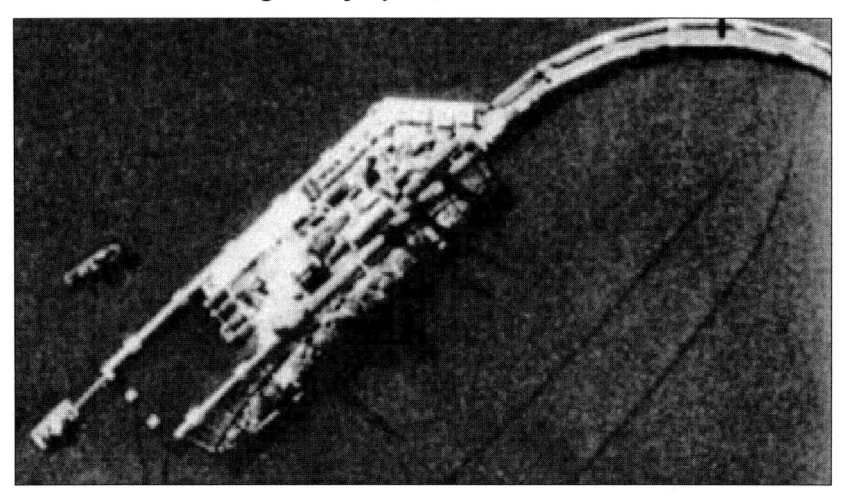

The Scharnhorst moored alongside the mole at La Pallice

Obviously with the Scharnhorst no longer at Brest, the 'Sunrise' plan was now in need of immediate revision. It was decided the attack against Brest would go ahead as planned, except the heavy bombers and the Whitleys would be withdrawn and redirected against the Scharnhorst at La Pallice. Because of the urgency, 15 Stirling heavy bombers would attack that evening, 23 July, and the Whitleys would carry out a normal bombing raid during that night followed the next day by the 15 Halifaxes mounting a daylight raid. La Pallice was beyond the range of our fighters, which meant these raids must be unescorted. The Stirlings had the cover of twilight; the Whitleys had the cover of darkness as usual. For the Halifaxes, however, attacking in the middle of the day there would be no cover – only the element of surprise. The Brest operation was timed to commence earlier than the La Pallice raid in the hope that some fighters would be drawn north away from the Scharnhorst. The only operational squadrons equipped with Halifax aircraft were 35 Squadron and Ken's 76 Squadron.

The first Ken knew something different was afoot would have been when Wing Commander Jarman called him in to discuss the prospect of an operation involving formation flying. How much Wing Commander Jarman knew of the planned operation at this point in early July and how much he took Ken into his confidence is not known. The discussion with Ken would have been about the defence of the formations against fighter attack and what was needed to achieve the necessary daylight operational efficiency. They would have debated the use of a fighting controller, deemed to be the most effective method of defence by organising the aircraft in the formation to act as a single unit. The fighting controller would be stationed under the astrodome (a perspex dome on the top of the aircraft behind the pilot, normally used for taking navigational fixes of the stars) where he would have a clear view of the aerial battlefield. When the group came under attack he would take charge of all the aircraft in the formation directing, by radio communication between the aircraft, both the gunners in collective defensive fire and the pilots by issuing orders for evasive action. Ken had received some training for this on his Gunnery Leader course at the Central Gunnery School earlier the previous year, but since then he had been involved in night operations only and therefore had no combat experience in this position. Ken was the only one with any such training and therefore the only candidate. Despite the lack of experience all round, Wing Commander Jarman decided to go ahead no doubt instructing Ken to organise a training schedule for him and his gunners. All the crews needed some training exercises and on most days from early July small formations of aircraft spent one or two hours practicing out over Bridlington Bay. The training involved groups of three aircraft flying in a close formation in the shape of a V called a 'Vic' (V for victory) and two or more Vics flying together in a squadron formation, with the gunners operating as a cohesive unit to defend the squadron formation and each Vic within it.

The crews were given no explanation for the introduction of these formation practices even though daylight bombing raids had been abandoned for some time because of the unacceptably high level of losses. The airmen of course wondered what was going on. Was this formation flying to be the new way of operations for heavy bombers in the future? Were daylight raids coming back – not good news – or was this for some special operation?

Normally squadron aircraft leaving base on a night operation took off within minutes of each other, and after take-off each pilot made his own way to the target independently from the rest of the squadron. Although each captain and navigator was given the same general route to and from the target, they did not fly together or as a group, and often pilots adopted their own individual tactics on the outward and return journeys. Flying in Vics of three, with the Vics then flying in a squadron formation, called for some very different flying techniques and discipline in the air, and also some detailed planning and careful briefing on the ground. All this did not come naturally. The fear of mid-air collision was very real; it was going to need some serious practice. Hence the series of training exercises over the North Sea.

It had been shown in the past just how vulnerable in daylight a single bomber was to a determined enemy fighter attack. For an unescorted formation to have any chance of success in a daylight bombing operation, it had to be able to defend itself much better than a single aircraft could. The Squadron's air gunners would have to work as a team, operating to a system of command and control and everyone had to understand his role and responsibility within the team. Just one hazard of flying in close proximity was the possibility of shooting aircraft in your own formation – so-called 'friendly fire'! As Squadron Gunnery Officer, Ken must have had much to do in planning and carrying out the training, including the arrangements for mock attacks by Hurricanes and Spitfires. Such mock attack training was inherently dangerous and required very careful planning. The fighter pilots would have had instructions to maintain the reality of an attack whilst minimising the risks. Head on attacks were particularly risky because the gap between the two aircraft closed at an alarmingly rapid rate compared to the more usual method of attack from the rear.

How vital these practical training exercises turned out to be. Because Ken would not be in a rear turret as usual, he must have been extremely nervous at the prospect of his changed role, so these practice sessions were vital to his preparation. The pilots were also particularly affected. Flying the huge Halifax in formation was extremely difficult, requiring the utmost concentration and considerable physical effort to maintain station especially over long distances.

But tragedy was to strike the Squadron during this special training period. Even if crews did not need reminding how dangerous flying exercises can be, the events of 21 July provided a shocking reminder. At 12.45 hours Pilot Officer Blackwell had just taken off in his Halifax. He had not been involved in the formation flying exercises as he was inexperienced and was simply setting off on a separate training flight. However, the pilot of one of the Hurricanes from the North Sea exercises, thinking the aircraft was part of his exercise, made a mock attack with disastrous results. Pilot Officer Blackwell took emergency avoiding action from which he was unable to recover and the Halifax crashed on the airfield killing all five crew aboard. Men from the base ran across to the scene of the crash but there was nothing they could do for anyone on board.

On the morning of 23 July orders came through to the Station Commander of RAF Middleton St George that six Halifaxes from 76 Squadron plus nine from 35 Squadron were to mount an unescorted daylight attack against the Scharnhorst at La Pallice the following day – time over target 14.00 hours to dovetail with the Brest operation. The raid was to be led by 76 Squadron's Officer Commanding, Wing Commander Jarman, and he decided Ken should fly with him as fighting controller. This put Ken in the lead aircraft. After the initial briefing there was a lot to do. Wing Commander Jarman needed to put together the remainder of his crew and Ken needed to organise his gunners. The aircraft needed air testing; bomb loads had to be organised, which included special armour piercing bombs; guns required testing and ammunition stored aboard; communications equipment had to be tested and the aircraft fuelled up. The navigators worked on the route which would take the formations well out to sea to avoid being picked up by German radar bases over northern France thus maximising the element of surprise. But at 15.30 hours information was received that all the Halifaxes were to fly that evening to RAF Stanton Harcourt, a satellite airfield of RAF Abingdon, just west of Oxford and some 200 miles nearer the target. This was to help achieve the timing and to ensure the aircraft could carry the optimum bomb loads. Wing Commander Jarman was not pleased at this very late change of plan as 1,000 gallons of fuel had to be drained from each aircraft and routes reworked; and also he had to take over 20 of his own ground crews with him because RAF Stanton Harcourt's ground staff had no experience of the Halifax. All this led to delays, and it was not till 22.00 hours that all aircraft landed at RAF Stanton Harcourt. And then crews had to be transferred to RAF Abington for overnight accommodation, which for some turned out to be in a hanger and for some others the station chapel. Hardly ideal preparation for a very difficult operation the next morning, but morale was high.

Ken and his fellow officers were woken at 05.30 hours. The final briefing was at 07.00 hours in readiness for take off at 10.30 hours. They woke up to a thick white mist with visibility only 30 yards. Spirits immediately dropped as initially it looked as though the operation would be affected but after breakfast and the briefing, spirits lifted again when the mist started to clear as the sun began to burn it off. Over night the Intelligence Officer and others had been gathering the latest intelligence information and weather reports in preparation for the briefing and from early on they worked with the navigation officers and senior officers to finalise the route. They learned the Stirling and Whitley raids over night were not successful and that one Stirling bomber had not returned. The crews gathered for the briefing in a makeshift hut where the scene was set by the Intelligence Officer who stressed the imperative of putting the Scharnhorst out of action, emphasising the need to press the attack home and to bomb accurately.

Ken would have been particularly keen to hear the assessment of the protection and defences surrounding the Scharnhorst which were known to be considerable. The group was shown photographs of the Scharnhorst lying alongside what looked like a large sea wall extending out to sea and it was explained that in order to penetrate her heavy steel decks the special armour piercing bombs needed to be dropped from 19,000 feet. The route was outlined. From RAF Stanton Harcourt the aircraft would fly at 1,000 feet to Lizard Point, then very low over the sea to 'Position A' about 50 miles out to sea from the north western tip of France where they would turn south east direct to La Pallice climbing to 19,000 feet. The return journey would be the reciprocal of the outward route. In all, the plot worked out at 1,228 miles and seven hours flying time. The six Halifaxes of 76 Squadron would take off first at one minute intervals starting at 10.30 hours and form two Vic formations of three aircraft before setting off southwest, followed by the nine aircraft of 35 Squadron which would assemble in three Vic formations. The two groups of formations would rendezvous over Exeter then proceed to Lizard Point.

After the briefing Ken no doubt brought his gunners together to ensure they all understood their respective roles and to give them encouragement. For them this operation would be something different; no staring into the blackness for hours on end in the cold, rarely seeing the enemy. They had been chosen for this special mission where they could really come into their own and would almost certainly have the opportunity to show their mettle.

At about 09.00 hours, coffee and sandwiches were brought over and there was time for the crews to relax a little and make their final preparations. What to wear was a bit of a conundrum. The forecast was for a scorching summer's day and for much of the trip the aircraft would be stiflingly hot, however at 19,000 feet it might be –20°C. But the crews were aware that as conditions changed they would be at 'Action Stations' and there would be little opportunity to make other than minor adjustments to their clothing. Intense cold can affect a person's performance much more than being too hot; but each crew would decide for himself what best to wear.

There was time, too, to think about what lay ahead. For some this sort of lull was when their nerves set in. Ken's new role must have given him more than usual food for thought. At this point was he thinking how more confident he might feel if he was about to climb into the familiar surroundings of the rear turret with its four powerful machine guns with which he could defend himself? As it was he would have no guns to fire on this trip – at least if all went to plan. Perhaps Wing Commander Jarman was also reflecting on his decision to put Ken in the fighting controller position for there was a consequent and significant risk. On balance he had adjudged it better to have improved defensive capabilities by taking a fighting controller, but the downside was there would be no second pilot on board – should anything happen to him there would be no one to bring the aircraft home. Just one of the many concerns on his mind at that time…

The aircrews made their way to their aircraft where the ground crews were finalising their pre-flight work. Some of the ground crew helped the airmen into their flying suits and lifejackets while the Group Captain and Intelligence Officer went from group to group, wishing them good luck. As they climbed into the aircraft the crews were immediately reminded how hot the day was going to be; the outer skin of their aircraft was warm to the touch and the interior felt decidedly sticky already. The crews settled to their positions. Ken sat next to Wing Commander Jarman in the second pilot's seat. The remainder of the crew were Flying Officer Brisbane, navigator and bomb aimer, Sergeant 'Taff' Gurmin, wireless operator, Sergeant Patterson, front gunner, Sergeant Sprigge, flight engineer and Flight Sergeant 'Timber' Woods, rear gunner. Sergeants Gurmin and Woods normally flew with Flight Lieutenant Christopher Cheshire, a very experienced pilot who would undoubtedly have been selected to fly on this operation had he not been on leave.

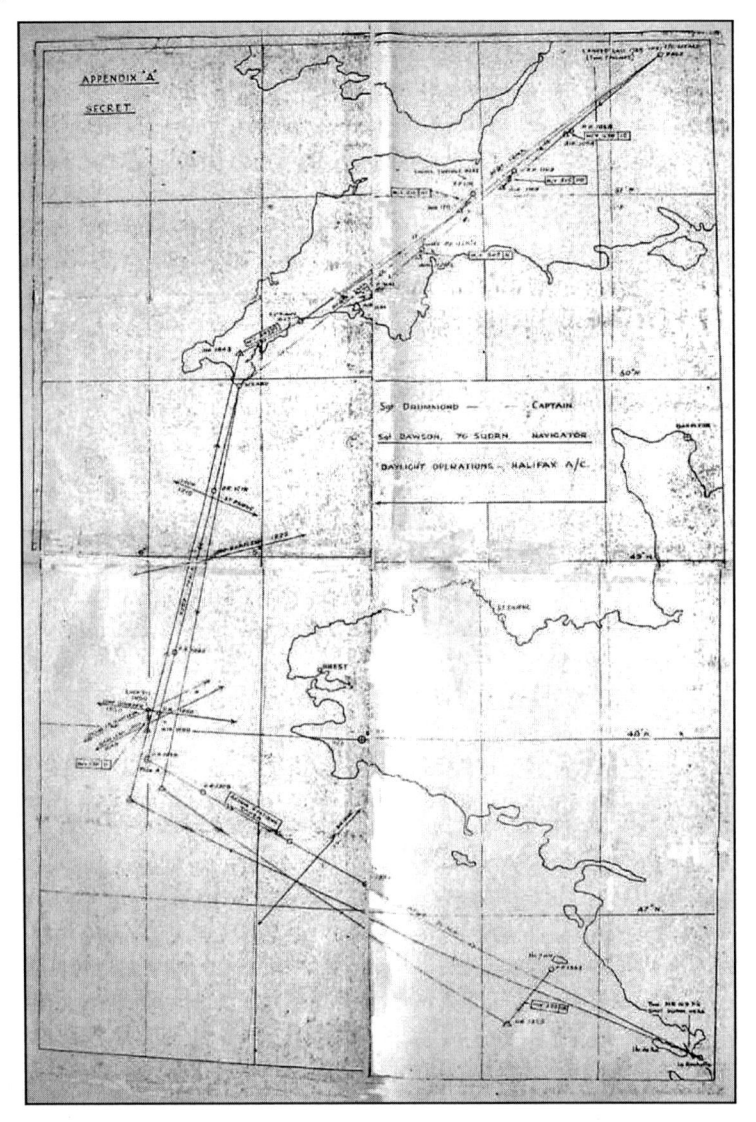

The original navigation chart of Sergeant M E H Dawson detailing the route to La Pallice – updated as the operation progressed. His aircraft flew in formation behind the lead aircraft in which Ken was fighting controller.
[Image: Courtesy of Cherry Dawson]

One by one the engines were started until there was a deafening roar as 60 Rolls Royce Merlin engines were powered up – the first time 15 Halifaxes had lined up for an operation. It was some sound and sight and a larger than usual crowd from the station had gathered to wave them off. At that time the

Halifax was largely unknown and those on duty would have been excited to see this new breed of heavy bomber take to the air.

The final checks were made and Wing Commander Jarman gave the order to remove the chocks and the huge, heavily laden Halifax gradually rolled forward to taxi to the end of the runway. At 10.33 hours he lifted off to take a holding position above the airfield to allow the other five 76 Squadron aircraft to form up behind him before setting course for Lizard Point. Next off at 10.34 hours was Flight Lieutenant Lewin followed at 10.35 hours by Sergeant Drummond. But there was a problem. The leader of the second formation of three, Squadron Leader Williams who should have followed immediately, was delayed because his aircraft became unserviceable as he was about to take off and he was forced to change to a spare aircraft. Over the radio telephone he agreed with Wing Commander Jarman to rendezvous over Swindon, and so the three airborne 76 Squadron Halifaxes set a south-westerly course at an air speed of 160 mph at 1,000 feet; it was 10.41 hours. Without delay the nine 35 Squadron aircraft took off at one minute intervals and were all airborne by 10.44 hours forming up in their three Vics of three before setting off for the planned rendezvous with the 76 Squadron formation over Exeter.

At 10.48 hours Wing Commander Jarman was over Swindon, but there was no sign of Squadron Leader Williams and his formation, so he pressed on for the Exeter rendezvous. Soon after take-off Sergeant Gurmin reported the wireless set had stopped functioning; a setback but not such a setback as the delay to Squadron Leader Williams, however it meant the leader's aircraft could not send or receive any important wireless messages until fixed. Sergeant Gurmin set about fixing it, grumbling under his breath because his own set in Flight Lieutenant Cheshire's aircraft was in perfect working order! 11.09 hours saw them over Glastonbury. They reached Exeter at 11.26 hours where they circled and duly picked up the 35 Squadron formations, but still no sight of Squadron Leader Williams. Wing Commander Jarman decided they could not wait so at 11.30 hours the 12 aircraft headed for Lizard Point. Squadron Leader Williams finally took off at 10.55 hours, followed by Pilot Officer McKenna at 10.57 and lastly Flight Lieutenant Hillary two minutes later. That delay was to have disastrous consequences for two of those three crews – they never did catch up with the main formation and consequently were much more vulnerable to fighter attack when they reached the target area.

Several of those aboard the Halifaxes well remember their thoughts as they sped over Devon and Cornwall watching the patchwork of fields and villages rush by below them. It was easy to make out the tors and streams as they flew low over Dartmoor. They could even make out people on the beaches enjoying the glorious summer's day. Many on the beaches waved as they recognised the RAF roundels on the planes as the formation of aircraft roared across the sky. On the minds of many of the airmen as they closed on

Lizard Point was, 'Shall I ever see these beautiful fields, these villages and shores again.' Was that what Ken was thinking too …?

Squadron Leader Williams and his formation ploughed on behind, while the main group crossed Lizard Point at 10.59 hours veering 40° to take a more southerly course to Position A out in the Atlantic.

Flying now at just 100 feet the sea shimmered below them as they headed almost directly into the sun. The run to Position A was about 150 miles, just under an hour; time enough to make those last minute equipment tests, to check again that everything was in its place, to have a bite to eat. Some of the gunners asked permission to test their guns, fired into the sea and watched the splashes.

By dead reckoning Flying Officer Brisbane reported at 12.56 hours they had reached Position A and gave Wing Commander Jarman a compass bearing of 133° to set course for the target. As all the aircraft swung onto the new course the atmosphere changed, the idle chatter ceased. 258 miles to the target; about an hour and a half. The note of the engines altered as the aircraft now climbed steadily and the sea receded further and further below them. Shortly afterwards a group of fishing vessels was sighted; at least the crews hoped they were all innocently fishing and that no one was reporting an RAF formation heading down the coast. At 13.10 hours Wing Commander Jarman ordered 'Action Stations'. Ken moved out of his seat and took up his position under the astrodome. Looking back he could see the other eleven aircraft in formation still – some sight. But Ken was more concerned with what else might be in the skies as they sped towards La Pallice. They needed that element of surprise. They had suffered two setbacks already; were they the extent of their bad luck or was more to come? Ken peered anxiously all around for signs of enemy aircraft. But then, 50 miles from the target, a threat appeared below them in the form of a destroyer dead ahead. Almost immediately the warship, expecting to be a target, put up a barrage of accurate anti-aircraft fire and began to zigzag its course. The formation, now at 12,000 feet, could see the puffs from the anti-aircraft shells exploding around them and felt the buffeting; but none of the aircraft suffered any damage and they pressed on taking no action. This encounter was cursed though because almost undoubtedly the crew of the enemy destroyer would report the engagement, giving the size and direction of the formation. To the German authorities ashore it would be all too obvious what the real target was for this formation of RAF heavy bombers – the Scharnhorst. The element of surprise appeared to have gone. What would their reception be now?

Their course was good; the navigators got a certain fix at 13.55 hours as they passed the Isle d'Yeu, just 15 minutes from La Pallice and the target. It was clear though the formation would not reach the intended 19,000 feet height in the time left; 13,500 to 14,000 feet looked like the level they would achieve. Ten miles from the target Wing Commander Jarman announced he was commencing his bombing run and Flying Officer Brisbane took his position at the bomb sight. Sergeant Gurmin would normally have been at one of the beam guns but Wing Commander Jarman had ordered that he stay at the wireless set throughout the operation so that any urgent messages could be sent or received by the attack's lead aircraft. In the event Sergeant Gurmin continued fixing his wireless, still in bits on the small table in front of him. Behind them Flight Lieutenant Lewin and Sergeant Drummond opened up the formation in preparation and the 35 Squadron aircraft veered to port as planned to make their approach from a slightly different angle.

It was now 14.10 hours and the outside temperature was −8°C. As Ken's aircraft made its final approach the scene emerging before his eyes would have made any man's blood run cold. A massive barrage of anti-aircraft fire was making the sky thick with smoke, pumped relentlessly upwards by guns from the fleet of six escort destroyers and from a host of ground batteries together with the 40 flak guns on the Scharnhorst itself. So thick was the flak that one airman said, 'You could put your hat on it'! Worse still, fighter planes were already up and more could be seen taking off or climbing. A reception party of over 30 enemy fighters was counted. Below all this the bomb aimer, Flying Officer Brisbane, could make out the Scharnhorst, toy-like, moored to the jetty as predicted. The aircraft was now being buffeted about by the flak, shrapnel rattled against the outside metal skin and an acrid smoke filtered into the fuselage.

It was here Ken's job really began. As the first fighter closed in from 400 yards with guns firing Ken ordered evasive action and the rear gunner to open up – at 300 yards the fighter arced away. Attacks on all three planes in the formation continued and time and again Ken ordered defensive fire and evasive action. At times the attacking fighters seemed to ignore the flak coming up, closing in to just 150 yards. But Flight Lieutenant Lewin had difficulty maintaining station through one of the evasion turns and was lagging behind 100 to 150 yards when shells from a fighter struck his aircraft damaging the undercarriage. Further bursts from the fighter hit the engines and vapour started pouring out. The formation slowed so Flight Lieutenant Lewin could catch up but he was unable to close and Ken must have watched briefly with a sickening feeling as the plane began to spiral down.

From his grandstand position Ken could see the whole battlefield. Fighter attacks were constant now. The other formations lost cohesion and became spread out through the accuracy and severity of the flak and the many attacks. Sergeant Drummond drew his aircraft closer to his leader's tail now there were just the two of them in formation. In the confusion one of the 35 Squadron aircraft released its bombs immediately above them – a heart-stopping moment as the cascading bombs miraculously missed them. Seconds later the two 76 Squadron aircraft simultaneously dropped their own bombs in one stick, holding course to see the results and take photographs.

Their bombs missed; some falling short by 300 yards or so, others exploding closely alongside the Scharnhorst.

Wing Commander Jarman made a left turn immediately the results of the bombing were seen, heading away from the area to pick up the return route. But still the attacks came, more aimed at Sergeant Drummond's aircraft than Ken's. Although fewer, the attacks at Ken's aircraft were mostly made at a very close range. But under Ken's direction they fought their way through, weaving and blazing away with their own guns – so successful were some of the evasive manoeuvres that return fire was not necessary. In all there were 21 attacks on the formation, six directly at Ken's aircraft and 15 on Sergeant Drummond's. And all the time the flak hosed up at them. As they turned away Sergeant Drummond's rear gunner Flight Sergeant Begbie was seriously injured in the shoulder by cannon fire and Sergeant Fraser, the radio operator, went aft, managed to get him out of the turret and took his place. Sergeant Dawson also went to help, dragged the injured gunner down the fuselage to the bed by the main spar and gave him a shot of morphine. He then manned the beam gun as they were under attack from all sides.

Sergeant Harry Drummond. He was commissioned in October 1941 and rose to the rank of Wing Commander
[Photo: Courtesy of Peter Cook]

Just then a fighter made a stall turn ahead of them and made yet another attack. Cannon shells and machine gun fire from the ME 109F fighter raked Sergeant Drummond's plane shattering the windscreen and much of the instrument panel, but miraculously missed the crew. Hands bleeding from shards of perspex from the holed windscreen Sergeant Drummond held on to the controls and managed to hold station a few feet from Wing Commander

Jarman's tail. During the encounter Ken's aircraft also sustained hits, putting the automatic pilot out of action. In returning fire against all these attacks several enemy fighters were hit, one of which appeared to go down slowly under control.

Looking back Ken could see the mayhem continuing with the aircraft of 35 Squadron being equally persistent in driving home the attack. He could see one Halifax aircraft that was in serious trouble about half a mile away to port, under attack from several German fighters and with smoke pouring from one engine. Ken directed Wing Commander Jarman's attention to it suggesting their formation should go to its assistance. Sergeant Gurmin remembers hearing this over the intercom and looked out of the nearby window and thought the aircraft was already doomed, saying so to his captain. Wing Commander Jarman considered the situation for a second and said, "You may have a point there, Gurmin". At that moment the stricken aircraft started to arc downwards. This may have been Flight Sergeant Godwin's aircraft. He had just released his bombs when the aircraft took a direct hit from some flak. Severely damaged and with most of the crew injured it came under attack by three fighters. With two engines smoking it began to spin downwards – only two parachutes were seen to open. Damage to Squadron Leader Bradley's bomb doors meant he could not release his bombs over the target but everyone else managed to do so. Sergeant Walters, the bomb aimer on Flight Sergeant Greaves's aircraft, reported he had released half their bomb load. Bravely they went round again and as they headed back through the blackened sky Sergeant Walters released the last of their bombs in a stick with remarkable accuracy. Five of the bombs were seen to score direct hits on the Scharnhorst. But Flight Sergeant Greaves and his crew were now surrounded by seven fighters who took it in turns to attack. Desperately defending their aircraft the rear gunner Sergeant Gillbanks thought he had shot down two fighters before he was seriously wounded in the face, and both Sergeant Constable and his colleague Sergeant Ogden manning the beam guns were hurt. The second pilot was also injured, and when the cockpit exploded Flight Sergeant Greaves too suffered lacerations. By now three engines were on fire. Sergeant Greaves still struggled to fly on, but with the fires spreading he was forced to give the order to bale out. Despite the injuries to five of the crew, everyone got out. Before jumping Flight Sergeant Greaves paused briefly, took off his flying helmet and put it on the control column. 'I shan't be needing that,' he said to himself, clipped on his parachute and dropped through the escape hatch. Only a few moments later, the aircraft exploded. During the rest of the combat many more 35 Squadron crew were injured, some fatally, and all the aircraft suffered damage.

All this fierce aerial battle lasted just 15 minutes or so. Shortly after 14.20 hours as the fighting subsided around him Wing Commander Jarman set course for Position A and home, still 600 miles away. Ken remained in the astrodome as they were not yet in safe territory. Sergeant Drummond doggedly held on behind. But soon after leaving the area Wing Commander Jarman's inner starboard engine spluttered to a halt. He feathered the airscrews and by boosting the power to the other three engines was able to maintain 155mph. By now Ken could not see any other Halifaxes as the battle had spread them far and wide, so the two aircraft headed for home on their own.

Ken may have had a moment to wonder where Squadron Leader Williams and his formation were. In spite of flying fast in an attempt to reach the target on time they were still about half an hour behind. But even more problems beset the formation when persistent engine trouble on Flight Lieutenant Hillary's aircraft left him lagging the formation and unable to climb. Eventually he aborted his mission about 40 miles from the target and turned for home, leaving Squadron Leader Williams and Pilot Officer McKenna to press on together. There were no fighters to greet them this time but the flak barrage soon resumed, just as accurate and as fierce as before. On the first bombing run they could not get a good sighting on the Scharnhorst, so turned over La Rochelle to make a second run. Just then Pilot Officer McKenna's aircraft took a direct hit and plunged into the sea. No parachutes were seen. It was witnessed on the ground by a local professional photographer called Robert Brochot who took a photograph just moments before it fell. Now aged 86 years he says he always remembers this aircraft, the image of which is engraved on his memory.

The Halifax of Pilot Officer McKenna and crew moments before it plunged into the sea
[Photo: Courtesy of Robert Brochot]

Squadron Leader Williams made his second run, but just after releasing his bombs he took a hit on his starboard side and one engine lost power. An enemy fighter appeared and attacked him as the second starboard engine failed. Unable to maintain height, he prepared his crew for a ditching, finally hitting the waves about seven miles off the French coast. No Halifax had ditched before but through Squadron Leader Williams's skill only one of the crew suffered any injury. The injured man just managed to get out and into the water before he lost consciousness, and fortunately for him the remainder of the crew managed to drag him into the dinghy. An enemy fighter made a couple of low passes but took no further action.

Not long after Wing Commander Jarman's aircraft lost an engine the inner port engine on Sergeant Drummond's aircraft gave up, damaged over La Pallice. By 15.00 hours they were down to 4,000 feet in a temperature of 20°C and by 15.41 hours, with Ken back in the second pilot's seat, Flying Officer Brisbane reckoned they had reached Position A. He gave Wing Commander Jarman a course of 028° which should see them back to Lizard Point again still some 150 miles and nearly an hour away. Sergeant Gurmin still struggled with his wireless but fortunately the wireless on Sergeant Drummond's aircraft was working and they were able to pick up a number of radio beacons to help Sergeant Dawson with his navigation. The minutes on this haul over the sea must have dragged. Ears must have been attuned to any change in the note of the engines. Would they hold out till they reached land? At long last land appeared. The wind had pushed them slightly east and they crossed the coast at Fowey at 16.43 hours. Everyone's spirits immediately lifted. They set course for the airfield at Stanton Harcourt, only 175 miles to go, estimated time of arrival 17.48 hours. Emergency airfields were available now if needed. Sergeant Dawson went aft to see to the injured Flight Sergeant Begbie and gave him some further first aid assistance. They radioed ahead for an ambulance to meet the aircraft when it landed. But a few minutes later over the town of Wellington their outer port engine began to give concern and they were now very low on fuel. The engine held out for a while but over Chippenham at 17.30 hours it gave up. Determined to make base Sergeant Drummond ploughed on. Swindon appeared at 17.36 hours ... would the two starboard engines still running make it? At 17.43 hours they could see the approach to Stanton Harcourt airfield, Wing Commander Jarman still leading them. But he moved into the circuit allowing Sergeant Drummond, on two engines, low on fuel and with an injured crew member on board, to land first. He touched down at 17.45 hours. Ironically, whilst in the circuit as Sergeant Drummond landed, Sergeant Gurmin finally mended the faulty wireless set and transmitted the 'Mission completed' signal. A few minutes later Wing Commander Jarman brought down his aircraft, taxied to a halt and shut down his three functioning engines. Ken and the other crew gradually emerged from the aircraft, unhurt but utterly fatigued and drained. Over by the other aircraft Sergeant Drummond had collapsed on the grass, totally exhausted.

For a while the crews stood around quietly discussing their experiences. Sergeant 'Taff' Gurmin turned to Sergeant Patterson, their front gunner, and asked him what he thought of all those German fighters. He jokingly replied with a mixture of relief and nervous tension, "I never could see much with my eyes closed, Taff!" Flight Sergeant Begbie was taken off in an ambulance and the Medical Officer began giving first aid to Sergeant Drummond who was coming round. But thoughts soon turned to the fate of the other crews. Two aircraft had already made it back to Stanton Harcourt. Flight Lieutenant Hillary who had turned back with engine problems was first back, all safe. Just before Ken's aircraft landed Pilot Officer Johnston and his 35 Squadron crew landed safely. They reported their bombs fell short of the target, their aim spoilt by a fighter attack. In all they recounted seven attacks, putting up stiff resistance with the rear gunner telling of one enemy fighter definitely downed and possibly a second. But the crew said they saw one Halifax going down.

News began to come through that four aircraft had earlier landed at the emergency airfield RAF St Eval, north of Newquay in Cornwall, and two more had just touched down at RAF Weston Zoyland near Bridgewater in Somerset, all from 35 Squadron. The news was not all good. Flight Sergeant Godwin's aircraft was seen to go down in a slow spiral with two fighters on its tail, smoke coming from its engines and a fire in the rear turret. All the pilots reported fierce fighting and the aircraft landing at RAF St Eval had two fatalities aboard with four more crew injured. There were still three aircraft unaccounted for and the crews waited anxiously for news of them, but eventually they too were reported missing. The toll was high; half the contingent of six aircraft from Ken's 76 Squadron was missing plus two of the nine from 35 Squadron. In all, five Halifaxes were missing from the fourteen that attacked the Scharnhorst.

The state of the returning aircraft was further testament to the ferocity of the aerial battle over La Pallice. All were damaged to one extent or another, only two not seriously. Apart from one engine not working, Ken's plane on examination had just six bullet holes; Wing Commander Jarman put down this small number to Ken's excellent fighting control. Sergeant Drummond's aircraft on the other hand had 35 holes in it apart from the smashed windscreen, damaged instrument panel and two lifeless engines. The extensive damage meant it had to remain at RAF Stanton Harcourt for repairs and it was not until 4 August that Sergeant Drummond and a crew could fly down to collect it. In all five aircraft were so badly damaged it was estimated they would each take three weeks to repair, and another two would be out of action for nearly a week.

Of course the aerial battle was not all one-sided. Flight Sergeant Woods on Ken's aircraft claimed one fighter hit and in all the tally of claims by the gunners was five fighters shot down, five or six more 'probables' and many others damaged. Inevitably these figures do not exactly match up with Luftwaffe records which appear to show only two fighters destroyed, three severely damaged and one pilot wounded.

And what of the Scharnhorst? This time her luck ran out as the five bombs from Sergeant Greaves's aircraft that struck her caused serious damage, and one account talked of two of her crew being killed and 15 injured. The damage would have been much more extensive had the three 1,000lb armour-piercing bombs detonated, but they holed the ship without exploding. Water flooded in and the battleship took on an 8° list, although prompt action by the crew soon stabilised this. Nevertheless the consequent flooding caused considerable damage particularly to electrical installations. The other two bombs exploded between decks causing local damage and some small fires which were quickly extinguished. Captain Hoffmann assessed the situation and deciding his ship was seaworthy and that it was too dangerous to stay at La Pallice gave orders to return to Brest that night. She left at 21.05 hours with 3,000 tons of flood water in her hull, tying up at the jetty at Brest at 09.30 hours the following morning. Repairs would take at least four months.

The Scharnhorst leaving La Pallice – smoke in the background, 24 July 1941
[Photo: Courtesy of Robert Brochot]

The Scharnhorst leading her escorts returns to Brest for repairs, 24 July 1941
[Photo: Courtesy of Robert Brochot]

Immediately the RAF bombers returned from La Pallice and from Brest reports of the results were quickly sent up the line reaching the Air Ministry and the War Cabinet. If Ken and his colleagues tuned in to the Nine O'clock News on the BBC that evening this is what they would have heard:

> *Here is the news, and this is Frederick Allen reading it. Daylight attacks on the German battleships Scharnhorst and Gneisenau are reported by the Air Ministry.*

It went on:

> *The following communiqué has been issued by the Air Ministry:*
> *"During the last twenty four hours extensive operations have been undertaken by Bomber Command against the German battleships Scharnhorst and Gneisenau. Yesterday the Scharnhorst was discovered by air reconnaissance to have been moved from Brest to La Pallice two hundred and fifty miles to the south. ... At two o'clock this afternoon a very strong force of heavy bombers developed simultaneous attacks on the Gneisenau at Brest and the Scharnhorst at La Pallice.*
> *The attack on Brest was supported by squadrons of fighters. ... Preliminary reports of the operations last night and today indicate that these attacks were successful."*

A similar report was carried on the midnight news, and each bulletin throughout the following day added more detail. The combined raids were described as 'the heaviest daylight attack since the war began.'

On the seven o'clock bulletin the next morning mention was made for the first time to the British public of the existence of the Halifax bomber.

> *...Meanwhile, Halifax four-engined bombers were after the already damaged Scharnhorst at her breakwater in the harbour of La Pallice. The huge bombers attacked in force each carrying a formidable load of great armour piercing bombs and at least one more direct hit was made on the Scharnhorst.*

The mention of 'one more direct hit' was a reference to the belief that one of the Stirling bombers had succeeded in the evening raid of the 23 July which was not the case.

The day after the raid *The Times* carried an article with the headline, 'Scharnhorst Hit Again – Heavy Attacks In New Refuge' and a fuller report appeared the day after with the headline, 'A Great Air Battle', that emotively talked of the Scharnhorst 'in her new lair' at La Pallice and that 'the attack was driven home in the teeth of heavy anti-aircraft fire and swarms of Messerschmitts'.

Also the following day Ken would have read a message from Sir Richard Peirse, Air Marshal, Commanding-in-Chief, Bomber Command, addressed to participating squadrons:

> *A magnificent day's work executed with that characteristic dash and courage which the world now knows is the tradition of Bomber Command. Well Done.*

Sir Richard accompanied his message with a message from the Chief of the Air Staff, Air Chief Marshal Sir Charles Portal:

> *Please convey to all who took part in yesterday's operations my warm appreciation of the efficiency and determination with which the attacks on the enemy warships was conceived and executed. I am sure all Units realise the supreme importance of keeping these German Cruisers inactive and the great contribution their attacks have made towards relieving the Royal Navy of some part of their heavy burden. It was most satisfactory that the number of enemy fighters destroyed by your gunners well exceeded your own losses.*

The raid was important enough to be mentioned in a telegram to President Roosevelt the following day, and to be carried in a separate paragraph in the War Cabinet's Weekly Résumé.

In writing his report on the raid, Wing Commander Jarman was typically forthright, no doubt still smarting from the Squardon's losses. He pointedly complained about the late switch of base to Stanton Harcourt and under the heading 'Lessons Learned' he drew attention to a number of issues including several impracticalities of trying to fly in one large formation, the inadequate notice for the operation, of using a base not used to the Halifax aircraft and to the poor quality of the radio equipment. However, in his report on the air battle he wrote, referring to Ken:

> *The Squadron Gunnery Leader was stationed in the astro dome and carried out the duties of fighting controller for both aircraft. Due to his excellent controlling a total of <u>six bullet holes only</u> were found in his aircraft upon inspection. It was not necessary to allocate fire to targets as at no time did the enemy carry out a twofold attack. <u>He gave the necessary evasive action to be carried out and the executive word of command for its employment</u>.*

A few days later, recommendations were put in hand to recognise the courage and determination of the operation's leaders and a number of notable aircrew, including Ken who was recommended to receive the Distinguished Flying Cross. The first signature to Ken's recommendation was that of Wing Commander Jarman. Further signatures were added up the chain of command; the final sign off was by Air Marshal, Commanding-in-Chief, Bomber Command, Sir Richard Peirse on 8 August.

The Distinguished Flying Cross was awarded to Officers and Warrant Officers for an act or acts of valour, courage or devotion to duty whilst flying in active service against the enemy. The equivalent award for other ranks was the Distinguished Flying Medal. The older, and higher, honour of the Distinguished Service Order was awarded to Officers for individual instances of meritorious or distinguished service in war.

CONFIDENTIAL.

RECOMMENDATIONS FOR HONOURS AND AWARDS.

Christian Names.	Kenneth Montague.	Surname.	Bastin.
Rank.	A/F/Lt.	Official Number.	75168.
Command or Group.	4 Group.	Unit.	76 Squadron.

Total No. of hours flown on Operations.   152.50 hrs.

No. of Sorties carried out.   24.

Recognition for which Recommended.   Immediate award of D.F.C.

Appointment Held.   Gunnery Officer.

Particulars of Meritorious service for which the Recommendation is made, including date and place.

This Officer was Gunnery Officer in the leading aircraft in a daylight attack on the Scharnhorst at La Pallice on 24th July, 1941.

On this occasion the section which he was controlling was heavily engaged over the target by flak and his aircraft sustained damage. Immediately after leaving the target, the section was engaged by a succession of Messerschmitt 109F fighters, which made at least twelve attacks during which all aircraft were hit and one shot down.

Throughout the engagement, F/Lt. Bastin controlled the fire of all guns and gave directions for avoiding action which resulted in the safe withdrawal of two of the section, and the certain damage of two fighters.

His coolness, precision and complete indifference to heavy fire, were an inspiration and a fine example to all members of the formation. I unhesitatingly recommend that his action be recognised by the immediate award of the Distinguished Flying Cross.

Date.   Signature of Commanding Officer.

Remarks of Station Commander.

Strongly recommended. During the heat of the action this officer's fire control orders and directions were given with the same clarity and accuracy he has shown when practising with friendly fighters.

Date. 26th July, 1941.   Rank. G/Capt.

Remarks of A.O.C.

Recommended for award of D.F.C.

Date. 31.7.41.   Rank. Air Vice Marshal.

Commanding, H.Q.No.4 Group

The recommendation for the award of Distinguished Flying Cross to A/F/Lt. Kenneth Montague Bastin. Note the details of the citation and the strong recommendation of the Station Commander
[Image: Courtesy of The National Archives, Kew (AIR2 8858)]

Ken doubtless heard confirmation of his award on 8 August as that is the day his award was signed off at the topmost level and is noted in the Squadron's records. He contacted his family as soon as he could to tell them the news. On Sunday 10 August, Ken's sister Phyllis wrote in her diary:

What a day. Heard in the evening that Ken has been awarded the DFC ... What a thrill – so excited we could hardly think of anything else. However Mum & Mary came over in the afternoon. Gardened. Heard the Queen in the evening on the radio.

In all, for the operation against the Scharnhorst at La Pallice, awards were made as follows:

Distinguished Service Order

Immediate Awards

- Wing Commander Geoffrey Twyford Jarman DFC (76 Squadron, Leader of the Operation & Pilot)
- Squadron Leader Terence Patrick Armstrong Bradley DFC (35 Squadron, Leader of 35 Squadron Formations & Pilot)

Distinguished Flying Cross

Immediate Awards

- Flight Lieutenant Kenneth Montague Bastin (76 Squadron, Gunnery Officer)
- Flying Officer Guy Maxwell Brisbane DFM (76 Squadron, Observer Officer)
- Warrant Officer George Walton Holden (35 Squadron, Pilot)

Non-Immediate Awards

- Flying Officer Richard Charles Rivaz (35 Squadron, Gunnery Officer)
- Flying Officer Peter Stanley James (35 Squadron, Pilot)

Distinguished Flying Medal

Immediate Awards

- Sergeant George Alexander Fraser (76 Squadron, Air Gunner)
- Sergeant Herbert Reginald Higgins (35 Squadron, Air Gunner)
- Sergeant Mark Antony Sachs (35 Squadron, Air Gunner)

Non-Immediate Awards
- Sergeant Henry Howard Drummond (76 Squadron, Pilot)
- Sergeant Montagu Ellis Hawkins Dawson (76 Squadron, Observer)
- Sergeant Thomas Neville Sankey (35 Squadron, Air Gunner)

And, belatedly, after the war in December 1947
- Flight Sergeant Stanley Desmond Greaves (35 Squadron, Pilot)

Mentioned in Despatches

Belatedly, after the war in December 1947
- Sergeant Alan Gillbanks (35 Squadron, Air Gunner)
- Sergeant Wilfred C Walters (35 Squadron, Observer).

And what of those airmen who did not return? In night operations when losses occurred these were generally termed 'missing'; aircraft that simply failed to return, their fate unseen. This time it was somewhat different. Ken and a number of others saw what happened to some of the 'missing' aircraft, could estimate whether the crew might have survived, hoping for the better, fearing the worst. Nevertheless, Ken may not have learned of the fate of those crews before his next posting because information on individuals killed or made prisoner of war would often take some months to come through.

From Ken's 76 Squadron, the casualties were:

- Flight Lieutenant Lewin's aircraft, part of Ken's formation, crashed into the sea just off the Pointe de l'Aiguillon. Flight Lieutenant Lewin, Sergeant Gourley, Flight Sergeant Horner and Sergeant Vickey were all killed; Sergeant Phillips, Sergeant Finlayson, who was slightly injured, and Flying Officer McLeod survived. Sergeant Phillips was captured immediately, but the other two were helped ashore and hidden by two local farmers, Fernand Neau and Alphonse Gouraud, with the help of Fernand Neau's two children, Fernand aged 20 and Rose aged 16 who spoke a little English. But the airmen were captured early the following morning at Fernand Neau's house.

- After Squadron Leader Williams successfully ditched his aircraft, all the crew of seven were rescued from their dinghy by a local fisherman, Pierre Brintin, in his small boat. But before the fisherman could reach a nearby port his boat was intercepted by the crew of a Kriegsmarine craft who captured the wet and bedraggled airmen.

- Pilot Officer McKenna's aircraft, one of the delayed formation, was hit by flak and crashed into the sea off La Rochelle. The crew of Pilot

Officer McKenna, Sergeant Ford-Hutchinson, Sergeant Summers, Sergeant Davis, Sergeant Pilbeam, Sergeant Rice and Flight Sergeant Hill all died.

Here should be recorded the tragic consequences for the Neau and Gouraud families for helping Sergeant Finlayson and Flying Officer McLeod. Fernand Neau senior and Alphonse Gouraud were arrested at the time and shot by the Germans the following February. The Germans also arrested Fernand Neau junior, his sister Rose, Alphonse Gouraud's son Michel aged 15, the local mayor and another local man. The latter three were released at the beginning of August but Fernand Neau junior was not released until November. Rose Neau, only in her mid teens, was imprisoned until the following February. A few days after her release she was given the news her father had just been executed.

The 35 Squadron casualties were:

- Flight Sergeant Godwin's aircraft came down on a farm near the small town of Angles. Flight Sergeant Godwin, Sergeant Esnouf, Sergeant Newstead, Sergeant Rudlin and Flight Sergeant Shirley all perished. Only two of the crew managed to bail out, Pilot Officer Eperon who was quickly taken prisoner and Sergeant Balcomb who attempted to evade capture with the help of some local people. He was given a bicycle and headed away from the area but after a while ran into a German patrol and was captured. During interrogation he told his captors he had stolen the bicycle to protect the identity of those who helped him.

- In the doomed aircraft piloted by Flight Sergeant Greaves only two of the crew were uninjured and it was miraculous they all parachuted out to safety and capture. The injured were taken to hospital for treatment. One of them, Sergeant Gillbanks, had been seriously wounded in the face but the skill of the German surgeons saved his sight. There is a wonderful sequel to the story of Flight Sergeant Greaves and his crew recounted at the end of this book.

- There were casualties too in the returning 35 Squadron aircraft. Squadron Leader Bradley's plane carried the body of Sergeant Bolton, killed instantly in one attack, and the injured second pilot, Sergeant Rowley-Blake, who had several shrapnel wounds. The first attack on Warrant Officer Holden's aircraft killed the rear gunner, Pilot Officer Stone, and injured both crew manning the beam guns; they were Sergeant Smith who was severely wounded and semi conscious and Sergeant Perriment who was in acute pain. And finally, Sergeant Walker the rear gunner on Pilot Officer Millar's aircraft was injured in the leg in the first attack he defended and his turret was put out of action.

The human toll makes grim reading. Eighteen airmen were killed, eleven from Ken's squadron. A further twelve were injured, some seriously, and nineteen made prisoner of war. And tribute should be paid to the local French people who offered help and shelter to our airmen, particularly the two who were arrested and executed, Fernand Neau and Alphonse Gouraud.

And the ultimate fate of the Scharnhorst …? In the autumn of 1941, when Admiral Raeder was planning to send his battleships back into the Atlantic to attack Allied convoys, Hitler became convinced the main Allied threat would come via Norway and wanted his main battleships back in home waters as protection and as a threat to the Russian convoys. The loss of the Bismarck gave him added reason for not wanting to risk his capital ships in the Atlantic. And so an audacious plan was hatched by the German Navy to bring the Scharnhorst, Gneisenau and the Prinz Eugen back to German ports. On the evening of 11 February 1942, the battleships broke out of Brest and accompanied by an array of protection vessels and aircraft made a daring dash through the English Channel to safety. Ken's colleagues at 76 Squadron and 35 Squadron were amongst a vast assortment of British forces sent out to attack them, some making truly heroic assaults. But a combination of atrocious weather, surprise, bad luck, poor communications and missed opportunities resulted in the warships making it through despite suffering some damage. Seen as a major coup for the Germans, nevertheless this turn of events meant that the main purpose of the La Pallice attack, which was to prevent the Scharnhorst causing havoc in the Atlantic, had been achieved. Later the Scharnhorst was moved to the Norwegian fiords. From there on Christmas Day 1943, ordered by Admiral Dönitz who was under pressure from Hitler to disrupt supplies reaching Russia, she set out to attack convoy JW-55B heading for Murmansk. But the Royal Navy had two large forces in the area north of Norway, which the Germans failed to properly identify, and when the Scharnhorst despatched her destroyer escorts to scout for the convoy she was pursued, attacked and finally sunk on 26 December 1943.

7. The King, the USA and the 1,000 Bomber Raids

The tragic losses at La Pallice left a very sombre mood at the station. Amongst the crews little was said, and only then when the subject could not be avoided. Operational flying did not resume until nearly a week later when four aircraft went to Cologne. After that though, it was back to business as usual with operations on eleven nights in August and a further seven nights in September.

But losses continued too – the night of 12/13 August being the worst with the loss of three aircraft. One of these, piloted by Flight Lieutenant Christopher Cheshire, was shot down near Hamburg. Flight Lieutenant Cheshire was flying with his usual crew, two of whom had flown with Ken on the La Pallice raid – Sergeant 'Taff' Gurmin, the wireless operator and Flight Sergeant 'Timber' Woods, the rear gunner. Most of the crew, including Flight Lieutenant Cheshire, landed safely and were captured, but Flight Sergeant Woods and one other did not survive. After landing Sergeant Gurmin remembers walking down a road whistling, 'There will always be an England,' in case any of his crew was nearby. Unfortunately for Sergeant Gurmin the first person he met was a Luftwaffe Officer and a squad of about ten men who promptly took him away.

By coincidence Christopher Cheshire's older brother Leonard, then a Flight Lieutenant with 35 Squadron, was also flying on the same operation. The charismatic Leonard Cheshire became one of the most famous pilots of Bomber Command and was decorated with the Victoria Cross in 1944.

At the end of August the cruellest luck befell one of the Squadron's senior officers, Squadron Leader Bob Bickford DFC. He and his crew were almost home from a raid on Frankfurt when their aircraft developed engine failure over Yorkshire. The crew were forced to bail out but somehow Squadron Leader Bickford's parachute caught up in the tail plane and he was dragged down to his death. Ken must have felt his loss keenly as they had also been together at 10 Squadron. On 14 September another survivor of La Pallice, Pilot Officer Hutchin, was killed when his aircraft came down near Bedford.

Meanwhile, Ken's mother went to stay with Ken and his wife, and she obviously learned more of the details of his Distinguished Flying Cross. When his mother returned home to Northampton the rest of the family were eager to hear more, and Ken's sister wrote in her diary on Saturday 6 September:

Did usual work and bottled.
Tony home to look after R while I went to Mum's house. Tea with Mary and then off to meet Mum at Kettering, back from staying with Ken. Heard all the

details of Ken's DFC — the Wing Commander said their plane would never had got back but for Ken's calm clear evasive and gunnery orders — only 2 out of the 5 from Ken's squadron got back. Stayed till 7.45 then home.

The official announcements of the decorations for the La Pallice operation had been made in *The London Gazette* and *The Times* on 2 September. These were in a group citation incorporating the awards for the simultaneous raids on Brest and Cherbourg. Even the local newspaper where Ken's family lived, the *Northampton Chronicle & Echo*, was not going to miss out on the story, although Ken was hardly local. His sister, Phyllis, pinned in her diary a short piece carried by the paper, which used some journalistic license to make the connection with Northampton.

> **ANOTHER D.F.C.**
>
> ANOTHER D.F.C. has come to Northampton, not exactly to a Northampton man, but at least to a son of one who is well-known to many Northamptonians.
>
> The award has been made to Flight-Lieut. K. M. Bastin, whose mother, Mrs. J. E. Bastin, lives in Meadway, Weston Favell. His sister is Mrs. L. P. Williams, who lives at Duston, and whose husband is on the Northampton staff of the National Provincial Bank.
>
> Young Bastin, who was articled to a city firm of auctioneers and estate agents, joined the R.A.F. and was given a commission at the outbreak of war. He was a well-known hockey player, turning out for the Tulse Hill club, and played international hockey in tours with a British team on the Continent, including Germany.
>
> Another sister, Miss Mary Bastin, who is now a nurse at St. Matthew's Nursing Home, is a well-known Oxford grouper, and was a member of the Northampton Amateur Operatic Society, taking the title role in "The Grand Duchess" a few years ago.

Article from the Northampton Chronicle & Echo pinned in Phyllis's diary Saturday 6 September 1941
[Image: Courtesy of Chronicle & Echo]

Operations continued through October, reflecting the task given to Bomber Command in July of greater emphasis on targets around the Ruhr to prevent supplies moving out of the main industrial areas. When poor weather over the Ruhr prevented operations there, Bomber Command was to continue the offensive against Germany's other significant centres of industry. The Squadron was involved in several more raids against the warships at

Brest, which continued to receive sporadic attention. But Ken was to fly on operations only once more with 76 Squadron. This was on the night of 12/13 October when four Squadron aircraft were detailed to Nuremberg and one to Bremen.

This was another record night for Bomber Command. Over 350 aircraft were despatched, of which just over 150 were allocated to attack the town of Nuremberg in southeastern Germany.

The entry in the Squadron's record book clearly suggests Ken's Halifax bombed Nuremberg that night. But was this so?

Possibly not, as we shall see …

Date: 12.10.41

Aircraft Type and Number: 9601 "F"

Crew: Sgt Turnbull, P/O Anderson, Sgt. Thompson, Sgt. Pearce, Sgt. Linton, Sgt Sprigge, F/Lt. Bastin.

Duty: BOMBING ATTACK ON NUREMBURG [sic]

Time Up: 1908. Time Down: 0310

Details: This aircraft attacked the primary target from a height of 15,000 feet at approximately 2355 hours. Little Flak was encountered on either outward or return journeys. On attacking the target fires were started and seen to grow with intensity. Visibility was fair with very little cloud. Balloons were up at 8,000 feet. Aircraft returned safely and landed at Docking.

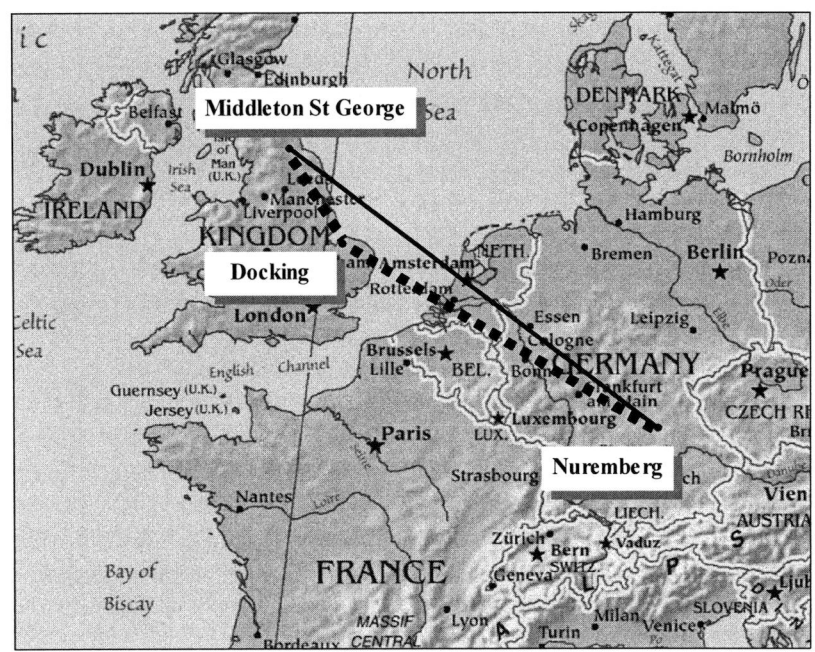

The Route to Nuremberg landing back at Docking, 12 October 1941

Yet another lonely eight-hour operation for Ken, much of it over enemy territory, reportedly completed successfully. They landed at Docking in Norfolk just after three o'clock in the morning. After some well earned rest and the traditional eggs and bacon breakfast, they doubtless flew the last hundred miles or so back to Yorkshire later in the day. Another Squadron crew that claimed to have bombed Nuremberg landed back at South Cerney, near Cirencester.

As usual, not everyone was so lucky. In all thirteen aircraft were lost on the continent that night, eight from the squadrons attacking Nuremberg. 76 Squadron lost one aircraft, the one despatched to Bremen, shot down over Holland. The pilot was killed and the remaining crew made POWs. In a wretched night, a further five aircraft returning from Nuremberg crashed in England, some crews fortunately survived.

The results of this raid were a notable example of the difficulties the crews faced navigating their way on a long flight through the night. Before an operation they were briefed with the forecast wind strength and direction, but it did not take much difference between the forecast and the true strength and direction for an aircraft flying over hundreds of miles to become tens of miles or more from its intended flight path. Crews struggled in the blackness to pick out distinct physical features, such as a coastline, lakes or rivers, to help them 'grope' their way to the target and back. The longer it became since a certain navigational fix was made, the greater the possible variance from their planned route.

Post war reports from the city of Nuremberg itself record only a few bombs fell on the city. Many more bombs fell on the town of Schwabach, 10 miles south of Nuremberg, where 50 buildings were destroyed.

So if Ken's crew had not actually bombed Nuremberg, they possibly dropped their bombs on Schwabach. It is also possible they mistakenly bombed Lauingen, a village of no military or industrial significance some sixty-five miles from Nuremberg, whose poor inhabitants suffered four hours of intense air raids with hundreds of high explosive bombs and incendiaries falling on it, with more in the surrounding countryside. Forty-four houses were destroyed and several people were killed. Or indeed they may have been even further off target since the small town of Lauffen, some ninety-five miles from the primary target, suffered a similar fate; here forty-six houses were hit.

The explanation for these events may lie in the fact that from the air at night, Lauingen and Lauffen could easily have been mistaken for Nuremberg as all three are situated on wide rivers. It may have only taken one or two 'off course' aircraft to bomb these two places, believing they had found Nuremberg, for other similarly wayward aircraft to be attracted to the fires. These 'stray' crews, thinking they too at last had found the target, dropped their bombs and incendiaries, adding to the confusion.

And of course after dropping their bombs these 'stray' crews would have thought they were navigating a route for home starting at Nuremberg. Perhaps Ken's crew was one of these 'strays' and that was why, instead of returning to Yorkshire, they landed in Norfolk. The Squadron aircraft that landed in Gloucestershire was even further astray!

The Nuremberg raid was a classic example of problems Bomber Command had experienced in the early part of the war, problems which were brought sharply into focus in the autumn of 1941 by the Butt Report. Those at the head of Bomber Command and the RAF were aware from various sources that the efficiency of their bombers was probably not as good as the somewhat optimistic reports coming up through the chain of command. But it was not the Air Ministry or Bomber Command itself that decided to make a close analysis of the effectiveness of night operations, a strategy forced on Bomber Command by the heavy losses of bombing in daylight. The report was commissioned by the Prime Minister's chief scientific adviser, Lord Cherwell, who asked a civil servant in the War Cabinet's office to conduct the survey. His name was Mr D M Butt. The Butt Report concluded from analysing over 4,000 aircraft photographs that only one in four of the crews that claimed to have bombed a target in Germany were found to have been within five miles of their target. This proportion improved on full-moon nights, but worsened in moonless periods, and was particularly poor over the Ruhr area, which was often covered in haze. Considering the samples taken by Mr Butt excluded the one third of crews who did not claim to have reached their target, the stark conclusions were both dramatic and disappointing. In truth they were only a reflection of the navigation equipment then available, the general standard crew training and the tactics Bomber Command were forced to adopt. Initially Bomber Command itself was in somewhat denial over the report, but eventually by mid-November it was informed after a War Cabinet meeting that during the coming months only limited operations should be carried out while the whole future of the Command was reviewed. In warfare, heavy losses may be justifiable when the objective is being achieved. But for Bomber Command this equation was now being seen as out of balance.

Excitement mounted in the Bastin family households when an invitation arrived for Ken to receive his decoration at an Investiture at Buckingham Palace on Tuesday 25 November 1941. Two guests were permitted and he wanted Teddie and his mother to be there. His mother had to buy a new hat!

Ken travelled down from Middleton St George to London the day before to meet up in London with his wife and mother. He was accompanied by some of his 76 Squadron colleagues who were also to receive their decorations at the same Investiture.

In her diary for the day before the Investiture, Phyllis wrote:

Dashed down to see Mum off at the station by 10.18.

The day finally arrived and Ken, his proud wife and mother took their places in the Investiture room at the Palace, awaiting the entrance of King George VI.

> # INVESTITURE
>
> AT
>
> BUCKINGHAM PALACE,
>
> On Tuesday, the 25th November, 1941, at 11 o'clock a.m.

The Heading of Buckingham Palace's Investiture List, 25 November 1941

Ken's mother was delighted at seeing the King in the flesh for the first time, but sat rather impatiently during the long wait before Ken's name was called, as the list of presentations was long. One of those receiving his decoration before Ken was a Squadron Leader being presented with a Bar to his Distinguished Flying Cross. Not conspicuous at that time, his name was to become one of the most famous of the war – Guy Gibson, who won the Victoria Cross for leading the Dams Raid. At long last, the moment came when Ken was called forward to be presented with his Distinguished Flying Cross.

The Distinguished Flying Cross

His sister wrote in her diary for that day:

Did the washing.
How prosaic compared with the Investiture at Buckingham Palace & Ken being decorated by the King. Mum & Teddie there! What a thrill.

But Ken's spell with 76 Squadron was coming to an end, with a rather unexpected and surprising posting. His eight months on the Squadron had been hectic to say the least. The Squadron had been formed from scratch and Ken's task had been to bring the gunnery contingent quickly up to operational level on the new Halifax, which was still having its teething problems. Of course the La Pallice raid was a hugely significant event for Ken; and although some of those who survived went on to complete two or even three tours of operation, La Pallice would forever stand out amongst their wartime memories too. During his eight months with 76 Squadron 47 colleagues had been killed and more than 30 made prisoner – each one a harsh reminder of the toll of war that must have weighed heavily against the undoubted pride Ken felt in the award of his Distinguished Flying Cross.

When the American Congress passed the 'Lend Lease' Bill in March it paved the way for a significant increase in the supply of arms from the USA. Before that the RAF and France had already ordered a number of B-24 type aircraft – a four-engine, long-range heavy bomber to be built by the manufacturers Consolidated of San Diego, which became known in the RAF as the Liberator. With the fall of France the RAF took over their contract and the early versions began to come through in the summer of 1941. The initial small numbers of these aircraft were mainly used as unarmed transports across the North Atlantic and by Coastal Command. The latest version, the B-24D, was expected to be produced in large numbers and was due to be delivered in the early months of 1942. But in October the Ministry of Aircraft Production in London was expressing to the Americans serious concerns about the suitability of the proposed armament for those aircraft destined for the RAF under the Lend Lease scheme. This concern was prompted by a report from a Wing Commander Spreckley following his visit to the States. These concerns were taken up through the British Air Commission in Washington – the British Air Commission was the agency through which aircraft were purchased from America.

The planned armament for the B-24D was to use three different makes of turret; a Martin upper turret, a Bendix lower turret and a Consolidated tail turret. Four areas of concern were identified and were being quite explicitly expressed. Whilst the Martin upper turret was considered 'fairly satisfactory', it was said the 'supply, maintenance and training problems incident to having three types of turrets on the same airplane render the situation almost hopeless'. The Bendix lower turret was called, 'completely hopeless due to improper control and poor design'; and the Consolidated tail turret was described as, 'too small'. Lastly the .50 calibre guns themselves were 'not regarded as satisfactory for night operations because of flash, and technicians are of the opinion that very little could be done without considerable reduction in muzzle velocity'.

On 7 November a quite strident cypher was sent from the British Air Commission to Air Marshal Linnell in London, who was the Controller of Research and Development for the Ministry of Aircraft Production. It read:

> To strengthen our arguments with the U.S. Services on essential requirements for future turrets, particularly as regards size and comfort, we urge you arrange for an experienced gunnery leader with recent extensive operational experience in Northern Europe to visit America. He would be able to test American turrets personally and should be available for the trials of the B-24D which are expected to start shortly. If you agree to this visit we will give you a firmer date for these trials. A gunner of reasonably large stature should be selected and he should preferably have some engineering knowledge to be able to discuss broadly the effect of turrets on aircraft performance.

How Ken came to be selected for this visit is not certain, but it is reasonable to think the Ministry of Aircraft Production requested Bomber Command to release someone who fitted the above criteria. Bomber Command in turn may have approached the commanders of the more experienced Halifax heavy bomber squadrons, 35 Squadron and 76 Squadron, for recommendations. Squadron Leader Bouwens, who was temporary Officer Commanding, would doubtless have put forward Ken's name immediately, and it was Ken who was selected. When he was told of his new duty it must have come as a total surprise to him. Initially he was probably very pleased at the thought of getting away from the war for a spell, and quite probably he felt proud to be called to represent the RAF on such a mission. He was officially transferred to the Ministry of Aircraft Production, Directorate of Armament Development on 10 December 1941.

As these arrangements were being put in hand, the whole outlook of the war changed with the historic attack by the Japanese on Pearl Harbour on 7 December. The following day the United States and Britain declared war on Japan, and three days later Germany declared war on the United States. This meant that as Ken set out for Washington, he was heading not for a neutral country, but for a military ally.

He arrived in Washington towards the end of January, just as the British Air Commission received advice that the US Air Corps had a B-24C 'equipped with the defensive armament as for the B-24D' ready for ground examination and ground and air firing tests at Eglin Field, Florida. In 1942 Eglin Field was the site for gunnery training for fighter pilots, as well as a major testing centre for aircraft, equipment and tactics. On the coast in western Florida, Eglin Field had immense ranges in the surrounding forest and out over the Gulf of Mexico.

Ken travelled there with Wing Commander A S Fletcher, starting their tests on 28 January. Over three days they conducted comprehensive ground and air trials on the three turrets. How Ken must have felt a world away from the war and England's winter! And surely he must have been a focus of attention for the American airmen at Eglin Field. Here was a decorated RAF officer with recent and considerable experience of the air war over Europe; here was someone who had been heavily involved in what they themselves could soon be facing; here was someone who could tell them what it was really like.

Following their tests, Wing Commander Fletcher and Ken prepared a detailed report which was sent by 'Air Diplomatic Bag' to the Director of Armament Development in London on 10 February. A few days earlier Wing Commander Fletcher sent a summary report outlining the conclusions, which were:

> (a) The Consolidated turret falls very far below the operational standard required and is therefore not acceptable for Lend Lease British aircraft. The outstanding faults are: space accommodation is much too small to allow for the gunner to occupy the turret for any required length of time; ingress, although possible, is difficult and egress is impossible with gunner in full flying clothing, unless assisted by another member of the crew. These facts, coupled with the non-rigidity of gun mountings and the amount of flexibility in the gun sight mounting and linkage, are sufficient in themselves to damn the whole turret.[2]

> (b) The mid-upper turret has very good controllability, adequate room for the gunner and air firing results were satisfactory. Azimuth power failed with the aircraft in the dive at speeds in excess of 250 m.p.h., but it has not been established whether this was due to insufficient torque power available or a faulty break circuit switch. There were several other points which require attention, such as difficulty of harmonizing and also removing the guns, but our report has been forwarded to the Air Corps recommending that the required modifications should be put in hand as soon as possible. This turret has therefore been accepted.

> (c) The Bendix retractable Under turret presents a very poor picture, and quite apart from the impossibility of having any search view and the very awkward position taken up by the air gunner, plus the fact that when the gunner's eye is behind the sight he has no idea or visual indication as to the directions in which his guns are pointing, the mechanical components are still in the experimental stage. Complete retraction of the turret takes no less than 1¼ minutes, and the ammunition feed arrangements need considerable redesign.

The summary report continued:

---

[2] The comment about getting into and out of the turret by an airman in full gear only confirmed what Wing Commander Fletcher had earlier told the Americans, pointedly supplying them with a photograph that appeared in The Aeroplane, an English magazine. This photograph showed a rear gunner in full flying gear climbing out of his Whitley rear turret. Underneath the photograph Wing Commander Fletcher had underlined the wording, 'After some 10 hours, with the temperature about 20 degrees below', emphasising the conditions under which the RAF's gunners had to operate.

> The Air Corps has expressed its willingness to make arrangements on Lend Lease B-24D aircraft for installation of the Boulton Paul Type E Mark II, and we have therefore accepted their offer, in view of the inacceptability of the Consolidated Tail turret for our operational use.
>
> The ammunition tracks and boxes, with their ancillary fittings, will therefore be utilized for Lend Lease B-24D aircraft.
>
> As stated above, the Martin Mid-Upper turret has been accepted and will be installed, but we are requesting that the Bendix Under turret should be deleted with the turret accommodation ring left in position and the hole faired over.

Wing Commander Fletcher ended his summary report with the following:

> Flight Lieutenant Bastin's arrival was opportunely timed for taking active part in the B-24D turret trials. He has been very well received by both Army and Navy armament personnel, and he has supplied just that link of conviction, previously lacking, to U.S. Authorities and turret designers, which can only be supplied by the "user". Arrangements have been made for him to visit Army and Navy establishments and principal turret manufacturers, and his personal contacts and talks during his tour will prove most valuable.

He wrote in a later report dated 11 April:

> Flight Lieutenant Bastin did a grand job of work over here and his visits to Army and Navy operational units were very much appreciated. As far as we know he left for England by sea on March 20th, and by this time he should be nearing the shores of England once more and will be able to give you his own story.

All in all it seems Ken's visit was deemed a success. He and Wing Commander Fletcher were able to convince the Americans of the validity of the original concerns and the armament configuration was amended accordingly. The British Air Commission also seemed pleased with the impression Ken had made with the American military and with the major turret manufacturers. After Pearl Harbour, and now that America was militarily involved, Ken doubtless received a warm welcome wherever he went. It may also have helped that he would have been able to wear his uniform – previously British military personnel visiting the States had to go about in civilian clothes in respect of America's neutrality. Without a doubt it must have been a rather pleasant few weeks away from the grim times at home.

Ken had missed the worst of the English winter, but not without some risk. It is probable that he sailed on a convoy ship out of Liverpool to Halifax, Nova Scotia finishing his journey to Washington by train. Crossing the North Atlantic at that time was fraught with danger. German U-Boats now operated right across the Atlantic and regularly patrolled the eastern coasts of Canada and America where they found easy pickings initially. Enemy submarines, operating in packs, targeted the slow-moving convoys. And the winter weather would have made for very uncomfortable crossings, although ironically poor weather helped to shroud the convoys from the eyes of the submarine captains. At least he would not be sunk on the way home by the Scharnhorst, then back in German waters. Ken's only previous experience of the sea was a few crossings of the English Channel before the war, so he must have been very relieved to step on shore at the end of these two long and dangerous voyages.

One notable person Ken may well have met at the British Air Commission in Washington was Air Marshal Arthur Harris, then head of the RAF Delegation. His role there was to speed up the supply of aircraft. But Air Marshal Harris's relationship with the Americans was not always smooth, and it is said that at times this led to them not listening to technical advice from the British. Given the plea that resulted in Ken's visit, was the issue of the B-24 turrets one where the Americans were 'not listening'? Towards the end of February Air Marshal Harris returned to the United Kingdom to take charge of Bomber Command.

An RAF Liberator of Coastal Command
[Photo: Courtesy of the Imperial War Museum, London (CH11798)]

In the end, Ken and Wing Commander Fletcher were listened to and the armament for the RAF's B-24D Liberators was changed accordingly. Altogether the RAF received over 350 of this version, some of which went to Coastal Command. The RAF flew many later versions of the legendary Liberator, which were used in a wide variety of roles and with an equally wide variety of armament.

Having returned from the United States, Ken's thoughts would have turned to his next appointment. Most airmen who completed a tour of operations moved to a training role, and so it was with Ken. Keen to make the most of his experience and his officer status, the RAF gave him his own command, and the promotion to go with it. It would seem he had demonstrated all the right qualities in his roles as a squadron gunnery officer, added to which were the favourable remarks about his spell in America.

The command was 1481 Target Towing & Gunnery Flight. His new rank was Squadron Leader. In just two and a half years as an RAF air gunner he had his own unit. By now Ken was one of a very rare breed indeed – an air gunner of senior rank. This latest promotion put him among the most senior air gunners in the whole of the RAF. Of course many of the gunnery officers who had qualified early on in the war had not survived.

On 20 April 1942 Ken arrived at RAF Binbrook to take up his new post and his new rank. Typical of many support units, 1481 Target Towing & Gunnery Flight had evolved over recent times. Originally it trained pilots and crews for target towing duties in specially adapted Lysander aircraft. In January 1942, shortly after the unit moved to RAF Binbrook, Bomber Command gave instructions for a Gunnery Training Flight to be established and combined with the Target Towing Flight. When Ken arrived the unit was about thirty strong with maybe ten aircraft; three Lysanders, two Defiants and five or so Whitleys. Essentially the purpose of the Flight was gunnery training, hence Ken's appointment there. It was called a flight rather than a squadron simply because it was a smaller unit than a full squadron.

RAF Binbrook was about nine miles south west of Grimsby in north Lincolnshire. The station was a modern airfield built in 1940 with five large hangers, although in early 1942 the runways were still grass. It was the home of 12 Squadron, which with its Wellington and Battle bombers was very heavily involved in bombing operations around the time Ken arrived; in fact it was involved in operations on eighteen nights that April, despatching 156 sorties; a record in its Group. It was a busy front-line station.

As Officer Commanding, Ken was in charge of the whole Flight, responsible for all its day-to-day activities. Much of his time would have been taken up with organising gunnery training sessions for various groups of air gunners and with some ground defence units. Of course the weather was the main determinate of events, frustrating many a day's organised training, which would then have to be rearranged. The gunners for training came from various RAF stations in the area, squadrons that needed to maintain a regular programme to keep their air gunners up to scratch.

The unit required two sorts of aircraft in order to function. There were single-engine aircraft, Lysanders and Defiants which had been fitted with apparatus that enabled them to tow a drogue at a suitable distance behind them so that the drogue could be used safely as a target. Then there were the Whitleys, which were pensioned-off operational aircraft needing tender loving care to keep them flying. They could carry several gunners under instruction who could practice firing from the rear turret under the supervision of a gunnery instructor in the aircraft with them. Possibly one Defiant had its power-operated upper turret retained for training purposes. There was one group of pilots to fly the 'tugs', as the towing aircraft were called, and crews to operate the drogue towing gear, which broke down quite regularly – another frustration. There was a separate group of Whitley pilots. Pilots who were qualified only to fly the single-engine Lysander or Defiant aircraft could not fly the multi-engine Whitley, so there was not a lot of interchange between the two pilot groups. The remainder of the unit was made up of instructors, other aircrew, ground staff, and administrative staff. Then there were the visiting gunners who would arrive in groups of ten or a dozen at a time.

Of course Ken would have operated under the immediate command of the Station Commander, Group Captain C D C Boyce. He had overall responsibility for the whole station, which included 12 Squadron, Ken's Flight, the airfield's defence units and all the support and ancillary units that made the place seem like a small town. Although 12 Squadron were flying night operations there was a good deal of associated daytime flying so Ken's daytime training sessions needed to dovetail in with their undoubted priorities. Occasionally Ken arranged night flying for his own pilots and crews to keep them in training. Some regular night flights were arranged with the local searchlight unit at Market Rasen to help them calibrate their searchlights. Another regular activity was ground to air firing exercises set up with batteries of anti-aircraft guns at Market Rasen and with other defence units around the area, both to calibrate their guns and for practice.

But the main business of the unit was air gunnery training practice for small groups of gunners. Typically, a Lysander would take off and fly to the designated firing area out over the sea. Firing was not carried out over land as the bullets could go anywhere! Once over the area, the crew on the Lysander would wind out a drogue on about 100 yards of cable. Meanwhile, a Whitley would take off with five or six gunners for training plus an instructor. Each of the gunners had a few hundred rounds of ammunition, specially tipped in coloured powders; the usual technique so the number of hits per gunner could be determined later. Once a rendezvous was made with the Lysander the two pilots would follow a well-practiced routine of parallel flying with each gunner taking it in turns to fire at the drogue with his differently coloured ammunition. As long as the weather held, each Whitley would take up one group of gunners in the morning, another group in the afternoon. Safety was of course paramount, but even so, it could not have been much fun flying the Lysander with someone always shooting in your direction. To illustrate the point, apparently that well-known radio and television entertainer the late Jimmy Edwards was a target-towing pilot at one point during the war and he is said to have regularly railed at the gunnery 'pupils', as they were called, "Shoot at the target and not me, you bastards!"

Almost inevitably accidents would happen. Just a few weeks before Ken's arrival a Lysander had crashed due to engine failure; fortunately both crew were unhurt. The ever present possibility of a serious accident must have been a constant worry for Ken. In that respect his responsibilities were not much different from other commanders whose units carried out flying duties, although with his unit there was the added risk of live firing by pupils – but at least it was not the enemy. And the vast majority of flying was in daylight under good weather conditions. Even so Ken doubtlessly took very seriously the responsibilities of his first command. At 1481 Flight one notable pressure was absent, and that was the pressure of warfare – but as we shall see that state of affairs did not last long.

Within a few days of Ken's arrival there were other new arrivals. Two officers were posted in to strengthen the unit; Flying Officer Rupert Astbury for flying duties and air gunner Pilot Officer Killick for instructor duties. A third arrival was Whitley V aircraft number Z.9149, which was collected from Ken's old 10 Squadron at RAF Leeming. This Whitley had been with 10 Squadron since it was new in September 1941 and the reason it was available was because all Whitleys were now being retired from operations. It was serviceable, even though it had been shot up a bit in December requiring several days' repairs.

Flying Officer Astbury was a very experienced pilot who had been flying operations in Halifaxes with 35 Squadron. He had arrived at 35 Squadron after the La Pallice raid had taken place, so whilst he knew of the attack, he recalled it was a sort of taboo subject amongst the crews there. Somehow when living close to death each night, he recalled, it helped not to talk of such events and the loss of friends if it could be avoided. He was transferred to 1481 Flight because he was being 'rested' from operations following a crash in a Halifax while on a training flight with a senior pilot. He was the unfortunate victim of a multiple engine failure – all aboard were lucky to get out of the wreaked aircraft.

When Flying Officer Astbury arrived he needed a few hours flying in a Whitley just to get the feel of it again as he had not flown one for a while. He remembers one such practice day when Ken had just visited a local airfield. The transport there had allowed Ken to take his bicycle with him, but he had had to leave it behind because the transport back could not carry it. Wanting his bicycle and seeing Flying Officer Astbury about to take off for a short familiarisation flight, Ken suggested to him a trip to the airfield he had just visited might be a suitable exercise. And whilst there, could he see if Ken's bicycle fitted through the crew door and if it did, could he bring it back with him. It did fit through the door, and so Ken got his bicycle back – possibly the only time the RAF had laid on transport just for a pushbike! Flying Officer Astbury also remembers that quite often groups of Polish airmen came for gunnery training – they would have been from a Polish squadron flying Wellington bombers at nearby RAF Hemswell.

Ken probably thought his operational days were over and that 1481 Flight would be a welcome relief from the stresses of operational flying. If so he was mistaken – for he was to fly on operations again within a matter of weeks. To understand the background to this unexpected turn of events, we need to go back to the high level developments within Bomber Command during the winter months.

The RAF was operating further and further afield both in the Mediterranean and in the Far East, stretching precious resources. In Europe, the strategic bomber campaign continued albeit at reduced levels because of the winter weather and also because a major review of the role of Bomber Command had been taking place, the background to which was the now acknowledged poor results from night bombing coupled with heavy losses in the late autumn. In January 1942 Bomber Command's Air Officer Commanding-in-Chief, Sir Richard Peirse, was relieved of his post, a judgement on his handling of the Command. The strength of Bomber Command had not really altered since the beginning of the war due to attrition and about 250 planes being transferred to Coastal Command. And in February, despite the largest Bomber Command daylight assault so far, the German battleships Scharnhorst and Gneisenau together with the cruiser Prinz Eugen succeeded in making an audacious escape from Brest to home waters via the Channel. Flying Officer Rupert Astbury had been one of the many pilots seeking the German flotilla in the Channel that day, but he like nearly everyone else was beaten by the atrocious weather that shrouded the German ships throughout their dash for their home ports and greater safety.

These were to be defining moments in the future of Bomber Command; its current major strategic role was under scrutiny and therefore at threat. Other service chiefs were calling for the RAF's forces to be deployed firstly in the fighter defence of Britain, secondly in supporting the needs of the Navy, then of the Army, with strategic bombing the last priority. They were also calling for control over the disposition of Bomber Command's forces, meaning effectively the break-up of the Command. Fortunately Churchill still favoured the strategic bombing offensive because he believed in taking the attack to Germany, and until conditions were ripe for a land offensive – still some way off at this point – Bomber Command was the only means of doing so. He approved a new overt 'area bombing' directive in February – in effect area bombing had been creeping in by the back door these last twelve months; now it was the stated primary objective. Churchill however could not add his weight to the proposed massive ten-fold increase in Bomber Command's strength thought necessary to bring Germany to heel in the short term.

What was needed next was a new commander to take forward the new directive, and he came in the form of Air Marshal Arthur Harris, just like Churchill an enthusiast for striking out at the enemy. He was appointed on 23 February 1942.

Air Marshal Arthur Harris,
Air Officer Commanding-in-Chief, Bomber Command
[Photo: Courtesy of the RAF Museum, London (P000577)]

Initially Air Marshal Harris was cautious in his approach, assessing the situation, conserving resources when the weather was poor. He was fortunate that the heavy bombers, the Halifax and the Stirling, were coming through in greater numbers; also the first Lancasters began arriving in March; and at the same time a new electronic navigation system called 'Gee' which used radio signals was being installed in new aircraft; all of which he could use to strengthen the hitting power and efficiency of his front line forces. He had some early successes, but the Command's detractors, including America, were far from silenced. He needed something – something spectacular. Something that would deal a major blow to the enemy, silence the critics permanently; something that would swing public opinion in his favour and strengthen his call for the industrial resources he needed. If only he could put up, say, a thousand bombers ... on one night ... a thousand over a key Germany city! Even if he had a thousand planes, was it feasible to put that number over a target in a single night?

And so in late April the idea was born. But nothing approaching it had ever been done before, and Bomber Command's front line operational strength was much less than half the target figure of 1,000; even adding reserve crews would only bring the total available to just over the halfway mark. Scratching around the conversion units (where crews from older bombers were trained on the new 'heavies') and various training units the number gradually grew to about 700. An initial promise from Coastal Command of the 250 planes recently switched to them from Bomber Command brought the total just short of the target. In propaganda terms reaching the target number was thought to be psychologically important. When announced, the figure of 1,000 aircraft would look impressive and provide a boost for the British public and shock Germany. The next problem was to reduce the very significant risks inherent in such an untried venture, risks that had increased over the winter by German aerial and ground defensive improvements, which included radar guided fighters operating in a series of dedicated areas of the sky, or boxes as they were called, across the approaches to Germany. Bomber Command's back room boys came up with a plan – to put our bombers in a single, concentrated stream over the target in the shortest possible time, overwhelming local ground defences. The new navigation system Gee could guide the stream straight through the minimum number of air defensive boxes confusing the German radar and providing mutual defence against relatively few night fighters, whilst intruder forces would harass and occupy other night fighter units to the north and south of the stream. Key to success would be accurate navigation. Gee had a range of 400 miles or so, beyond which planes would inevitably begin to spread out. So a suitable target within Gee range, or close to the end of it, was needed – Hamburg or Cologne. Reducing the time over target, however, simply increased the crews' greatest fear – that of collision. To address this, the target area would be split into three so there would be three parallel streams operating at different heights and to strict timing. The calculation was this scheme would reduce the risk of collision to just one. Total losses including the minimal risk of collision were estimated at fifty aircraft.

    Air Marshal Arthur Harris took his 'Thousand Plan' to Churchill. In military terms such a plan, which committed all front line and reserve forces to a single operation, was highly dangerous. Added to that, the future of Bomber Command itself was on the line and with it the strategic bomber offensive. Yet Churchill approved it, saying he would accept losses of a hundred aircraft. The risks were high; but so were the rewards – a significant blow landed against the enemy, a huge propaganda coup and the critics silenced.

    Planning went ahead at full speed. Secrecy was paramount and it was vital to go during the next full moon phase starting on 27 May. Air Marshal Arthur Harris decided he could capitalise on the assembly of his force, which entailed moving large numbers of men and aircraft to eastern airfields, by sending them out again within the same moon phase; in effect getting a double benefit. Group commanders were advised on 20 May, and asked for their total commitment. This is probably when Ken knew of the plan from his station commander, Group Captain Boyce, who would have asked him what he could contribute. He had a number of old Whitleys; they had not flown operationally for some time but getting the flight engineers to work flat out on the best Whitleys he could probably put up three or four aircraft. Crews were more problematical; he would need some help even to make up three crews. He could fly the Whitleys with a crew of four, rather than the usual five in his 10 Squadron days, by dispensing with a second pilot but that would still leave a few gaps to fill after using his own instructors and staff.

Thus started a period of intense activity in which Ken was in effect acting as an operational commander. By 25 May he had decided his captains would be Flying Officer Astbury, Sergeants Mead and Harrison, and with some outside help he had three crews. Of course he had enough rear gunners from his own staff, but he had a decision to make. Did he go? He did not have to. In considering this question, did he think back to his operational days when his commanders would invariably show their leadership by putting their names down whenever a particularly difficult raid came up, not asking their men to do anything they were not prepared to do? Ken put his name down as one of the three rear gunners.

Now Ken had just a couple of days to fashion what he had into three fully operational crews capable of reaching Hamburg or Cologne without Gee which was not fitted to the Whitleys. On 25 May air tests on the aircraft were carried out in the morning and a short practice of local night flying circuits and landings was performed at about 23.00 hours. The following afternoon crews made a cross-country flight lasting an hour and forty minutes to get used to one another. That day, 26 May, Air Marshal Arthur Harris had issued his final operational orders. At the last moment, but not totally unexpectedly, The Admiralty withdrew the 250 aircraft of Coastal Command. However, by calling on every possible reserve the deficit was nearly made up from within Bomber Command itself and the revised order put 940 aircraft on standby. From now on the order to go would be weather dependant, not just over the target area but also of equal importance over the eastern airfields for the returning bombers.

The weather forecast for 27 May was not favourable. At RAF Binbrook, Ken ordered his pilots to practice a take-off fully loaded and to carry out a short local night flight. Again on 28 May the weather forecast meant the raid was still on hold. Ken took the opportunity to give his crews some much more thorough preparation. After an air test in the afternoon, they went on a lengthy cross-country night flight for nearly three and a half hours; but only two were able to go as one aircraft became unserviceable. On 29 May the crews carried out a short night flying test on their aircraft. But at Bomber Command HQ Air Marshal Arthur Harris was becoming frustrated as the weather was again not suitable. However the delays worked in his favour in one respect, because the extra time allowed squadrons and units to prepare yet more non-operational aircraft and the total available gradually crept up.

At HQ on the morning of 30 May the forecast was better, not clear-cut, but it was predicted that there was a 50-50 chance the cloud would break up over Cologne by about midnight. Hamburg, Air Marshal Arthur Harris's preferred target was still impossible. UK bases looked pretty good. He made his decision – "Thousand Plan tonight. Target Cologne."

Around one o'clock in the afternoon Ken's crews carried out a short night flying test on the aircraft. Work bombing up and preparing the aircraft carried on through the afternoon. Then at six o'clock Ken and his crews were called across to 12 Squadron's briefing room, just as 6,000 or so airmen were called to their briefings. Whilst necessary secrecy had been maintained, by then everyone knew 'something big' was in the offing because of all the activity and the security limitations imposed at the time. Many had feared a daylight operation and were quietly relieved to hear the target for 'tonight' was Cologne. It has been reported that at some briefings when they were told that more than a thousand bombers would be over the city that night there was a gasp and spontaneous cheering. They had been waiting for something like this. There was a lot of information to get through though; a single route leaving the coast at Aldeburgh in Suffolk in three parallel streams, initial incendiary bombing, strict timings, heights, gunners not to shoot until absolutely certain the target was an enemy fighter, diversionary intruder raids, return route, North Sea rescue patrols and much else. Imagine the excitement and anticipation as the briefings broke up.

Although Rupert Astbury does not recall an enthusiastic reaction to the 1,000 Plan among the crews in the briefing room at 12 Squadron, he does remember a response to the briefing officer's announcement of take-off times. He said 12 Squadron were to take off at 23.30, and then with a deadpan face that 1481 Flight were to take off at 23.00 in order to arrive over the target at the same time. This caused a gust of sympathetic laughter from the crews of 12 Squadron who realised the implication that the Whitleys of 1481 Flight were much slower than their Wellington aircraft and would be much longer exposed to enemy attack.

It seems that Ken was just one of many commanders who took part. For instance Group Captain Boyce, the Station Commander at Binbrook flew as a second pilot with a 12 Squadron crew and one of Ken's old 10 Squadron pilots John Russell, also now a Squadron Leader and who like Ken had charge of a small training unit, led a contingent of five Whitleys from his 1502 Beam Approach Training Flight at RAF Driffield.

Ken's crew was comprised of Flying Officer Astbury, pilot; Sergeant Thomas, navigator; a young Canadian Sergeant Guinn, wireless operator; and Ken, rear gunner. Ken had chosen to fly with Flying Officer Astbury who remembers feeling honoured that his Officer Commanding had chosen him rather than another more senior pilot. Sergeant Guinn was doubtless very nervous. He had just about finished his operational training and had been sent to RAF Binbrook only a few days before. This was his first operation.

The first to take off into the darkness was Sergeant Harrison at one minute to eleven o'clock, followed by Ken and Flying Officer Astbury in 'P' for Peter at three minutes past eleven and lastly Sergeant Mead and his crew six minutes later. 'P' for Peter was the Whitley number Z.9149 that had come from 10 Squadron at the same time Ken had arrived at the Flight. He may have thought he had chosen the best pilot, but he was mistaken if he thought he had chosen the best of his aircraft because of the three aircraft that took off for Cologne his was the only one not to make the target. In fact they had flown less than 100 miles before Z.9149 developed engine trouble over north Norfolk. The problem was with the supercharger on the port engine and having reached only as far as Bircham Newton Flying Officer Astbury made the decision to turn back. He turned and headed north just off the coast in case he needed to dispose of his bombs quickly in order to maintain height, then having reached Saltfleet decided it would be safer to offload his bombs before turning due east for home.

All through this Ken would have been aware via the intercom of the problems as they unfolded and even though he was the most senior officer aboard the decision to abort and the subsequent decisions to get them home were the responsibility of the captain. So with a mixture of frustration and relief, the crew landed back at RAF Binbrook at 00.48 after an hour and three quarters in the air.

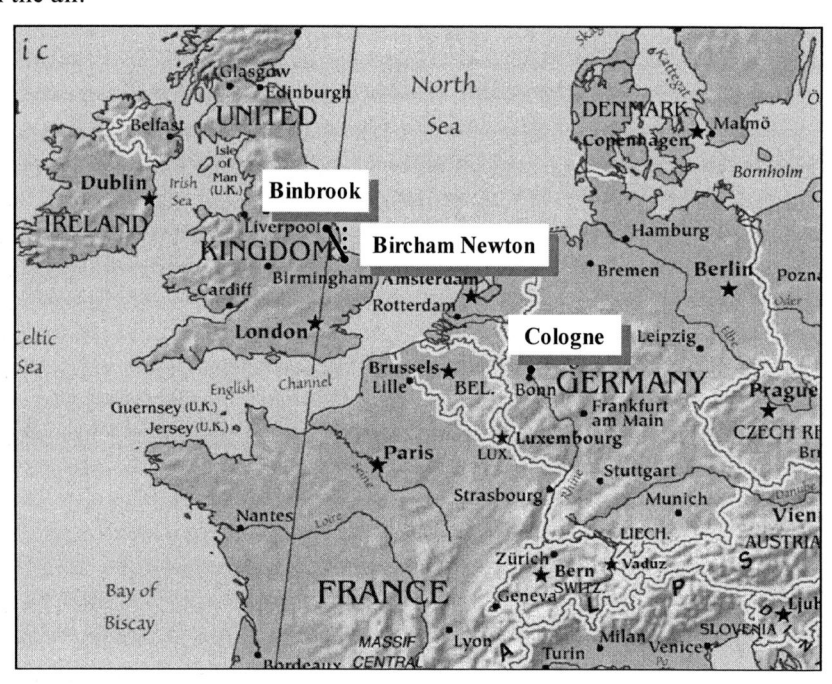

A long Way Short of Cologne, 30 May 1942

According to the Operational Record Book for the Flight each aircraft was carrying six 250lb incendiary bombs, two 250lb small bomb containers, two 500lb general purpose bombs and 170 4lb incendiaries, plus nearly 450 gallons of aviation fuel. The Operational Record Book also tells of the other two aircraft:

> Aircraft "M" (Captain, Sgt. Harrison) and aircraft "O" (Captain, Sgt. Mead) reached the target area and dropped all bombs, extensive fires and H.E. bursts were observed which seemed to be concentrated on N.W. of town and in the town area. Weather conditions were perfect,

there being no cloud and observation and visibility was good. On the return journey each aircraft was approached by enemy night fighters but after the rear gunners ("M" P/O Killick and "O" F/Sgt Jones) had fired short bursts and evasive tactics had been used the encounters were broken off. Both aircraft returned safely to base, Sgt. Harrison at 04.35 and Sgt. Mead at 04.49.

Ken had an anxious wait of four hours, ending in huge relief as his two aircraft called in seeking permission to land. He would have congratulated the crews at the debriefing, particularly the two gunners for their part in seeing off the German night fighters. All in all, it was not a bad outcome. Certainly it was rather a better outcome than his old colleague Squadron Leader John Russell and his contingent of equally frail Whitleys managed to achieve. Four of his five turned back, mostly because of severe icing; only Squadron Leader Russell himself was able to press on. But he became the sole Whitley casualty of the night after an encounter with a German night fighter over Belgium on the return journey. He survived the crash in the suburbs of Antwerp – but only just. The first attack resulted in a fire in the port engine but, as the crew began to bail out, the port wing was blown off in a second attack, sending the aircraft into an inverted spin. Squadron Leader Russell was trapped, pinned against the cockpit roof by the force of the spin, clutching his parachute in his hand. As the ground approached a sudden explosion seemed to cast him free but he could get only one of his parachute clips on his harness. With no time to spare he pulled the ripcord, just hoping the one clip would hold. It did and his chute opened enough to break his fall, although he fell heavily and badly broke a leg. He was of course captured, but sadly three of his scratch crew, who were still under training and on their first operation, lost their lives. Despite the trauma of being shot down and breaking his leg, his captors carried him around the crash site to identify the bodies of his dead crew. Later John Russell was to say this was the worst moment of his war.

The heaviest air attack ever made in a single night was deemed a great success by the Air Ministry. Nearly 900 aircraft bombed the target in the space of 90 minutes causing considerable damage and dislocation. The number of aircraft missing was forty-one, a record loss, but below that expected. Inevitably the authorities sought to make as much propaganda out of the success as possible with communiqués released immediately to the press. On 1 June *The Times* carried a major headline, 'Over 1,000 Bombers Raid Cologne' – the article that followed included the congratulations of the Prime Minister to everyone in Bomber Command, quoting Churchill's words that the raid was the herald of what Germany will receive "city by city" from now on. In the House of Commons the next day Churchill talked of the raid as a triumph of skill, daring and diligence against the enemy with all previous records of night bombing having been doubled and excelled. It goes without saying that the warm glow of the success and congratulations spread throughout Bomber Command giving a much-needed boost to morale.

This historic raid secured the future for Bomber Command, making Air Marshal Arthur Harris a household name – he received a Knighthood in June 1942. Most of the new tactics employed became standard for the remainder of the war. Air Marshal Harris however was not done. Whilst he had his force assembled he wanted to press home his advantage. A second major raid was planned for the following night; this time the target was Essen. Ken received his orders to put up three Whitley aircraft again, which he did, selecting the same crews as before.

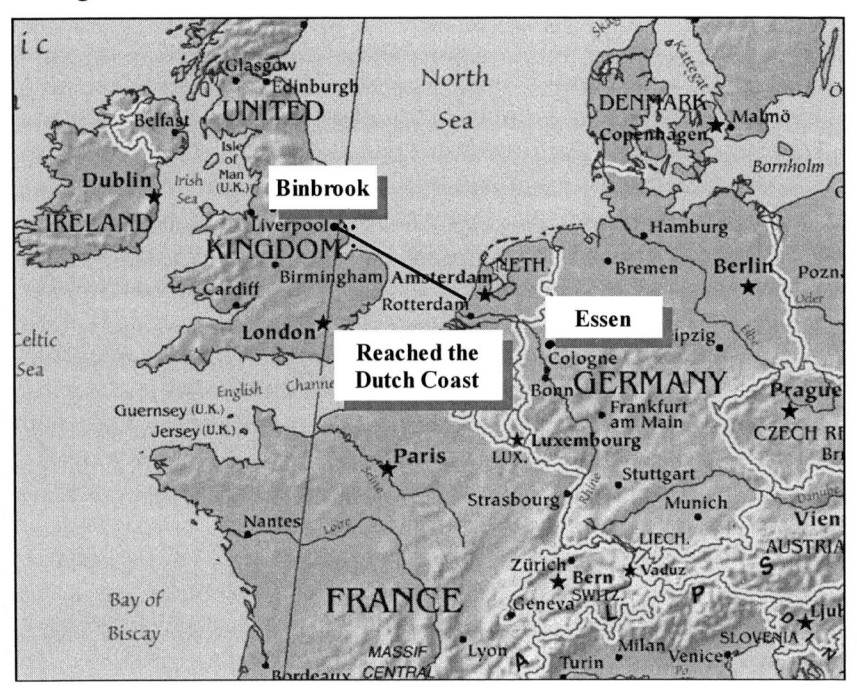

Target Essen – turned back at the Dutch Coast, 1 June 1942

In preparation the mechanics had worked on Whitley Z.9149 during the morning of 31 May to correct the problems encountered during the previous night's operation. In the afternoon Flying Officer Astbury took the aircraft and crew up for a lengthy air test and night flying test following which the aircraft was considered 'OK'. All three aircraft and crews were made ready for the operation that night, but in the event it was cancelled in the evening.

A further half hour night flying test on Whitley Z.9149 was undertaken on the morning of 1 June; again the aircraft passed. Later the order came through that the major raid against Essen was on for that night. Ken would have made particular note of Section XVIII of the Group orders which said, 'All Air Gunners are to positively identify apparently hostile aircraft before opening fire, to prevent shooting at our own aircraft'. Also, crews were warned to be on the outlook for enemy aircraft with headlights on. Other sections gave instructions to avoid collisions by not flying in cloud if possible and captains were warned to keep clear of large twin and four-engine aircraft. Again it was stressed that timing was of the essence and all aircraft were to turn for home at zero hour plus one hour and forty-five minutes whether they had dropped their bombs or not. The aim was for the raid to last no more than 90 minutes, like the Cologne raid.

For 1481 Flight the operation was due to get underway at the same time as the Cologne raid and Flying Officer Astbury and his crew in 'P' for Peter Whitley Z.9149 with Ken in the rear turret took off at 23.05. This time the aircraft managed to get further than the two other Flight aircraft, but still did not reach the target. Aircraft 'O' for Oboe captained by Sergeant Mead did not even take off due to a broken airscrew. Sergeant Harrison in 'N' for Nuts abandoned his mission and landed back at Grimsby at 01.26. Out over the North Sea the crew of 'P' for Peter were no doubt nervous as they headed for the Dutch coast. Ken must have been jittery because Rupert Astbury remembers an urgent report coming over the intercom from Ken that he had spotted a fighter aircraft with a great headlight on it, just like the earlier warning. He recalls advising Ken to tell him if it closed in and that he intended to take evasive action by pulling sharply across and towards it and to dive as fast as possible. Immediately Ken's response was, "Sorry, pilot. I can now see it is the moon." That emergency was soon over, but as they approached the Dutch coast and tried to climb the Whitley's engines could just not cope with the load. Flying Officer Astbury consulted with Ken about what to do. Ken's response, quite correctly, was that the decision was entirely his to make as captain and that Ken's seniority had no significance in the air. With the Dutch coast in sight and no improvement in the aircraft's performance, Flying Officer Astbury decided to abandon the mission and return to base. On the journey back the bomb load of 6 x 250lb incendiaries, 2 x 250lb small bomb containers, 16 x 30lb incendiaries and 2 x 500lb general purpose bombs were all jettisoned. RAF Binbrook was made shortly before two o'clock and Flying Officer Astbury made the required circuit of the landing area seeking and receiving permission to land. Half way through his approach routine he saw a bright white light just ahead of his aircraft. Taking it to be another aircraft that had nipped in front of him to land, he swore and went round again to make another attempt. At the same point in the circuit he saw another white light ahead of him. It seemed to him he had lost his landing spot yet again which made him even more annoyed. At this point the navigator came forward to see what the trouble was and said, laconically, "Well, if you are going to turn off the circuit every time you see the planet Venus, then we are going to be up here for a very long time." Finally they landed at 01.55. So the efforts of 1481 Flight on the night of 1 June were not quite so good – thankfully however all the crews were safe. *The Times* of Wednesday, 3 June 1942 carried the headlines, 'Great Fires In Essen And The Ruhr. Pilots Report Widespread Damage'. It reported, 'In the second great blow within 48 hours against German war industries the RAF sent out

1,036 bombers on Monday night'. Officially the total aircraft involved was 956 with 31 lost, and the results were much poorer than at Cologne due to scattered bombing, the result of haze and low cloud over the target area.

As far as can be discovered that was the last operational flight Ken took part in.

Young Sergeant Bert Guinn, the wireless operator who had been detached temporarily to the Flight, joined 12 Squadron after the Essen raid where he completed a tour of operations. Later he was made an officer, completed a second tour, flying on 54 operations in all and was awarded the Distinguished Flying Cross. He survived the war, afterwards returning to Canada.

Even though Ken was not to fly on operations again, he was still in charge of 1481 Flight at RAF Binbrook for two more '1,000' bombing operations, the first of which was on the night of 25 June 1942 to attack Bremen. The Flight's records show three Whitley and five Wellington bombers ordered for the operation. His usual three Whitley pilots were again selected to take part; Flying Officer Astbury of necessity had a new wireless operator and rear gunner. It seems Ken had borrowed two Wellingtons plus crews from 142 Squadron. With further Wellington crews attached from 12 Squadron and 103 Squadron, he was able to contribute a total of five Wellingtons in addition to his three usual Whitleys. So on this occasion he was responsible for eight operational aircraft and crews. Take-off for the Whitleys was 23.00 hours with the Wellingtons shortly afterwards. As usual technical problems arose to disrupt the detailed plans. Firstly, one Whitley's operation was cancelled prior to take-off due to magneto problems. Then one of the Wellingtons developed engine trouble, and unable to climb, returned after two hours its bomb load intact. Flying Officer Astbury's aircraft again developed a mechanical fault and turned back after attacking a target just over the Dutch coast. Three Wellingtons bombed Bremen successfully and landed back between 05.00 and 05.30 hours. The other Whitley, losing height with an airscrew control broken, dropped its bombs just short of Bremen and limped home just after 05.30 hours. Then Ken waited in vain for the return of the last Wellington. As time ran out and it did not appear, and no report came in of it landing elsewhere, Ken was forced to report the crew missing. Sadly it had crashed into the sea off the north coast of Holland with the loss of all the crew. Although the crew were not from his Flight, he must nevertheless have felt the loss, no doubt hoping they had somehow survived. Three of the crew were young Australians from 103 Squadron. It is not clear why the pilot Squadron Leader Matthew Atkinson was involved at RAF Binbrook; he was not from 103 Squadron but from a technical Flight in Bedfordshire testing Gee. As fellow Squadron Leaders he and Ken must have got to know each other briefly before Squadron Leader Atkinson took off into the night – the briefest of acquaintances.

The Bremen raid, in which 960 aircraft took part, was deemed more successful than the second 1,000 bomber raid on Essen but less successful than the first on Cologne. Ken's Wellington was one of 48 aircraft lost that night.

A week later Ken effectively stood down from day-to-day control of the Flight and probably was hardly at RAF Binbrook again. The Operations Record book for 1 July 1942 reads, 'F/Lt. R.M. Pinkham assumes command, vice S/Ldr. K.M. Bastin (on duty and leave)'. 'On duty and leave' was a euphemism meaning Ken was on his way to another posting, which indeed he was.

During his few months at 1481 Flight the unit had changed considerably. New Whitley and Wellington aircraft had come in to increase the strength and there were now 'A', 'B' and 'C' Flights within the unit. Five-day gunnery courses had been established with ground turret training at a nearby range, and even a flight engineers course had commenced. Pilots originally trained on single-engine aircraft were given conversion training on the two-engine Whitleys. More importantly, the Flight had become operational, regularly contributing to bombing operations over Germany. Three Whitleys were again put up for an operation to Düsseldorf on 31 July, unfortunately with the usual results – all turned back with various mechanical problems! Further significant changes happened in August and September. Firstly, on 4 August the unit was notified of Ken's posting and on 5 August Squadron Leader A H S Brown arrived to take command with the unit being renamed 1481 (Bomber) Gunnery Flight. By the end of September the Flight had moved to RAF Blyton and contractors had moved on to RAF Binbrook to lay concrete runways.

Ken's posting was Chief Instructor at the Central Gunnery School, RAF Sutton Bridge. The Central Gunnery School came under the control of Flying Training Command, which meant that Ken was leaving Bomber Command after two years nine months having survived nearly thirty operations.

8. School & 'University' – Chief Instructor & Officer Commanding

In the summer of 1942 the main newspaper headlines were about North Africa and Russia. Rommel had captured Tobruk and had reached El Alamein near Cairo in Egypt, and the German army had taken Sebastopol and was driving towards Stalingrad. In Europe, Bomber Command, buoyed by the successes of the 1,000 Bomber raids and with the political support to carry on the strategic bomber offensive, pressed ahead in the advantageous summer weather conditions. A wonderful and versatile new aircraft was introduced about this time, the de Haviland Mosquito, which proved a real if somewhat unexpected winner largely due to its speed, enabling it to out-run anything the Luftwaffe had at the time. Also, August saw the establishment of the new Pathfinder Force, the brainchild of Wing Commander Bufton which stemmed from his days in 10 Squadron when Ken was in his crew. But the Germans were not standing still; they were improving their ground and air defences and RAF losses continued to grow. The previous winter the loss rate was 2.5%; it was now 4.3% and would go higher in the coming months. The Halifax squadrons suffered a rate over 6% partly due to the technical difficulties with the aircraft in the early days. A rate of over 4% was not really sustainable, as too few crews would survive their first tour to provide squadrons with the leadership and experience they would need. Such was the demand for aircrew that new crews were introduced to full operations much earlier than hitherto, which in itself was a factor in the rising losses. The Germans were using greater numbers of fighters in their defence systems and to counter this increasing threat more and better-trained aircrew were needed, particularly air gunners and gunnery leaders.

It was in this climate that Ken arrived at the Central Gunnery School at RAF Sutton Bridge on 4 August 1942, still as a Squadron Leader. RAF Sutton Bridge was in a quiet backwater of The Fens, just on the southern edge of The Wash on the border of Norfolk and Lincolnshire; in fact it straddled the border with the landing area in Norfolk and the domestic site in Lincolnshire. The RAF had used it since about 1926 mostly for summer armament training until it became a full-time station in 1936. Although some operational units were based there in the early part of the war it was mainly used for training. It had a grass airfield and extensive ranges out over The Wash. Despite its rural location, it still suffered frequent air-raid warnings and a week or so before Ken arrived the station was bombed in the night with several men injured, one seriously, and several buildings damaged. Defence exercises were a regular feature.

On arrival Ken was met by the station commander Group Captain C H Keith. He was an armament specialist of immense technical knowledge, had considerable flying experience particularly during the inter-war years in Iraq and who had run the RAF's first Air Gunnery and Bombing School in Canada. He wrote in his book 'I hold My Aim' about his posting to RAF Sutton Bridge in the spring of 1942. He recalled that at the briefing before taking up his new command he was told it was a dirty, unhappy and inefficient place. He said that after the briefing he flew on to RAF Sutton Bridge and, 'confirmed the truth of this!'

Here was Ken back at the Central Gunnery School for a second time but in a very different role. At the end of 1939 he had been on the very first course the School ran when it was established at RAF Warmwell. The School had two intermediate moves before coming to RAF Sutton Bridge; and now had a motto – *I Hold My Aim* – the title Group Captain Keith adopted for his book. Since inception, training at the School had been for aircrew gunnery leaders, like Ken; but on its move to RAF Sutton Bridge in April it had developed an additional course for fighter pilot gunnery instructors delivered through a new Fighter Wing. The courses catered for 10 or so fighter pilots and 32 air gunners and because courses overlapped there were twice these numbers training at the School at any one time. For Ken this meant 64 so-called 'pupils' at a time under instruction on his Gunnery Leader Wing. In fact when Ken arrived this Wing was called the Bomber Wing – it was re-named the Gunnery Leader Wing the following month. The two Wings each had their own Officer Commanding. When Ken arrived, the Officer Commanding the pilots' Wing was Wing Commander 'Sailor' Malan, one of the most celebrated fighter aces of the war. In charge of Ken's Gunnery Leader Wing was Wing Commander J J Sutton. Next in seniority on the Gunnery Leader Wing was Ken, his role being Chief Instructor, Flying, and third in line was the Chief Instructor, Ground.

In describing the Central Gunnery School at this time, it is probably easiest to quote directly from Group Captain Keith's book *I Hold My Aim*.

The Central Gunnery School provides "post operational" training for fighter pilots and air-gunners. Its pupils are those who have already had experience on active service operations and have shown themselves sufficiently successful to justify being given an advance course in air gunnery, lasting a month. ... The fighter lads went to Fighter Wing, under the famous Battle of Britain pilot Wing Commander A.G. Malan. "Sailor" Malan was a South African who had started life in the Merchant Navy. When he was with me he wore a DSO and bar, a DFC and bar and also the highest Polish decoration. He was a first-class exponent of air-gunnery and lived up to it, but he was not ever interested in what the air-gunners of bombers did. The latter were trained in a Bomber Wing, commanded by Wing Commander J.M. Warfield, who had been decorated for good work in the defence of Malta. Inappropri-

ately, he was really a fighter pilot, but he was soon replaced by an old hand on bombers, Wing Commander J. Sutton. The school was equipped with nine types of aircraft, ranging from Spitfires to Wellingtons. The maintenance of this variety in good flying condition was no easy matter. Life was further complicated by the station being within the zone of anticipated enemy invasion, and much time had to be spent upon practices with my own RAF Regiment personnel and the local Army forces.

The motto of the CGS is "I Hold My Aim" – which I have chosen for the title of this book. The school is intended to be the last word in everything to do with air gunnery, but in some respects we were expected to turn out lovely bricks without sufficient straw. Although instruction was never as complete as I would have liked it to have been, undoubtedly pupils did benefit considerably and could go back to operational stations to preach their added knowledge to good effect, and into the air to tackle an enemy with added confidence. All the instructors had had outstanding success in air combat. People like "Sailor" Malan knew exactly how they had achieved their successes, and what to do in an air scrap. At the CGS they passed on their knowledge, first hand, to those who had shown promise in the air. The training was arduous, complete and comprehensive. Air Gunners, manning the turrets of a bomber, were "attacked" by fighter pupils, whilst an instructor inside the bomber watched what was done. Miles of ciné-gun film were exposed, and the most exhaustive resurrection talks were held after each mock attack.

There was no one on the station with the necessary mathematical knowledge to unravel some of the problems which cropped up, so I managed to get 'Gunner' Hill attached for a limited time. Long before this was up he had proved himself to be invaluable. When dealing with the abstrusities[3] of air firing it is not possible to go far without getting into terms of 'X' and 'Y' and the result, when plotted on squared paper, is often the best means of 'seeing' the solution of the problem.

Only a month after his arrival Ken attended a high level conference at the Air Ministry on 5 September, held 'to consider whether any improvements or alterations in the courses at the Central Gunnery School could be made with advantage'. Chaired by Air Commodore E S Goodwin, Director of Operational Training, there were senior representatives from the Air Ministry and all the Commands at this conference. The Central Gunnery School was represented by Group Captain Keith, Wing Commander Malan, Wing Commander Sutton, Ken and three instructors. By then Ken would have familiarised himself with the content of his course and the routine at the School which included flying every day. From this conference, however, he

---

[3] things that are hard to understand.

would have learned a great deal about the wider issues surrounding the School. At the outset the conference was supportive and generally agreed the School had proved its worth. Of particular interest to Ken, the conference agreed the Gunnery Leader Wing intake of 32 pupils every two weeks was the maximum possible under present conditions, but that it would need to increase in future as Bomber Command expanded. And Ken was no doubt very glad the conference gave approval for an improvement in the aircraft establishment for his Wing; notably the number of Wellington bomber aircraft was agreed at 30 and an acceptance that really another eight Lysander towing aircraft were needed although the additional eight were unlikely to be available in the short term. In conclusion the conference did not see the need for any major changes to the structure or content of courses but it did acknowledge the general difficulties under which the School operated at RAF Sutton Bridge and it looked to Flying Training Command to find solutions.

A Spitfire and a Wellington of the Central Gunnery School,
RAF Sutton Bridge in a mock attack exercise, June 1943
[Photo: Courtesy of *Aeroplane* magazine/www.aeroplanemonthly.com]

Just after the conference Group Captain Keith, who suffered from a bad hip, was replaced by Group Captain Charles Beamish DFC. What a surprise Ken had when Group Captain Beamish booked himself on the next Gunnery Leader course starting on 17 September! Nevertheless this may well have played into Ken's hand because it was clear from later comments that Ken was distinctly unhappy with the quality of some of his instructors; and by joining the course the new Commander would be able to judge the instructors for himself. Ken felt that at least five were quite unsuitable and would never set the standards or example required – there was even an officer amongst this number. Ken made representations to Wing Commander Sutton and Group Captain Beamish but was told the men could not be replaced. This was not a new situation however; similar concerns had been raised before the School came to RAF Sutton Bridge. Another problem Ken had was the generally low quality of 'pupils' coming forward for the courses – there was a sense that the standard of gunnery in operational units was still poor. Supposedly units should have been sending their most suitable and experienced gunners but only 20 on average were passing out as gunnery leaders from each course of 32, and then only eight or ten were thought really up to the required standard. This may well have been what Group Captain Keith meant when he wrote, 'but in some respects we were expected to turn out lovely bricks without sufficient straw'. Added to these problems sometimes the maintenance crew was able to make serviceable only a third of the station's 60 or so aircraft.

On top of these frustrations, the School itself was not really settled. There were continuous debates about what the Central Gunnery School's primary function should be. Also the establishment was under constant review, improvements were much needed to the accommodation and there was continual speculation the School would be moved to a more suitable location. On occasion Group Captain Beamish called together his senior officers to discuss these issues – Ken, of course, would have been there.

At least an updated Gunnery Leader Wing syllabus was agreed at a meeting on 28 December. Again the meeting of senior officers was at the Air Ministry, this time chaired by Group Captain C W Busk OBE MC, Deputy Director Training (Armament) who had been at the 5 September conference. Group Captain Beamish, Wing Commander Sutton and Ken attended for the Central Gunnery School. Other topics discussed at the meeting included the methods of assessing pupils and the introduction of an arrival examination paper for pupils. Interestingly there was an officer from the US 8th Air Force in attendance. He asked about the teaching of fighting control of formations of aircraft as his unit considered it impracticable for formations of more than three. He was assured the instruction was given for formations of up to three aircraft. At the 5 September conference it had been agreed that the US Air Force should have access to the Central Gunnery School.

Ken, who was more interested in practical matters, must have found some of these administrative aspects tiresome and a distraction from the immense stimulus of being at the epicentre of air gunnery in the RAF, of being amongst the best of his field (although not everyone was up to scratch) and of holding a senior position in what some called the 'Air Gunnery University'. For the reputation of the Central Gunnery School went far and wide, reflecting the spread of pupils, who came from all arms of the service, from all the Dominions and from our Allies, particularly Poland and in due course the USA.

Essentially the confirmed purpose of the School was still to turn out gunnery instructors to work in operational squadrons and training units –

graduates of the Fighter Wing would be responsible for training pilots in all aspects of fixed gunnery training – and graduates of the Gunnery Leader Wing would be responsible for training air gunners and wireless operator/air gunners in all aspects of free gunnery training with an emphasis on tactics. It is worth listing here the duties and responsibilities of the newly qualified Gunnery Leader when he returned to his unit:

1) To serve as an air gunner in the air and personally maintain a high standard of marksmanship.

2) To know and understand his Air Gunners, to stimulate their interest, improve their operational efficiency and maintain their morale; and to ensure their physical fitness.

3) To initiate and control training in gunnery and aircraft recognition.

4) To check, but not technically supervise, gun and turret maintenance and the harmonisation of sights.

5) To advise Air Gunners and other members of the Squadron on gunnery equipment and its uses.

6) To help Squadron and Flight Commanders in administration and disciplinary matters affecting Air Gunners.

7) To discuss, collate and explain all facts and principals relating to air fighting tactics.

The duties of a Pilot Gunnery Instructor from the Fighter Wing were similar, with perhaps more emphasis on instruction than leadership.

A Lysander aircraft out over The Wash – used for towing target drogues, June 1943
[Photo: Courtesy of *Aeroplane* magazine/ www.aeroplanemonthly.com]

For both Wings the major part of the training was done in the air. Hence Ken's role was the senior of the two Chief Instructors of the Gunnery Leader Wing. Nevertheless there were considerable ground facilities for training in such aspects as turret manipulation, sighting and tactics. Quite an emphasis was made on understanding the tactical measures needed to make an operation successful. Such things as German night fighter tactics were discussed together with the use of the latest electronic devices. Ken's responsibilities included the planning and supervision of air-to-air live firing at drogues towed by Lysander aircraft and the more exhilarating yet inherently dangerous mock combat between fighter and bomber. Also, a key element of his role was to keep abreast of the latest developments in tactics and equipment and to introduce these into the course – this would involve keeping in close liaison with Headquarters of Training Command and with the operational squadrons. And Ken would have had to manage his instructors and oversee their assessment of pupils.

Models in use at the Central Gunnery School, RAF Sutton Bridge during ground instruction on aerial tactics, June 1943
[Photo: Courtesy of *Aeroplane* magazine/ www.aeroplanemonthly.com]

Pupils were under constant assessment. Their progress on the course was logged and shooting exercises were plotted on a graph. In the drogue exercises the well-tried method of marking the gunner's bullets with a coloured paint or powder was still used. Considerable use was made of ciné-gun film in discussing and assessing performance.

Whilst each Wing of the School had its own syllabus, one section of each syllabus brought the two Wings together, and this was the mock combat between fighter and bomber. Here Ken needed to work closely with the Officer Commanding of the Fighter Wing. Initially when Ken arrived this was the famous 'Sailor' Malan. It is clear from the remarks in C H Keith's book that 'Sailor' Malan had little time for liasing with the Gunnery Leader Wing, probably concentrating on the fighter-to-fighter combat part of his syllabus. Even so, Ken must have had discussions with him, and maybe in the mess they talked about their respective trips to the USA. 'Sailor' Malan had been there and to Canada recently with a group of the RAF's most notable pilots on a goodwill mission. It was while at the Central Gunnery School that 'Sailor' Malan developed his so-called 'Ten Commandments' for fighter pilots, which started with, 'Wait till you see the whites of their eyes …' and ended with, 'Get in quickly, punch hard, get out smartly.' Subsequently these were printed as billposters and pinned up in all fighter stations. Having established the Fighter Wing 'Sailor' Malan moved on in September after fittingly taking command of the parade to celebrate National Thanksgiving Day for the Battle of Britain victory.

Aerial combat exercises were a vital part of the syllabus for both Wings and whether it was planning these with 'Sailor' Malan or his successors Ken needed to prepare them very carefully because of the dangers involved. Ken himself or his deputy managed the exercise until the bomber took off; then the instructor in the bomber controlled it. These exercises were carried out in the wide skies over the surrounding fenland and the ranges on The Wash. Both aircraft used ciné-guns for taking films of their combat for later analysis – there was a Photographic Section on the station where WAAFs developed miles of ciné-film. But the risks of combat conditions could not be eliminated if the exercises were to be anything like realistic. Mistakes were almost inevitable and the threat of a mid-air collision was always there.

These aerial combat exercises covered two aspects of Ken's syllabus. Firstly air practice for the gunners in the turrets and secondly for the fire controller gunner who stood in the astrodome controlling and directing the aircraft's gunnery defences as well as giving orders to the pilot for evasive action – just as Ken had done over La Pallice. The instructor taking the exercise would be in the second pilot's seat observing and listening on the intercom. The bomber pilots would not stint in throwing their aircraft around in response to evasion instructions. So violent were these manoeuvres that often the Wellington was pulling two or three 'G' of gravity, such that the crew would be pinned down and it was hard for them even to lift an arm. The Wellington bomber was the workhorse for these exercises and was well suited to this purpose.

There were standing instructions for these aerial combat sessions. Each session lasted about an hour and the bomber would have four pupils aboard. The initial exercises would be on Range Estimation followed by Quarter Attacks, then Varied Attacks. The latter would include attacks from quarter, half-roll from above and from below, then all angles and head-on. The later stages of the course would involve full evasive action of the bomber and all the variety of fighter attacks. Normally these exercises would take place at 3,000 feet, but there would also be attacks on low flying bombers. Of all these the head-on exercises were the most dangerous because of the high closing speed. The initiative for these attacks lay with the fighter pilot who had to thoroughly work out his approach and most importantly his breakaway. At the end of the course the fighter pilots would have the chance to take a trip in a bomber and try the turrets, to give them an idea of the air gunner's point of view. These combat exercises sparked a great deal of friendly rivalry between the two Wings – the air gunners having the opportunity to test themselves against highly experienced staff fighter pilots and the most able pilots from operational fighter squadrons. This all led to an exciting atmosphere for those involved.

With so much flying there was the inevitable crop of mishaps and crashes, often it seems involving Spitfires. One pilot was killed a few days after Ken arrived and an instructor and pupil successfully baled out of a Master when the control column jammed in mid-exercise. Flying was almost uninterrupted in the summer, although air raid warnings were common around the time Ken arrived. But through October, November and December rain and fog, then early snow, began to disrupt the regular pattern of flying.

Efforts were made to improve the lot of the airmen and WAAFs on the station. A number of concerts and cinema shows were staged, which proved very popular, and a new cookhouse and mess was opened and deemed a great success. Also on Christmas Day a special dinner was served to the airmen and airwomen by Group Captain Beamish, Ken, the other officers and the NCOs, followed in the evening by a free cinema show.

Snow returned after the Christmas festivities were over and flying was restricted, but by mid-January the weather was really foul with rain, hail, frost and snow all interrupting flying. In fact the airfield was pretty soggy by the end of January and totally waterlogged and unserviceable on 1 February. One distraction on 27 January was the sight of nearly 60 Flying Fortresses going over the station, possibly on their way to Wilhelmshaven on what was the USA's first bombing operation over Germany.

All the time there was a stream of official visitors to the School, mostly by various liaison and other officers from the Headquarters of Flying Training Command but also from some of the normal gunnery training schools and from some of the Commonwealth Air Forces interested in the training methods. Some of the visits were to do with the introduction of clay pigeon shooting into the training programme.

Arguably the most important visitor whist Ken was at RAF Sutton Bridge was Air Chief Marshal Sir Edgar Ludlow-Hewitt, the RAF's Inspector General. He arrived on 2 February 1943 to discuss the future policy of the Central Gunnery School and made further visits on 10 and 18 February before preparing a comprehensive report dated 23 February. As mentioned earlier Sir Edgar had been the Air Officer Commanding-in-Chief of Bomber Command at the beginning of the war and had been the architect of the new class of officer gunner and of the Central Gunnery School in 1939. He had then argued the School was needed to turn out Gunnery Leaders to help address the poor quality of gunnery at that time. Now he was no doubt very interested to see the progress the School had made and keen to continue his promotion of it. When introduced to Ken he was probably more than delighted, for Ken must have represented exactly what the Air Chief Marshal had envisaged when he introduced his new breed of officer gunner and pushed for a Central Gunnery School to be established. Ken probably reminded him they met when the Air Chief Marshal visited the very first course the School mounted at the end of 1939; and now here was Ken a Chief Instructor at the School.

The Inspector General opened his report with these remarks:

> *This school has improved out of all recognition since I last visited it [the previous March]. But I am still not satisfied that the best use is being made of the school in respect of its functions as the centre and "hub" of Royal Air Force gunnery technique. The fault does not lie with the school itself; within the limitations imposed from outside the training courses at least are excellent.*

In his report he set out his views on the functions of the School, which were to set the highest standard in air gunnery for the whole service and to be the focus of the latest information of new developments, covering practical experience of developments in method. He added he believed the functions should also include technical development, but at a subsequent meeting this was not agreed by the Director-General Training (Air) who stated the School should concentrate on training in the most efficient use of weapons immediately available to both Operational Squadrons and Training Units. So it was that the main functions of the School were finally settled.

Ken took the opportunity of the Inspector General's visits to voice yet again his concerns at the quality of some of his instructors. He complained he had raised this before but that nothing had been done. To emphasise his point he gave the Inspector General a list of five names, one officer, one flight sergeant and three sergeants. This time something was done – the Inspector General backed Ken and included the complaint in his report. Subsequently at high level discussions it was agreed that as Instructors were due for replacement (generally after nine months) the School itself would generate a list of recommended replacements from former top pupils. From this list of names Fighter Command, Bomber Command and the other Commands were to fill vacancies in proportion to the number of pupils they sent to the School. It was also agreed the Officer Commanding the Central Gunnery School should submit the names of those Instructors identified by Ken as unsuitable to the Director General of Personnel for immediate posting and replacement. So Ken finally achieved his aim of getting rid of his weaker Instructors and improving the quality of rotational replacements.

The Inspector General's report and consequent high-level meetings settled a number of other outstanding issues. The School would remain at RAF Sutton Bridge for the time being with a suitability review of RAF Catfoss to be undertaken – the School did move to RAF Catfoss a year later. Also, the capacity of the School would be four-week courses for 64 Gunnery Leaders and 28 Fighter Instructors.

But not all the Inspector General's recommendations were adopted. He wanted Ken's course extended to make the pupils better marksmen, he thought gunnery practice at night should be introduced despite the difficulties and he did not agree with the recent withdrawal of the shotgun turret trainer in favour of clay pigeon shooting. These proposals were later discussed but not pursued.

One of the ground training exercises the Inspector General saw involved practice in turret manipulation. This required the pupil to follow with his guns a dot projected on a screen representing an attacking fighter. The dot moved rapidly and very erratically mimicking the relative position of an attacking fighter to a gunner during a violent evasion manoeuvre. The Inspector General thought this an excellent piece of equipment.

An essential element of the School was to keep abreast of technical developments and to bring them into its training at a very early stage of their introduction. Ken would have been particularly excited about one such new piece of technology that had recently arrived at the School – the gyro gunsight. Considerable scientific effort had gone into the development of this new gunsight, which promised to revolutionise the air gunner's efficiency in combat as well as to provide a marvellous training tool. This amazing development was the result of much research into solving the gunner's main problem – where to aim ahead of a fast moving target, 'deflection' or 'aiming off' as it was known. In simple terms, the gyro resisted movement causing a lag between the static ring of the gunsight and the gyro ring. The design of the sight makes this lag equal to the deflection needed. The faster the turret is rotated to track the fighter the more deflection is required. In resisting the greater speed of movement the gyro shows a greater distance between the two rings. The School had taken delivery of 10 of the Mark I gyro gunsights before the Inspector General's visit and he readily recognised their importance for training, particularly when linked to a ciné camera. He very strongly recommended the School receive the first of the new and much improved Mark II version ahead of its general rollout expected later that year. In the hands of a trained gunner the Mark I produced results 50% better than the currently used reflector gunsight, but this first version had a number of drawbacks; one being the moving sight was far too sensitive and its movement needed to be damped, another was it could not be used at night. After trials it was decided the Mark I would only be issued to training establishments whilst a better version was developed. The answer to the problems with the Mark I was solved by combining the gyro system with the existing reflector gunsight. At the time of the Inspector General's visit the new Mark II was nearing its test stage. The innovation of the gyro gunsight would have been of considerable importance to Ken and his other senior colleagues and they would have spent much time and thought introducing the Mark I into the School's training, both on the ground and in the air. The advent of the Mark II would have been eagerly awaited.

Of course the School was a place where the pupils could voice their concerns. One common gripe was about the efficiency of the .303 gun versus the more powerful .5 used by the Americans. The Inspector General had picked up these concerns elsewhere and Ken and his colleagues were able to confirm that nearly all the gunners coming to the School were asking when they were going to get the .5 guns. Instructors at the School regularly had to emphasise there was nothing wrong with the .303 if used properly. Often they had to correct the perception amongst the general ranks of air gunners that the maximum range of the .303 was 600 yards; probably a misunderstanding that 600 yards should be regarded as the opening range. The Inspector General raised these concerns in his report and later discussions disclosed that the introduction of .5 guns into the heavy bombers was being planned for the early part of 1944, although this timescale proved over optimistic.

All in all, the Inspector General's visits proved very helpful to Ken and his colleagues, enabling some of their issues to be raised at a high level; indeed Ken was to benefit later from the results of this inspection when he rejoined the Central Gunnery School at a later date. The final outcome of all the high level conferences, meetings, the Inspector General's Report and consequent deliberations was the issue in May 1943 of Air Ministry Order A.475 Central Gunnery School – Training Policy which substituted the original 1939 Air Ministry Order when the School was established.

From February 1943 the weather gradually improved and flying was possible on most days. Since Ken's arrival the Gunnery Leader Wing had been virtually accident free but their run of luck ran out on 22 March. On a routine exercise a Wellington suffered catastrophic engine failure; first the starboard engine cut out then the port engine. The aircraft came down at Terrington Marsh and burned out. One of the pupil gunners was killed and all the others on board were injured. That accident must have dampened the atmosphere of the 25th Anniversary celebrations of the formation of the RAF held on 1 April. Events that day included a visit by Air Training Corps cadets in the afternoon and a Gala Dance in the evening; as a special concession work at the station ceased early at 16.30.

Tragedy struck both Wings on consecutive days in April. On the 9th a Spitfire pilot dived straight into the ground near Wisbech while practising attacks on a Wellington bomber. The party sent to the site found very little of the aircraft or its pilot despite digging deep down into the silty soil. And worse was to follow the next day, when a mid-air collision between a Spitfire and a

Wellington killed the pilot, the instructor and all four pupils in the bomber. The Spitfire pilot managed to bale out but was injured and taken to hospital. Both pilots were judged blameless. Just five days later a Wellington made a forced landing after engine failure in mid-air and on the same day a Lysander made a heavy landing at the nearby Holbeach Landing Ground, severely damaging the aircraft. Fortunately neither of these incidences led to injury, but on 26 May a further Wellington attempted a difficult landing, this time with hydraulic failure to the flaps. It careered off the end of the airfield and hit a building on the perimeter breaking in two and injuring one of the crew. The month of June also saw a number of incidents. Tragically, one of the gunners from the station's ground defence unit fell off a lorry and suffered fatal head injuries. A few days later during an air exercise one of Ken's pupils lost his footing while acting as the fighting controller in a Wellington that corkscrewed away from a fighter attack; he sustained a broken left leg and minor injuries to his face. And the Fighter Wing did not escape without incident. A new Instructor arrived at the end of May who was one of the most famous names from the air battles over Malta, Flying Officer Beurling DSO, DFC, DFM. He managed to severely damage or write off three Spitfires in the space of two months! Luckily he survived all three accidents.

Instructors of the Gunnery Leader Wing, Central Gunnery School, RAF Sutton Bridge June 1943 with one of the instructional Wellington Bomber aircraft.
(From left to right) Flight Sergeant V.I. Jones, Warrant Officer R.C. Hillebrandt, Flying Officer W.W. Cumber, Flight Sergeant H.A. Matthews, Sergeant R.F. Crabb, Flight Sergeant E. Saunders, Group Captain C.E.St.J. Beamish DFC (Officer Commanding Central Gunnery School & Station Commander), Wing Commander J.C. Claydon DFC (Officer Commanding, Gunnery Leader Wing), Squadron Leader K.M. Bastin DFC (Chief Instructor, Gunnery Leader Wing), Flight Lieutenant W.E. Nicholas DFC, Flight Lieutenant M.C. Cleary DFM, Flight Lieutenant V.W.C. Taylor, Flight Lieutenant A.J. Savage DFC, Pilot Officer R.L.A. Woolgar, Flight Lieutenant H.S. Griffiths DFC, Pilot Officer E.J. Law, Warrant Officer E.J. Saunders.
[Photo: Courtesy of *Aeroplane* magazine / www.aeroplanemonthly.com]

Ken's time at the Central Gunnery School, RAF Sutton Bridge was coming to an end and one of his last duties was to show a contingent from the national press how the Gunnery Leader Wing carried out its training, arranging a number of flights for the photographers to get some dramatic aerial shots. On 25 June 1943 Ken left to take up his new post of Chief Instructor, No1 Air Gunners' School at RAF Pembrey on promotion to Wing Commander. During his spell at RAF Sutton Bridge nearly 600 airmen had passed through his Gunnery Leader Wing.

If the Central Gunnery School was to some the 'University of Air Gunnery', the No.1 Air Gunners' School at RAF Pembrey was the equivalent of a large technical college. The new pupils came here after about fifteen weeks in the RAF, having been through a Personnel Reception Centre, their Initial Training Wing and passing out from an Elementary Air Gunner School where they learnt the basics of gunnery and turrets. They were now about to embark on a six week course, later extended to seven weeks, to make them into air gunners. Until now the pupils had not flown and they would arrive very excited at the prospect, but they had to wait for a week or so into the course before air training began. In all they would gain about 15 hours flying. From here the successful pupils would go on to an Operational Training Unit where they would become part of a crew, training together for 10 weeks – or longer for crews destined for the heavy bombers. They would then join an operational squadron.

RAF Pembrey was one of the larger gunnery schools and was well sited on the eastern coast of Carmarthen Bay in southwest Wales. The station was opened in May 1940 and had three concrete and tarmac runways, two large hangers, the usual assortment of station buildings and a domestic site. It was an important fighter station providing air defence cover for the significant industrial area of south Wales until that role was taken over in the middle of 1941 by a new station at RAF Fairwood Common, Swansea, and its forward base at RAF Angle on the very western tip of Pembrokeshire. RAF Pembrey was then handed over to Flying Training Command who established one of the major air gunnery schools there under 25 Group.

Staff on the station in June 1942 witnessed a most extraordinary event. A German officer pilot flying the latest FW190 fighter became disoriented after an engagement with Spitfires from Exeter. He mistook RAF Pembrey for a French airfield and decided to land as he was short of fuel. In his approach he performed some victory rolls, extended his undercarriage upside down and landed off a steep turn. When he realised his mistake he intended to destroy his aircraft but before he could do so he was quickly surrounded by a group of very excited airmen. The station Armament Officer heard the commotion going on outside the hanger where he was working and went to investigate. The German pilot, seeing the arrival of an officer, climbed out of his aircraft, shrugged his shoulders, grinned and shook the Armament Officer's hand in surrender. The RAF had been very keen to examine a FW190 intact and at the time of this bizarre event a commando raid was actually being planned to steal one from northern France. The commando raid became unnecessary when a fully working aircraft was delivered to the RAF's doorstep, courtesy of the unfortunate pilot!

In the early summer of 1943 the tide of the war against the European Axis powers was turning. German and Italian troops had surrendered in North Africa in May. U-boat losses forced Admiral Döntiz to restrict operations in the North Atlantic and the Allies landed in Sicily on 9/10 July. On the night of 16/17 May, Bomber Command delivered one of its most spectacular operations of the war – the Dams Raid, led by Wing Commander Guy Gibson who was at the same Buckingham Palace Investiture as Ken in November 1941. In Russia the Germans would see their advances halted in the coming months and would be forced to retreat. The RAF's part in the struggle at this stage was the strategic bombing of Germany, specifically the aviation industry and the general disruption of German industry. All this was aimed at reducing the effectiveness of the Luftwaffe and of Germany's ability to support its ground troops in advance of an Allied land invasion of 'Fortress Europe' – Operation Overlord. Under Air Chief Marshal Harris the RAF was expanding with bigger aircraft carrying more armament needing more trained gunners. But there was also a continual drain on front line resources with surviving aircrew moving to other duties after completing their tour of operations and, of course, aircrew losses. So the need for trained air gunners continued apace. In the UK this need was met by 10 Air Gunners' Schools which operated under a new directive from July 1943 providing for an increase in the number of gunners under training – this meant there would be four schools each with a capacity of 360 pupils, including No.1 Air Gunners' School at RAF Pembrey, five with a capacity of 240 pupils and one for 120 pupils.

Ken arrived at RAF Pembrey on 28 June 1943 and his official promotion to Wing Commander came through on 6 July. Here was Ken a Wing Commander Chief Instructor at a major gunnery school less than four years since his initial gunnery training at RAF Manby.

Ken's principal responsibilities as Chief Instructor were the development and the day-to-day management of the courses running at the School together with turning out gunners trained to a high standard. The station itself was under the control of Group Captain A H Fear, a New Zealander who had commanded 27 Squadron in India. He was, however, soon to be replaced by Group Captain G P MacDonald, a career man in his mid-forties, who a few years earlier had been in the Technical Branch and had attended a specialist armament course, qualifying him for his new role. Ken was the second senior officer, and directly under Ken was a group of instructors for the ground and air elements of the course. The School's aircraft were mainly Lysanders and Martinets for towing and Blenheims – a light bomber with a mid-upper gun turret – for gunnery training; however, soon after Ken arrived the Blenheims were replaced by Ansons. It was not until the autumn of 1944 that Wellington bombers and Spitfires became available for more realistic air combat training. RAF Pembrey was a large station with nearly 1,000 personnel including the new capacity of 360 pupils; and with the pupil population regularly turning over the station was a busy place. Ken's first main task was to gear up the School to the new directive which increased the number of pupils under tuition from 240 to 360. A course consisted of 90 or so pupils and at any one time the four courses running would be at different stages. Each new intake would attend an opening address given by Ken and at the end of each course the station commander would present successful pupils with their Air Gunner brevet. Ken understood as well as anyone how vital a highly trained gunner was to the survival of an aircraft's crew and on average about one in eight pupils failed to make the grade. In order to maintain a high standard, pupils at the School were subject to regular assessment and sat a final examination. An example of this is evidenced by the results from No.107 Course which were as follows:

- 71 pupils successfully completed the course
- 8 were withdrawn at the Intermediate stage as unsuitable for further training
- 1 was withdrawn as being generally unsuitable for aircrew
- 2 were withdrawn sick
- 3 were withdrawn and transferred to No.109 Course
- 10 failed to reach the required standard at the final examination stage.

On the following page is the end result for one airman, Aircraftsman First Class Ron Powers, who completed his course in May 1944, approved and signed by Ken himself. After passing out as an Air Gunner Ron received the usual promotion to Sergeant.

The course was very intensive; seven and a half hours of instruction a day, six days a week. There would be half an hour's physical training or drill each day and one afternoon each week there would be two and a half hours for organised games. The pupils worked in squads of about 12 and their time on the ground was split more or less evenly between lectures and practical work. In the air they would take part in about 20 exercises. Ron Powers remembers his air exercises in the Anson. As usual, the four under-training gunners would have their bullet tips painted in different colours so the hits on the drogue could be allocated. He recollects particularly that after their first flight in an Anson the gunners tried not to be first on board on subsequent flights as they had learnt the first one on the aircraft sat by the pilot and had to hand crank the undercarriage up and down – hard work as it needed some 300 turns he recalls!

There was a long list of topics to get through on the course covering all aspects of air gunnery; the main subjects being machine guns, turrets, sighting and aircraft recognition. The many practical exercises included firing on the ranges as well as in the air. There was even three hours set aside for what was called, 'Dinghy, life-saving jacket, and parachute drills. Action stations for landing in the sea.' There was no night air firing, but efforts were made to give preliminary night vision training on the ground.

Exercise	Rounds Fired	% Hits	Type of Aircraft
25 yds. range 200 400	200 200 N/A	N/A	—
No. of G. 28 films. Cine footage.	185	N/A	Anson
Air to Ground	600		"
Beam	600	2·33	"
Beam R.S	600	3·16	"
Under Tail	300	2·66	"
Quarter PLAIN	1500 300	1·74 2·00	"
A TD	300	—	"
Night	—	—	
Exam. Marks 75·5%		15 Hrs 30 min	

REMARKS: PASS
Average cadet. Hard worker and keen.

Extract from the logbook of Sergeant Ron Powers, detailing the exercises he completed during 15½ flying hours. It shows Ken's signature below his remarks, 'Average cadet. Hard worker and keen.'
[Image: Courtesy of Ron Powers]

Promotion to Wing Commander meant Ken was due for a Senior Officers Course and on 18 August 1943 he joined 55 other officers at the School of Administration, RAF Stannington near Morpeth in Northumberland. RAF Stannington was in fact an old children's sanatorium. There Ken attended the first of a newly revised course lasting three and a half weeks and focussed on administrative planning from the staff point of view – some timely training for Ken as he was now responsible for a large team of instructors.

An array of training turrets – typical of a gunnery school. Here pupils are using aircraft movements around the airfield for sighting practice.
[Photo: Courtesy of *Aeroplane* magazine/ www.aeroplanemonthly.com]

At No.1 Air Gunners' School Ken's duties seemed to include the inevitable round of conferences and meetings at the Headquarters of Flying Training Command and liaison visits to other schools, often travelling by air. One such trip was to the Central Gunnery School, RAF Sutton Bridge in October, reciprocated in November by his former colleague there Wing Commander Claydon. These meetings took Ken away from the station at least twice a month, and he was equally busy with regular visitors coming to see him at RAF Pembrey. Also, at times there were public duties for Ken to attend. For instance on 20 November he presented a Wings for Victory trophy under the national savings scheme at a ceremony at Kidwelly, a small town nearby.

Sadly, serious flying accidents were never far away. On 24 July a Martinet towing aircraft and a Blenheim bomber collided in mid-air off Caldey Island near Tenby. Both crew of the Martinet died; the pilot's body was never found. When Ken returned from a conference on 13 August he learned that a Blenheim bomber with a pilot and three gunners under training was overdue presumed lost at sea. A week later the bodies of the pilot and one of the gunners were washed up on Marros Beach just along the coast to the west. And on 20 November another Martinet crashed near Burry Port a few miles east of the station – both crew died. But there was a lucky escape for the crew of a Stirling bomber from RAF Lakenheath that overshot the runway and crashed outside the perimeter track; this time no one was hurt.

The Stirling bomber was just one of a regular stream of aircraft stopping off at RAF Pembrey for one reason or another. Many carried important visitors going on to the nearby Ministry of Defence Small Arms Experimental Establishment at Pendine, and there were routine liaison visits to and from the many RAF stations in neighbouring Pembrokeshire, particularly those at Carew Cheriton, Angle, Dale, Manorbier and the very large and important Sunderland Flying Boat station at Pembroke Dock.

Towards the end of 1943 proof of the build-up of an invasion force appeared in a big way at the station when a detachment of the 112th Regiment of the US Army's 28th Division arrived just before Christmas and took over the Beach Camp. These were mostly young men who until recently had never been out of their home state of Pennsylvania. Other regiments of the Division were stationed nearby and the Divisional headquarters was established in a hotel at Tenby. Over the coming months the troops took part in intensive training exercises in the area in preparation for the invasion of Europe. Just before they left the men of the 112th Regiment took part in a boxing tournament against the RAF held on the station and in a rifle shooting challenge against the Pembrokeshire Home Guard, which surprisingly the Home Guard won. On 27 March 1944 the US troops left the Beach Camp at RAF Pembrey; but before they and the rest of the Division left the area altogether General Eisenhower came to inspect them and Churchill too came to watch them take part in rehearsals for the invasion. Although the 112th Regiment did not take part in the landings on D-Day itself, just over a month later they crossed Omaha Beach and fought their way north. By the end of August they were marching down the Champs-Elysées in newly liberated Paris. Later as the Allies pushed north they were involved in the heavy fighting of the German offensive in the Ardennes Forest on the Holland/Germany border that began on 16 December 1944, which became known as The Battle of the Bulge.

Soon after the Americans departed full postal censorship was imposed on the station; another sign that perhaps the invasion was not far off. Meanwhile training at the School continued apace. Instructional flying hours for March and April 1944 averaged over 110 hours per day. Ken would have been particularly interested in one unusual visitor in April, a USAAF Liberator that landed on route from Marrakech to RAF Valley on the Isle of Anglesey, the first of a number stopping off on that route. Ron Powers remembers the Liberator as he was allowed aboard to have a look round. He recalls the crew had pure white sandwiches with ham, not spam. The Americans, taking pity on their visitors, shared the sandwiches around. Ron also recollects an experimental Warwick aircraft arriving for tests on a novel gunnery arrangement. The month of May saw the crew of another Martinet sadly killed in a crash near Carmarthen and an Anson overshot the runway and crashed but fortunately no one was injured. There was an unusual mission for the crew of an Anson at the end of May when they were despatched to shoot down a barrage balloon that had broken loose from a ship in Swansea Harbour; they succeeded in bringing it down 10 miles north of Pembrey.

A group of air gunners discuss a training session by an Anson aircraft
[Photo: Courtesy of *Aeroplane* magazine/ www.aeroplanemonthly.com]

May also saw Ken off on another course, this time on a Senior Officers Course at the splendid staff college at RAF Cranwell in Lincolnshire. An Officers Advanced Training School had been established there a few months earlier. There were 13 on the course and it certainly was for senior officers; Ken's course group consisted of two Squadron Leaders, ten Wing Commanders and a Group Captain. The course lasted four weeks ending on 14 June.

One notable visitor during Ken's absence was none other than the Inspector General, Air Chief Marshal Sir Edgar Ludlow-Hewitt. Maybe he was disappointed Ken was not there as recently he had inspected a number of gunnery training units and had formed some views on which he would no doubt have welcomed Ken's thoughts. Always keen to improve the standard of air gunnery he had concerns about turret manipulation training, better use of ciné-gyro film and the length of the course at air gunners' schools not allowing time to coach the slower learners. These he voiced in a general report on gunnery training in which he also called for more scientific research into which methods of training produced the best results. The only specific comments he made on RAF Pembrey were to do with over-manning and better organisation of station staff.

Ken was at RAF Cranwell when the momentous and dramatic news of D-Day, the Allied Invasion of Europe, was announced officially at 09.30 on 6 June. At noon Churchill made a statement to an expectant House of Commons, confirming that, "... the first of the series of landings in force upon the European Continent has taken place ... the liberating assault fell upon the coast of France ...", and he presented the House with an impression of the vastness and complexity of the operation without of course giving away any vital details. Loud cheers regularly interrupted his speech. Later on the same day he made a second statement to the House relaying news of the latest situation declaring, "... this operation was proceeding in a thoroughly satisfactory manner. ... The resistance of the shore batteries has been greatly weakened by the bombing of the Air Force ..." Churchill, however, went on to warn, "... the enemy will now probably endeavour to concentrate on this area, and in that event heavy fighting will soon begin ..." He ended, "It is, therefore, a most serious time that we enter upon. Thank God, we enter upon it with our great Allies all in good heart and all in good friendship." This brought loud and prolonged cheers from a packed House.

The initial elation at the news soon gave way to a sense of relief that the long awaited invasion had begun at last. Quickly though, people's thoughts turned to the men fighting their way over the invasion beaches and along the hedgerows inland and to the servicemen in the navies and air forces providing vital support. The mood became solemn and serious, no more so than for those in uniform. Church services were organised and prayers offered. At RAF Pembrey a special service of Intercession was held in the station chapel during the afternoon.

Previous experience had demonstrated that air superiority was absolutely vital if the invasion of Europe was to succeed. For the RAF the build-up to D-Day and the support for the D-Day landings was a most intensive time. Prior to D-Day itself the RAF together with the USAAF carried out wide ranging sorties. In particular these attacks were on communications and coastal defence targets aimed at deceiving the Germans into thinking the invasion would be in the Calais to Dieppe area whilst at the same time severely damaging the defences in the Normandy region. Then during the first, most dangerous 24 hours of the invasion, fighter cover succeeded in providing a virtual 'no-go' area for the Luftwaffe over the Channel ports and the invasion area whilst transport air forces brought in vast numbers of men and equipment to the beachhead. Intensive day and night patrols over both ends of the Channel by Coastal Command ensured no U-boat got amongst the D-Day fleet. Close support was given to the ground forces and this close support moved its bases over the Channel as soon as airfields became available. All this effort was made while the strategic bombing of German industrial targets and patrols against U-boats continued.

Meanwhile, the necessary training at RAF Pembrey continued unabated. In June the total of instructional flying hours was 2,560. Over the next few months Ken worked on an experimental course, possibly introducing some new technology and methods of tuition and maybe adopting some of the Inspector General's ideas. The development of this experiment seemed to necessitate all sorts of visitors from the Air Ministry, the Headquarters of Flying Training Command and 25 Group, the Central Gunnery School and many other interested parties. Eventually the experimental course started on 7 October with 90 pupils. The start had been delayed possibly until the arrival of the first batch of Wellington bombers that were to replace the Anson aircraft. Only a few days after this course began a severe gale hit the area, with gusts up to 80 mph and before the aircraft could be headed into the wind seven Wellingtons were slightly damaged. Oh dear, Ken would not have been pleased! When the experimental course ended towards the end of November, a whole panoply of top brass descended on the station to review the experiment, including Air Marshal Sir Philip Babington KCB, Air Officer Commanding-in-Chief, Flying Training Command and Air Vice-Marshal E D Davis OBE, Air Officer Commanding, 25 Group. Unfortunately the experimental nature of the course and the review results were not written down in the station's records. During his visit Air Vice-Marshal Davis proudly presented Group Captain MacDonald with the newly approved badge for the No.1 Air Gunners' School sporting the motto 'Watchful And Sure'.

No doubt October and November was a rather anxious time for Ken under the spotlight of the experimental course but he soon knew he was on his way again after nearly 18 months at No.1 Air Gunners' School, his longest posting so far. In the middle of November he had made a quick trip to the Central Gunnery School, now at RAF Catfoss, where the current Officer Commanding Gunnery Leader Wing, Wing Commander A E Lowe MBE DFC was being posted to the RAF Staff College. Wing Commander 'Lofty' Lowe was the first air gunner to command a squadron and a very popular leader. Ken was his obvious replacement, and so it was that at the end of 1944 Ken left RAF Pembrey to join once again the Central Gunnery School. During his time as Chief Instructor at the No.1 Air Gunners' School some 3,200 trainee gunners had attended courses there providing an essential supply of aircrew gunners to operational squadrons.

Christmas 1944 came and went without the end of the war in Europe as many had hoped, and some had even expected, after the D-Day landings in June. Indeed victory in Europe was still some months away. German resistance on the ground was stubborn and the Germans even mounted a counter-offensive in December in the Ardennes region – the Battle of the Bulge – not retreating until the early half of January 1945. The RAF and the US Air Force had managed to gain air superiority over the battlefield despite massive Luftwaffe support for the offensive, and also in spite of heavy Allied losses in a surprise low-level attack on our forward air bases in Belgium and Holland. While these battles raged, Bomber Command continued its campaign against German oil resources and transportation systems. Bomber Command's front line strength had risen by 50% in 1944, mostly due to new Lancaster aircraft. Bombing sorties, now both by day and night, were running at three times the rate of a year ago – all this with improved effectiveness through better tactics and new electronic equipment. The supply of air gunners and gunnery leaders needed to keep apace.

Thus there was no let up in the courses being run at the Central Gunnery School at RAF Catfoss when Ken arrived on 5 January 1945 to take up his new position as Officer Commanding Gunnery Leader Wing.

When Ken had previously been at the Central Gunnery School, at RAF Sutton Bridge, a review had been instigated to see whether RAF Catfoss was a more suitable place for the School. Following that review the School did move to RAF Catfoss in February 1944. The airfield was situated just five miles inland from the coast at Hornsea, in the East Riding of Yorkshire, and its ranges out over the North Sea had been used before for gunnery and bombing practice. The site itself had been considerably expanded in 1940 with three concrete runways, new hangers and buildings. There were two satellite landing sites to the north at Lissett and at Carnaby. Carnaby had a long emergency runway equipped with a system called FIDO, paraffin burners on each side of the runway to clear fog and mist. The station commander was Group Captain M H Dwyer who had been there for just over a year – he was a pilot but with a considerable armament background.

The structure and function of the School was still the same as it was when Ken left RAF Sutton Bridge 18 months ago. The Gunnery Leader Wing produced gunnery leaders for operational and training units and the Fighter Wing trained experienced fighter pilots to become flight commanders. Wellington bomber aircraft were flown by the Gunnery Leader Wing; the Fighter Wing used Spitfires, Masters for dual flying exercises, and a few Beaufighters. Some fighter pilots brought their own aircraft, particularly from the US Air Force who brought Mustang and twin-engine P-38 Lightning aircraft. In fact it was only a few days after Ken's arrival that a Mustang crashed when its engine cut out during a low-level exercise with a Wellington; the American pilot baled out but was hit by the tail-plane and was lucky to get away with a broken leg.

That January saw atrocious weather with heavy snowfalls and deep drifts, five feet deep at times, that required the station's 'Snow Plan' to be put into operation. The frosts at night were severe; 28 degrees of frost was recorded one night, too cold for a planned night-flying programme which had to be cancelled. On more than one occasion courses were stood down due to the bad weather.

But whilst Ken was no doubt concerned at the weather's disruption to the smooth running of the Gunnery Leader Wing, in his new role he was not really involved in the organisational side of day-to-day training; this was in the hands of his next in command Squadron Leader P B White DFC. Squadron Leader White managed two teams of instructors each headed by a Course Leader, about 20 or so instructors in all – one team ran the odd-numbered courses and the other team the even-numbered courses. The courses were staggered; for example on 17 January 1945 Course No. 91 ended and Course No. 93 commenced while Course No. 92 was half way through. (Readers will remember that Ken himself was on Course No.1.) Each course lasted seven weeks now, having been extended from four weeks, and comprised 30 or so experienced air gunners from all quarters of the Allied air forces. All the instructors were officers as were nearly all those under instruction. In addition to the instructors, Ken was responsible for the staff pilots on the Gunnery Leader Wing, the armourer and his staff, plus administrative officers and their support staff.

Obviously Ken's prime responsibility was the management of the Gunnery Leader courses but he delegated much of this duty to Squadron Leader White and the team leaders who operated to an established syllabus. One instructor, Flying Officer Alan Lacy, who remembers Ken as a most likeable and unassuming person, recalls seeing little of him during the courses themselves; even the end of course conference assessing the final markings for the trainees was conducted by Squadron Leader White. Nevertheless Ken must have spent a certain amount of time managing his senior team. Other elements of his duties were keeping abreast of the latest developments that might impact on the course syllabus, and also helping to frame future air gunnery training in the RAF itself, both elements needing him to attend the inevitable conferences and meetings, and working closely with the RAF's main armament training units. Although the Fighter and Gunnery Leader Wings operated independently the two Wings co-operated as before over joint exercises and no doubt this very important aspect of training for both Wings required his attention from time to time. He was of course part of the senior management of the station and would have been regularly involved in station matters. And as he was regarded as the next senior officer to the station commander Ken deputised for Group Captain Dwyer whenever he was away – a significant elevation in responsibility for Ken. This happened on a number of occasions, notably in early March when Group Captain

Dwyer went to France for ten days on a visit to the Tactical Air Force over there.

The Officers' Mess for the Gunnery Leader Wing was in a large country house just a mile away called Brandesburton Hall, formerly a mental institution ... which led to the inevitable comparisons with the war-time RAF occupants! The house had a grand staircase, a dining room, a bar, large bedrooms usually with four beds, and it was set in very pleasant grounds much enjoyed by the officers many of whom would cycle to and from the airfield. Whilst this separation of the Gunnery Leader Wing Officers' Mess from the other Officers' Mess on station was not ideal from a cohesion point of view it was probably the only practical solution because the nature of the Central Gunnery School meant that far more officers needed to be accommodated than would be the case on a normal RAF station.

The routine of the Gunnery Leader course was much the same as when Ken was at RAF Sutton Bridge, although the length of the course had been extended. There was however the perennial problem of the poor quality of gunners being put forward for the course; for example 15 of the 34 candidates for course No. 97 in April 1945 failed the initial tests and were returned to their units. The course content was generally the same as it was when Ken left eighteen months ago with a mixture of theory and practice and a considerable emphasis on tactics. The theory on all aspects of gunnery was advanced with lectures given by staff instructors who were undoubtedly the RAF's top tutors and by experts in their field like Professor Hill, a ballistics advisor to the Air Ministry, referred to earlier by Group Captain Keith as 'Gunner' Hill. Practical exercises took many forms, the most exciting being the full-scale combat manoeuvres using camera guns with Spitfires from Fighter Wing, which still gave rise to intense rivalry between the two Wings. Ken would quickly have brought himself up to date with the course content changes introduced since he was last at the School. Among those changes were the use of the Mark II gyro gunsight; infra-red and electronic aids to gunnery and manoeuvres; controlling fire power on daylight raids; and the introduction of night flying exercises. Ken's approach to running the courses was typically pragmatic, similar to his predecessor Wing Commander Lowe. They were able to promote an atmosphere among their instructors which made their staff feel valued and special, not always the case elsewhere according to one.

The foul weather continued well into February and although Ken was forced to extend one of the courses the work of the station pressed on. Poor weather brought its crop of strays to RAF Catfoss as it was one of the main northeast coast airfields. In mid January several aircraft landed at the Carnaby satellite airfield and because there was no accommodation there 27 aircrew had to be ferried in the early hours to the base at Catfoss, all hoping for a bed. That was nothing compared to the 180 American aircrew that had to be put up for the night at the end of January when their Liberators were forced down by extremely adverse weather. On one occasion a Russian aircraft arrived complete with a supply of vodka; it left behind an awful lot of hangovers.

Accidents though were never far away. In January Ken lost one of his Wellington aircraft which caught fire when it was started up and burned out, fortunately without anyone being injured. Pilots from the Fighter Wing came away unhurt after three accidents on the ground while taxiing their Martinet aircraft, twice hitting fuel bowsers and on the other occasion hitting another Martinet. The Fighter Wing had a really poor day on 16 March when two Master aircraft crashed on landing and a glider trial went wrong – a new 32 foot experimental glider was being towed as a target by a Martinet aircraft when the cable broke in the air and the glider crashed two miles away. Fortunately all the crews survived; the glider did not. And only a few days later two Spitfires collided in mid air over the Lissett satellite airfield, one crash-landed on the airfield itself with its wheels up, the other crashed on a nearby beach after the pilot bailed out. This time the pilot who bailed out received slight injuries, but both Spitfires were written off. At the end of March a Wellington aircraft on a low level exercise hit a tree but landed safely.

Group Captain M H Dwyer, centre middle row, with Ken on his left and Ken's predecessor Wing Commander Lowe on his right with some of the officers of the Gunnery Leader Wing outside Brandesburton Hall, December 1944
[Photo: Courtesy of Alan Lacy]

Flying Officer Lacy remembers those low level exercises were really low level; one time his Wellington brought back some telephone wires. Far more serious though was the time he was involved in a mid-air collision a few months before Ken arrived. He recalls:

Shortly after I completed my first operational tour I was invited to become a Gunnery Leader instructor at C.G.S. This was a prestige posting for which you were interviewed and subsequently accepted or rejected.

C.G.S. was an exhilarating place with considerable competition between the Fighter Wing and the Gunnery Leader Wing. They fought, albeit with camera gun; nevertheless aircraft flying towards each other are quite dangerous. I knew that there had been mid-air collisions and I was always a little apprehensive during combat manoeuvres. On October 14th 1944 I was in the second pilot's seat of a Wellington bomber listening to the gunnery leader trainee in the astrodome giving instructions to the pilot to climb starboard into the attack from our starboard quarter by a Spitfire. Then, 'Bang' it had happened – the Spitfire hit our starboard engine about four feet from my right shoulder. The Spitfire pilot had left his breakaway too late. His plane cartwheeled away as it disintegrated.

Flying Officer Alan Lacy
[Photo: Courtesy of Alan Lacy]

I asked our pilot if the plane could be controlled and he moved the control column. This resulted in enormous vibrations. I called, 'Stand-by!' over the intercom. This word was reserved for use in a bale out situation. The pilot and I agreed we should bale out and I called 'Bale Out!' over the intercom. I reached for my parachute which was stowed near my seat and clipped it on to my harness. I then climbed down to the hatch between the pilots' seats and I opened the hatch. The other escape positions were a hatch halfway down the fuselage and escape directly from the rear turret doors.

I looked through the hatch at the earth below and immediately felt the pilot's foot on my back. There was no time to hesitate. I left the air-

craft and saw the tail plane and rear turret flash past. I moved my right hand towards the ripcord handle and I immediately realised that I had clipped the parachute on with the ripcord towards the left hand and I pulled the handle with that hand. There was then an almighty impact as the chute opened and I grabbed the harness. From a feeling of hurtling downwards there was now a sensation of floating upwards. I thought I was in an updraft that was going to take me to some oxygen sparse height!

As I was contemplating the situation an American Mustang started to fly circles around me in no doubt a friendly gesture. I thought any moment now his slipstream will hit my parachute. In less than no time the ground was coming up fast and crash-bang – and I was being pulled through a hedge by my parachute. I was OK except for a few scratches on my face from the hedge. I hit the parachute release and the harness fell away. I started walking and eventually found a farmhouse. I knocked at the door expecting to be confronted by a suspicious Yorkshire farmer. After a while a young man appeared from behind the house and in a very upper crust accent said, 'Hello old boy couldn't you make my aunt hear.'

He phoned the police who contacted the base and the CO Gunnery Leader Wing came and collected me. We went to the base sick bay and the MO checked me over and gave me two sleeping pills and said, 'Take these before you go to bed.' I went to the mess and was greeted by, 'You lucky bastard!' I had a pint then went to bed. I woke up the next afternoon.

One of the other survivors had a different reception when he approached a farmhouse. He was a Dutchman wearing his black Dutch Airforce uniform and speaking with a Dutch accent; he got the pitchfork treatment until the RAF rescued him!

Tragically the two other trainees did not get out of the Wellington. They were particular friends and I can only think that perhaps the one in the rear turret could not get out and the other one went to help him. Sadly the Spitfire pilot died too.

In March there were several close reminders that the Luftwaffe was not yet defeated although it was in its last gasps, severely crippled through lack of aviation fuel and replacement pilots. On the night of 3 March an intruder 'shot up' the No.1 Hanger damaging three aircraft and later in the month there was an air raid alert. But on the evening of the 17 March an intruder brought down a Lancaster of 550 Squadron on a training exercise which crashed on the sea front at Withernsea with the loss of all but one of the crew. Two of the bodies that were recovered were brought to the station. The body of the navigator was washed up on the shore six weeks later and was also brought to the station mortuary – one body was never found. A few days afterwards when Ken was in charge of the station in the absence of Group

Captain Dwyer another body was brought in, this time of an Australian airman from 466 Squadron washed ashore at Aldbrough just to the south.

During the early months of 1945 there were a number of events in which Ken would have been heavily involved. In January several of Ken's senior instructors were looking at a new method of examining, testing and assessing air gunners called Standard Efficiency Tests, based on a USAAF system called Phase Checks that employed a series of standardised 'drills'. In April there were two conferences at RAF Manby, the first a syllabus conference that all the senior officers from the Central Gunnery School attended and a second on 'Synthetics' (training on simulators) when Ken took Flight Lieutenant Hathaway (seen bottom right in the group photograph on p.173). One trip Ken would have enjoyed was a flight over to RAF Pembrey to visit his old station, strictly a liaison visit of course.

By the end of March, however, the course of the war in Europe was drawing to a close. The Rhine had been crossed in strength, the threat from the V1 and V2 weapons was over as sites were either bombed by the RAF or over-run by advancing Allied armies, and in the east the Soviets had Berlin in their sights. Surely the end could not be far away.

Extract from the Operational Record Book of RAF Catfoss showing Ken's distinctive signature, April 1945
[Image: Courtesy of The National Archives, Kew (AIR29 605)]

On 3 May Group Captain Dwyer was called away to preside over a court martial and again Ken was acting station commander. The following day Squadron Leader Scott from 124 Squadron flew over from RAF Hutton Cranswick to discuss co-operation over celebrations for Victory in Europe Day – VE Day – so Ken knew something was in the wind. Group Captain Dwyer was back on the 6 May and the next day took a call late on in the afternoon from Group Headquarters giving him instructions for VE Day which was to be officially announced the following morning – Tuesday, 8 May 1945. The plan was for the station to work as normal till noon then for everyone to assemble on the parade ground for an address by Group Captain Dwyer who would confirm the momentous news and explain arrangements

176 ~ *Gunnery Leader*

for the ensuing celebrations. But on the morning the rain came down and the assembly was hastily rearranged in the station concert hall. After Group Captain Dwyer's address, everyone then dispersed to listen on the radio to the official declaration by Churchill. Whilst Ken had advance notice of the German surrender, what emotions must he and all his colleagues have felt after nearly six years of war as Churchill made the following broadcast:

German armed forces surrendered unconditionally on May 7. Hostilities in Europe end officially at midnight, May 8, 1945.

Yesterday morning at 2.41 a.m. at Headquarters, General Jodl, the representative of the German High Command, and Grand Admiral Dönitz, the designated head of the German State, signed the act of unconditional surrender of all German land, sea, and air forces in Europe to the Allied Expeditionary Force, and simultaneously to the Soviet High Command.

General Bedell Smith, Chief of Staff of the Allied Expeditionary Force, and General Francois Sevez signed the document on behalf of the Supreme Commander of the Allied Expeditionary Force, and General Susloparov signed on behalf of the Russian High Command.

To-day this agreement will be ratified and confirmed at Berlin, where Air Chief Marshal Tedder, Deputy Supreme Commander of the Allied Expeditionary Force, and General de Lattre de Tassigny will sign on behalf of General Eisenhower. Marshal Zhukov will sign on behalf of the Soviet High Command. The German representatives will be Field-Marshal Keitel, Chief of the High Command, and the Commanders-in-Chief of the German Army, Navy, and Air Forces.

Hostilities will end officially at one minute after midnight to-night (Tuesday, May 8), but in the interests of saving lives the "Cease fire" began yesterday to be sounded all along the front, and our dear Channel Islands are also to be freed to-day.

The Germans are still in places resisting the Russian troops, but should they continue to do so after midnight they will, of course, deprive themselves of the protection of the laws of war, and will be attacked from all quarters by the Allied troops. It is not surprising that on such long fronts and in the existing disorder of the enemy the orders of the German High Command should not in every case be obeyed immediately. This does not, in our opinion, with the best military advice at our disposal, constitute any reason for withholding from the nation the facts communicated to us by General Eisenhower of the unconditional surrender already signed at Rheims, nor should it prevent us from celebrating to-day and to-morrow (Wednesday) as Victory in Europe days.

To-day, perhaps, we shall think mostly of ourselves. To-morrow we shall pay a particular tribute to our Russian comrades, whose prowess in the field has been one of the grand contributions to the general victory.

The German war is therefore at an end. After years of intense preparation, Germany hurled herself on Poland at the beginning of September, 1939; and, in pursuance of our guarantee to Poland and in agreement with the French Republic, Great Britain, the British Empire and Commonwealth of Nations, declared war upon this foul aggression. After gallant France had been struck down we, from this Island and from our united Empire, maintained the struggle single-handed for a whole year until we were joined by the military might of Soviet Russia, and later by the overwhelming power and resources of the United States of America.

Finally almost the whole world was combined against the evil-doers, who are now prostrate before us. Our gratitude to our splendid Allies goes forth from all our hearts in this Island and throughout the British Empire.

We may allow ourselves a brief period of rejoicing; but let us not forget for a moment the toil and efforts that lie ahead. Japan, with all her treachery and greed, remains unsubdued. The injury she has inflicted on Great Britain, the United States, and other countries, and her detestable cruelties, call for justice and retribution. We must now devote all our strength and resources to the completion of our task, both at home and abroad. Advance Britannia! Long live the cause of freedom! God save the King!

With the afternoon off everyone could relax and take in the news, thinking what it meant for them and their families, talking about life back in civvy street. They had a dance to look forward to in the NAFFI that evening and the whole day off tomorrow – what luxury! Amongst the relief and excitement, many were mindful of Churchill's words about the unfinished war in the Far East. Some feared they might even be moved out there as military resources were switched away from the European theatre to help bring an end to the fighting in the Far East. But those thoughts were for later; now VE Day celebrations could begin.

For Ken the reality of returning to civvy street had just come a lot nearer. No doubt he and his wife Teddie had talked at length about what they would do when the war was over. Everything pointed to Ken leaving the RAF. For a start Teddie certainly did not want him to stay on and because his current rank of Wing Commander was for the duration of hostilities, should he sign on as a regular he would revert to the rank of Squadron Leader. Peacetime in the RAF would be rather different and Ken's pragmatic and somewhat laid back approach, which in wartime had got the job done, would not fit in so well with a regular force. One thought Ken may have had was that if he stayed on might he be able to fulfil his original dream, to learn to fly? However, Teddie was dead against him learning to fly, so that was that. When the opportunity arrived he would leave without delay. But that day was still some months away.

The celebrations continued with a Thanksgiving Service held at Brandesburton Parish Church and a further day's holiday on 21 May. Meanwhile the routine of the Gunnery Leader courses continued. And with the better weather and lengthening evenings there was plenty of sport arranged for the men and the women on the station; perhaps Ken had time to watch some of the cricket and hockey matches.

One visitor at that time came from a Middle East Training School – doubtless he was questioned to see if gunnery instructors were needed out there. And at the end of the month Wing Commander Kerr visited the station to deliver a lecture to all personnel on 'Japan and the Far East', a reminder of the perils still being faced by the Allies on the other side of the world. On the lighter side in the middle of June a cricket match between the Instructors of the Gunnery Leader Wing and No. 98 Course ended in a resounding win for the Instructors – certainly Ken would have been involved in that somehow.

Training continued as before once the brief celebrations were over. Japan was as yet undefeated and it was far too early to assess what the RAF's future gunnery training requirements would be, so the courses needed to resume. On 27 June Ken assumed command of the station again as Group Captain Dwyer went on leave. In the event Ken was in charge for the next month because Group Captain Dwyer did not return after his leave; he was posted to Senior Armament Staff Officer, HQ British Air Forces of Occupation. Unfortunately during July there were a series of flying accidents, the worst resulting in the death of a pilot on a Fighter Wing course whose Spitfire crashed at Market Weighton. The same day a Wellington crashed but the pilot escaped injury and later in the month another Wellington caught fire over the airfield and crash landed near the perimeter, amazingly with no one injured. And engine trouble caused a Master aircraft to crash near Driffield injuring the pilot and passenger. One Leading Aircraftsman from the station found himself in trouble of a different kind, charged by the Police in Hull with assault. Ken approved the Adjutant to speak at court on the aircraftsman's behalf, but he was still fined 6 shillings plus £1 costs. A more pleasant duty came when Ken welcomed 100 Belgium Forces officers and men on a visit, the sort of event at which Ken, a charming host, would excel.

With the arrival on 29 July of the new Officer Commanding, Group Captain E S Butler OBE, Ken's release date came a step nearer. Two Australian airmen on the station had already been released for repatriation. Ken formally handed over command on 1 August, and then events moved quickly. On the world front, the first atomic bomb was dropped on Hiroshima on 6 August and the second on Nagasaki on 9 August, following which Japan agreed to unconditional surrender on 14 August. The news was announced by new Prime Minister Clement Attlee at midnight thus:

Japan has today surrendered. The last of our enemies is laid low.

Let us recall that on the 7th of December, 1941, Japan, whose onslaught China had already resisted for over four years, fell upon the United States of America, who was then not at war, and upon ourselves, who were so pressed in our death struggle with Germany and Italy. Taking full advantage of surprise and treachery, the Japanese forces quickly overran the territory of ourselves and our Allies in the Far East, and at one time it appeared as though they might even invade the mainland of Australia and advance far into India.

But the tide turned, first slowly, then with an ever-increasing speed and violence, as the mighty forces of the United States and of the British Commonwealth and Empire and of their Allies, and finally of Russia, were brought to bear. Their resistance is now everywhere being broken.

At this time we should pay tribute to the men from this country, from the Dominions and India and the colonies, to our fleets, armies and air forces, that have fought so well in the arduous campaign against Japan. Our gratitude goes out to all our splendid Allies and, above all, to the United States, without whose prodigious efforts this war in the East would still have many years to run.

We also think especially at this time of the prisoners in Japanese hands, of our friends in the Dominions and Australia and New Zealand, in India, in Burma and in those colonial territories upon whom the brunt of the Japanese attack fell. We rejoice that their sufferings will soon be at an end and that these territories will soon be purged of the Japanese invader.

Here at home you have a short rest in the unceasing exertions which were all borne without flinching or complaint for so many dark years. I have no doubt that throughout industries generally the Government's lead in the matter of victory holidays will be followed, and that tomorrow – Wednesday – and Thursday may everywhere be treated as days of holiday.

There are some who must necessarily remain at work on these days to maintain essential services, and I am sure they can be relied upon to carry on. When we return to work on Friday morning, we must turn again with energy to the great tasks which challenge us. But for the moment let all who can relax and enjoy themselves in the knowledge of a work well done.

Peace has once again come to the world. Let us thank God for this great deliverance and for His mercies.

Long live the King!

At last it really was all over. The station had the whole day as a holiday with a dance in the evening, and before the dancing commenced many would have listened to the King addressing the nation on the radio. Across the land people crowded onto the streets of every village, town and city singing, dancing, lighting bonfires and letting off fireworks. On Sunday a further

Thanksgiving Service for the station was held at the local church. Soon after that, one of Ken's senior instructors left to be demobbed at his local Personal Dispersal Centre. But Ken did not have to wait long for his release papers to come through – he had been granted a Class 'A' release. Class 'A' meant his demob was based on his age and service, and since Ken had been called up at the very beginning of the war and he was now aged 32 he was one of the earliest to be granted release. The other two categories were 'B' – Ministry of Labour essential worker for reconstruction and 'C' – Compassionate.

On 31 August 1945 Ken left RAF Catfoss and the Central Gunnery School for the last time and drove down to London. The following morning he attended No.100 Personnel Dispersal Centre at RAF Uxbridge. There he was duly 'processed'; through the records section, the medical section, the Ministry of Labour section, the Ministry of Health section, the accounts section, an advice section and the final departure section before driving down to Wembley where there was a vast clothing centre. Having chosen his full demob outfit and no doubt filled with mixed emotions, Ken walked out to his car … it was Saturday, 1 September 1945 and he was a civilian, his duty done.

9. Epilogue

Having survived nearly six years of war, what did post-war, post-RAF civilian life hold for Ken? Well, initially he faced a situation similar to the vast numbers of people who came out of the services in the immediate post-war period – the question of what to do. Many were able to go back to their old trade, resume a university education, find work in a new trade acquired in the services or rejoin a family business or farm. For many others it was not so easy. Ken's heart had not been in his articled auctioneer and estate agent position before the war and he had not completed his qualifications nor did he have a university degree; and outside the RAF his undoubted skills in air gunnery were not really marketable. Therefore nothing obvious beckoned. So at the age of 32, what to do?

There were agencies set up to help ex-servicemen find work, and all sorts of skills were required as there was much needed reconstruction work to be done and the government's policy was for rapid transformation from a war-economy to a peacetime export-led economy. Two factors were in Ken's favour however, time and rank. Time was available because his wife Teddie was sufficiently wealthy that he did not need to earn an income immediately to support them. He was paid by the RAF for a couple of months, but money was not an issue. Teddie had independent means and already owned a lovely cottage in Horsted Keynes in Sussex which was where they lived for a number of years after the war. For half the war he was a senior officer in training establishments reaching the rank of Wing Commander; any potential employer would know those duties and rank required considerable leadership and management abilities. Perhaps his future lay in some sort of managerial position. Finding something suitable would not be easy but there was no hurry to sort anything out.

Because Ken did not confide his feelings to his family or friends, what his thoughts were on his release from the RAF are unknown. Countless thousands of ex-servicemen would find some difficulty adjusting to their new life and Ken was probably no different. The immediate loss of status, having been a senior officer and just recently in charge of a large RAF station, was just one change he would have to get used to. Maybe he was not too bothered because he never appeared to be particularly status conscious. He was entitled to call himself Wing Commander K M Bastin DFC, but he never did. In many ways he seemed immediately to put the war years behind him, closed the door on them and turned the key. Perhaps like most leaving the services he just wanted to get back to a normal life, where plans could be made for next week or next month with some certainty, unlike wartime service life. When in Bomber Command, Ken had no certainty of even being alive the next day.

Since he kept his feelings to himself it is not easy to say how the war affected him. Before he joined up he was open and friendly, sociable, gregarious, looking for some fun and not too serious about anything, except playing sport. After the war, whilst he was respected, well liked and always very polite, he was to some extent less outgoing, comfortable only with a very small group of close friends and he became somewhat distanced from his family. Those who did know him were well aware of his enjoyment of a glass or two of gin or whiskey, but always the correct drink for the right time of day or occasion.

Certainly he had painful memories – the loss of so many friends and colleagues. A particular loss was the death of his close friend and best man at his wedding, Raymond Lumb, who died just three months after the wedding. In Bomber Command losses happened almost daily; even in Flying Training Command fatal accidents were a regular occurrence. Perhaps he never could become inured to the constant pall of death around him. Very nearly half of Bomber Command's 125,000 serving aircrew lost their lives, another 10,000 were made prisoners of war and over 8,000 were wounded. Including Fighter Command, Coastal Command and others the RAF's total fatalities in the Second World War were some 76,000. One of the saddest statistics is that over 20,000 of those who died have no known grave – nearly all of whom are commemorated on the Air Forces Memorial at Runnymede.

Prior to the war, career-wise Ken was drifting, he was not committed to his work and at times his father despaired he would ever achieve anything: only sport inspired him. The war gave him a direction, a purpose and initially, but only briefly, excitement. The RAF suited him by not being overbearingly strict, and it also gave him immediate responsibility by granting him a commission. Undoubtedly he was influenced by his experiences serving in nearly a dozen different postings and, of course, by his senior officers and fellow airmen. For instance, at 10 Squadron his Officer Commanding was the larger-than-life Wing Commander Bill Staton, a memorable figure. His nicknames 'Bull' and 'King Kong' summed him up. Renowned for his courage, skill and indomitable resolution, in this character was the spirit of the RAF writ large, but a character impossible to live up to!

Often a pilot had a major influence on those who regularly flew with him and was often very highly regarded by his crew. Ken's first regular pilot was Flying Officer Nelson; although young, he too demonstrated the true spirit of the RAF. William Nelson was determined and courageous, and experienced enough to be successful. Ken flew with him half a dozen times and after their last flight William Nelson was awarded the Distinguished Flying Cross 'for gallantry and devotion to duty in the execution of air operations'. Soon afterwards William Nelson transferred to Spitfires but sadly died in action before the end of 1940. Bill Staton, however, survived capture by the Japanese after the fall of Singapore to continue his illustrious career in the RAF, eventually becoming an Air Vice-Marshal.

Probably the most influential of all was Ken's next pilot, Wing Commander Sydney 'Buf' Bufton. They flew together on seven operations. Sydney Bufton had a pragmatic approach to the job in hand, decisive and quickly getting things done; but he was also a thinker and innovator with a determined streak, prepared to argue his point uninhibited by rank. He was devoted to his duty and a brave, 'press-on' captain who cared deeply about his men. Ken must have seen much to admire in Sydney Bufton; and doubtless 'Buf' Bufton was someone he could far more easily relate to than Bill Staton. Closer in age, they were of similar character and obviously got on well together, sharing a love of sport – Sydney Bufton was a gifted all-round sportsman who played hockey for Wales, the combined services and the RAF. Ken could well have seen in Sydney Bufton, his Officer Commanding for nine months, the type of officer he could aspire to be. In turn Sydney Bufton saw in Ken the type of officer he wanted when he was asked to re-establish 76 Squadron with the new Halifax heavy bomber, as he took Ken with him to be his gunnery officer.

Not long after his short spell at 76 Squadron Sydney Bufton went on to be Deputy Director and later Director of Bombing Operations at Bomber Command, and it was here he further developed his ideas for a Target Finding Force to improve bombing performance. These ideas were based on his experiences at 10 Squadron and also from listening to other operational and station commanders. He pressed for his proposal to be adopted but found fierce opposition from the Air Officer Commanding-in-Chief of Bomber Command, Air Marshal Sir Arthur Harris and Group Commanders too who were totally opposed for sound historical military reasons to any sort of elite force. However following the Butt Report in August 1941 which highlighted the inaccuracy and ineffectiveness of bombing operations in the early years of the war, events were on Sydney Bufton's side and he eventually prevailed. In June 1942 Air Marshal Sir Arthur Harris was overruled and the famous Pathfinder Force established. 'The little Air Commodore' – as Churchill called Sydney Bufton – continued in a long and distinguished career in the RAF, retiring with the rank of Air Vice-Marshal.

There was one further colleague at 10 Squadron who should be mentioned. He is Pilot Officer John Russell, remarkable in his own inimitable way. He and Ken were fellow officers for six months, flying together on a number of bombing operations. For five of these operations Pilot Officer Russell was second pilot to Wing Commander Bufton and there were two operations when he was captain, although on one of these they got bogged down on the airfield before take-off. People who knew John Russell could not fail to see he was very meticulous in everything he did. He was methodical and thorough, everything in its place, everything done properly. Described by some as 'reliability personified' he was someone who strove to achieve in himself and in others the highest standards – the 'perfect performance'. He was a quiet, thinking man, very self-reliant. He learned this self reliance at a young age when he became a proficient yet adventurous yachtsman, often sailing alone, even around the Isle of Wight aged ten or eleven. His love of sailing came from his parents, and he was also an artist like his father and grandfather. Indeed his grandfather was acquainted with a number of the French Impressionists, working with Monet and Matisse and regarded as a close friend of Rodin and Van Gogh of whom he painted a portrait. Originally John Russell thought it obvious he should join the Navy at the outbreak of war, but a friend who knew him well told him he would not take to being cooped up in the confines of a warship, rather he should aim for the freedom of the open skies with the RAF. But in war even the most precise preparation was no defence against bad luck and John Russell was shot down and badly injured in 1942. By then he was a Squadron Leader with the Distinguished Flying Cross. Captured, he whiled away his imprisonment by drawing and attempting to escape. After repatriation he could not settle and spent time in his native Scotland living on a barge and earning a living designing and painting theatre scenery, but later went back into the RAF as a flying instructor. When he retired from the service he turned to his real love, the sea, and became one of the earliest charter skippers operating on the west coast of Scotland. He was a highly regarded Royal Yachting Association Yachtmaster Examiner and wrote two books on seamanship. He died at sea in 1995 taking delivery of a new boat. He was close to his second cousin Timothy Laurence, now a Vice Admiral, and his wife Anne, Princess Royal, both of whom attended his funeral.

The other strong personality among Ken's early superiors was New Zealander Wing Commander Jarman who recommended Ken for the Distinguished Flying Cross. Tough and somewhat abrasive by nature, yet again his leadership and bravery could not possibly be doubted, particularly when one imagines the terrifying scene at La Pallice into which he led his formation. He obviously placed a great deal of faith in Ken's ability, but perhaps Ken found him less easy to get on with than, say, Sydney Bufton. Geoffrey Jarman had many significant achievements in the RAF but left in 1953 with the rank of Group Captain after a strange episode. He was court martialled for using RAF property for a boat he was converting and for improperly employing RAF personnel on the boat – an astonishing blemish to an otherwise extremely distinguished record.

By contrast there was a rather different and very late post script to the La Pallice episode for one of the other pilots, Flight Sergeant Stan Greaves. He and his crew were lucky to survive being shot down that July day in 1941. After the war Stan continued to fly as an instructor and he often wondered what happened to his crew. In 1979 he decided to find out and managed to trace all of them. He arranged a reunion on 23 July 1981 and the following day Stan himself flew them to their old base at RAF Linton-on-Ouse where he landed, bringing his crew back 40 years to the day they took off for La Pallice. They were greeted on the tarmac by the station commander with the words, "Welcome back even though it took you 40 years. Better late than never." A plaque in the Sergeant's Mess commemorates their return; it says, 'Mission Completed'.

Returning to Ken, in all probability one other source of motivation for him during the war was his long association with the Central Gunnery School. It may seem strange that an establishment could be a stimulus, but the Central Gunnery School had a cachet. Here not only did Ken brush shoulders with some of the RAF's aces and famous names, but there was often a high intellect and a cutting edge to the work at the School. He must have been buoyed by his two spells on the staff there, particularly his final months when he was often acting as the School's Officer Commanding. Without doubt he left the RAF on a high note.

There was a sense that Ken's wife Teddie too had a strong influence on him. Her background was very obscure as she seemed to have no family and few friends. One might have imagined she would have readily embraced Ken's family in the absence of any of her own, but she made no effort to fit in: rather the opposite. Her manner was even more surprising when you consider they had no children of their own. Whether deliberate on her part or not, Ken became increasingly removed from his family, a drift he appeared to let happen. Maybe he had changed, or perhaps there were other reasons. There were visits to Northampton to see his mother and sister but these became infrequent, brief and stilted. And later when he found a permanent position he kept his private life very separate from his work life; Ken neither talked about his home life nor did Teddie accompany him to company functions.

Eventually, through his wife's connections, Ken secured the position of senior administrative trainee at the division of Gallaher Limited that made Senior Service cigarettes. In all he spent 22 happy years with Gallahers retiring in 1974 as Head of Production Programme Planning. The company magazine, *Smoke Signals*, started the report on his retirement, 'Scattered around Britain and the Commonwealth there must be some hundreds of former wartime RAF men who remember with fondness the former Wing Commander Ken Bastin, because of his genuine concern for the dignity and feelings of people'. The report also remarked, 'Typically, Ken considered that *Smoke Signals* should concern itself only with his career in the company and took some convincing that colleagues were genuinely interested in the RAF years which he has always been loath to talk about'.

Ken had managed to survive everything the Germany military threw at him yet, bizarrely, a bee sting very nearly killed him one day on the train commuting to London. He suffered an anaphylactic shock which fortunately was recognised by a doctor in the carriage who rushed Ken to hospital from the next station. That episode prompted Ken and Teddie to move away from the Sussex countryside to a seaside flat in Hastings.

The death of his wife Teddie in May 1973 from liver failure had a profound effect on Ken. He was due to retire in a few weeks time but stayed on at Gallahers a little longer. Strangely, the day after his wife died the caretaker at the block of flats where they lived found Ken's RAF uniform in the dustbin; and at some point Ken cleared out practically all his personal affects, including papers and photographs. He even sold his medals comprising the Distinguished Flying Cross, the 1939/45 Star, the Air Crew Europe Star, the Defence Medal and the War Medal 1939/45. These he had promised to leave to his sister Phyllis so why he sold them is a mystery as he didn't need the money. In the years that followed his wife's death his family and friends became progressively concerned about his welfare. He became more and more introverted and seemed to go into a shell, unwilling or unable to lift himself out of it despite the encouragement of those close to him. He died of a stroke on 14 June 1987 two days after his 74th birthday.

Bibliography

The following works were those chiefly consulted in the preparation of this book. Other articles, papers and manuscripts too numerous to mention were also consulted fully or in part.

Action Stations series by various authors, Patrick Stephens Ltd, 1982 onwards.

AIR series at The National Archives, Kew.

Bomber Command by Max Hastings, Book Club Associates, 1980.

Combat Ready by Alastair Goodrum, GMS Enterprises, 1997.

From Hull, Hell & Halifax by Chris Blanchett, Midland Counties Publications, 1992.

Guns In The Sky by Chaz Bowyer, J M Dent & Sons Ltd, 1979.

I Hold My Aim by C H Keith, George Allen & Unwin Ltd, 1946.

Only Owls And Bloody Fools Fly At Night by Tom Sawyer, Goodall Publications Ltd, 1985

Personal Diaries of Phyllis Williams, 1939 -1941.

Raider: The Halifax And Its Flyers by Geoffrey Jones, Wm Kimber & Co, 1978.

Royal Air Force Bomber Command Losses series by W R Chorley, Midland Counties Publications, 1992 onwards.

Tail Gunner by R C Rivaz, Jarrolds, 1943.

The Bomber Command War Diaries by Martin Middlebrook & Chris Everitt, Penguin Books Ltd, 1985.

The Other Few by Larry Donnelly, Red Kite, 2004.

The Papers of Air Vice-Marshal Sydney Osborne Bufton at Churchill Archives Centre, Cambridge.

The Pendulum and the Scythe by Ken Marshall, Crecy Publishing Ltd, 1965.

The Whitley Boys by G L Donnelly, Air Research, 1998.

To See The Dawn Breaking by W R Chorley, W R Chorley, 1981.

We Act With One Accord by Alan W Cooper, J&KH Publishing, 1998.

Index

Advanced Air Striking Force, 34, 49, 53
Air Forces Memorial, Runnymede, 183
Air Gunners:
  as wireless operators, 13, 46
  development, 9-13
  sergeant rank, 47
  standard of, 13, 152, 157
  training, 14-16, 18-19, 21, 134, 135, 163-165, 167, 168
  see also Machine Guns
  see also Turrets
Aircraft:
  Anson, 163, 167, 169
  Battle, 134
  Beaufighter, 170
  Blenheim, 162, 166
  Consolidated type B24 (Liberator), 129-133, 167, 172
  Defiant, 134, 135
  Flying Fortress, 156
  Halifax, 89, 91-96, 99-101, 103, 104, 106, 107, 111, 112, 114, 116, 125, 129, 136, 138, 148, 184
  Hampden, 29
  Hurricane, 103
  Lancaster, 138, 170, 175
  Lysander, 134-136, 151, 153, 154, 160, 162
  Martinet, 162, 166, 167, 173
  Master, 156, 170, 173, 179
  Mosquito, 148
  Mustang, 170, 175
  P-38 Lightning, 170
  Spitfire, 99, 103, 150, 151, 156, 159-161, 163, 170, 172-175, 179, 183
  Stirling, 101, 104, 116, 138, 166
  Warwick, 167
  Wellington, 21, 29, 78-79, 100, 134, 141, 146, 147, 150, 151, 155, 159, 160, 163, 169, 170, 173-175, 179
  Whitley, 11, 18, 19, 21, 22, 24, 27-30, 36, 37, 47, 48, 51, 53, 55, 60, 67, 75, 76, 78-80, 84, 87, 88, 90, 91, 93-95, 99, 101, 104, 134-136, 139-141, 143-147
Anderson, Pilot Officer, 125
Andrew, Pilot Officer, 76
Angles, France, 121
Astbury, Flying Officer Rupert, 136, 137, 140-142, 144-146
Atkinson, Squadron Leader M, 146
Attlee, Prime Minister Clement, speech, 179-180

Babington, Air Marshal Sir Philip, 169
Bagshaw, Flying Officer, 37, 38, 76
Balcomb, Sergeant, 121

Barratt, Air Marshal, 53
Bastin, Charles Montague (father), 1-5, 183
  death, 1933, 7
Bastin, Jessie (mother), 1-4, 7, 8, 46, 49, 77, 85, 87, 91, 123, 127-129, 186
Bastin, Ken:
  Air Gunner training, 9, 14-15, 18-19
  birth, 3
  death, 187
  demobilisation, 178, 181
  Flight Lieutenant, promotion to, 89
  Flying Officer, promotion to, 47, 78
  Gunnery Leader training, 14, 17-18
  injury, 19
  marriage, 22-24
  medals, 98, 117-119, 123, 124, 128, 129, 187
  nickname, 'Cliff', 27
  Pilot Officer, commissioned, 9, 14, 17
  RAFVR, joins, 8
  Squadron Leader, promotion to, 134
  Wing Commander, promotion to, 161, 162, 165
Bastin, Mary (sister), 2-4, 7, 8, 85, 123
Bastin, Peggy (sister), 2-4, 7, 85
Bastin, Phyllis (sister), 3, 5-8, 20-23, 70, 77, 85, 87, 186, 187
  diary entries, 7, 8, 19, 36, 40, 42, 46, 50, 56, 60, 70, 77, 85, 87, 91, 119, 123-124, 127, 129
Battle of the Atlantic, 89
Battle of Britain, 47, 51, 75, 155
Beamish, Group Captain C E St J, 151, 152, 156, 160
Beeston, Pilot Officer, 76
Begbie, Flight Sergeant, 110, 113
Berlin, see Bombing Operations
Bessell, Sergeant, 67, 69-71, 73
Beurling, Flying Officer, 160
Bickford, Squadron Leader Bob, 34, 97, 123
Bismarck, German battleship, 63-65, 99, 122
Blackwell, Pilot Officer, 103
Bligh, Pilot Officer, 21
Bolton, Sergeant, 121
Bombing Operations:
  Berlin, 58-60, 73-75
  Bremen, 34-36, 60-62, 85-87
  Cologne, 140-142
  Ehrang, 66-70
  Essen, 144-146
  Givet, 40-42
  Hal, 42-43
  Hamburg, 63-64
  La Pallice, 103-117
  Lorient, 71-72
  Mannheim, 79-84
  Merseburg, 96-97

Gunnery Leader ~ 189

Nuremberg, 125-127
Oise, River, bridges 37, 38
Rheinfelden, 54-55
Rheydt, 38-39
Ruhr marshalling yards, 44-45
Stavanger, 30-32
Bouwens, Squadron Leader, 130
Boxwell, Pilot Officer, 76
Boyce, Group Captain C D C, 135, 139, 141
Bradley, Squadron Leader T P A, 111, 119, 121
Brandesburton Hall, Officers' Mess, 172, 173
Brant, Pilot Officer, 76
Bremen, *see* Bombing Operations
Brest, France, 65, 89, 97, 99-101, 103, 115, 116, 122, 124, 125
Bridson, Pilot Officer, 76
Brintin, Pierre (French rescuer), 120
Brisbane, Flying Officer G M, 105, 108, 109, 113, 119
British Air Commission, Washington, 129, 130, 132, 133
British Expeditionary Force, 43, 46, 49
Brochot, Robert (French photographer), 112, 115
Brown, Squadron Leader A H S, 147
Buckingham Palace, Investiture, 127-129, 162
Bufton, Wing Commander Sydney, 'Buf', 53-55, 58-60, 63-65, 67-76, 89, 94, 148, 184
   letters to his father, 57-58
Burgess, Guy (Cold War spy), 5
Busk, Group Captain C W, 152
Buster Hill, radio beacon, 56
Butler, Group Captain E S, 179
Butt Report, 127, 184

Central Gunnery School, 17-18, 27, 147-161, 169-181, 186
   Fighter Wing addition, 149
   formation, 14, 17, 157, 159
   function, 13-14, 17, 157, 159, 170
   Gunnery Leader courses, 14, 17, 150, 151, 153-156, 158, 159, 171, 172, 179
   move to Catfoss, 158, 170
   move to Sutton Bridge, 149
   quality of Instructors, 151, 157
   quality of pupils, 150, 152, 172
Chalmers, Aircraftsman George, 33
Chamberlain, Prime Minister, 7
Cheshire, Flight Lieutenant Christopher, 91, 105, 107, 123
Cheshire, Flight Lieutenant Leonard, 123
Churchill, Prime Minister Winston, 34, 36, 87-89, 99, 137, 139, 143, 166, 168, 177, 178, 184
   speeches, 49-50, 168, 177-178
Claydon, Wing Commander J C, 160, 165
Cleary, Flight Lieutenant M C, 160
Cohen, Flight Lieutenant, 76
Cologne, *see* Bombing Operations
Constable, Sergeant, 111
Cooney, Pilot Officer, 76
Cowie, Sergeant, 69, 71, 73
Crabb, Sergeant R F, 160

Cumber, Flying Officer W W, 160

Davis, Air Vice-Marshal E D, 169
Davis, Sergeant, 121
Dawson, Sergeant Monty E H, 106, 110, 113, 120
Dickinson, Pilot Officer, 76
Donnelly, Larry (Air Gunner, author), 26, 36, 41
Drummond, Sergeant 'Harry' H, 107, 109, 110, 112-114, 120
Dupe, Sergeant, 21
Duston, *see* Northampton
Dwyer, Group Captain M H, 170-173, 176, 177, 179

Eccles, J R (headmaster), 4
Edwards, Jimmy (entertainer, pilot), 135
Eglin Field, Florida, *see* USA
Ehrang, *see* Bombing Operations
Elcoate, Sergeant, 54
Eperon, Pilot Officer, 121
Esnouf, Sergeant, 121
Essen, *see* Bombing Operations

Fear, Group Captain A H, 162
Ferguson, Squadron Leader, 76
Fields, Pilot Officer, 33, 46
Finlayson, Sergeant, 120, 121
Flares, target identification, 72-73
Fletcher, Wing Commander A S, 130-133
Flewelling, Pilot Officer, 84
Flights:
   1481 Target Towing & Gunnery Flight, 134-147
   1502 Beam Approach Training Flight, 141
Ford-Hutchinson, Sergeant, 121
Formation flying, practice, 101, 102
Fraser, Sergeant G A, 110, 119

Gallaher Limited (post-war employer), 186, 187
Gamble, Mr (teacher), 4
Garraway, Group Captain, 94
Gayhurst, preparatory school, 3
Gee, radio navigation system, 138-140, 146
Gerrards Cross, 3, 8
Gibson, Squadron Leader Guy, 128, 162
Gillbanks, Sergeant A, 111, 120, 121
Givet, *see* Bombing Operations
Gneisenau, German battleship, 65, 89, 98, 99, 116, 122, 137
Godwin, Flight Sergeant, 111, 114, 121
Goodwin, Air Commodore E S, 150
Gough, Pilot Officer, 84
Gouraud, Alphonse (French rescuer), 120-122
Gouraud, Michel (French rescuer's son), 121
Gourley, Sergeant, 120
Greaves, Flight Sergeant S D, 111, 114, 120, 121, 185-186
Gresham's School, 4-7, 34
   Officers Training Corps, 6, 15
Griffiths, Flight Lieutenant H S, 160
Guinn, Sergeant, 141, 146
Gunnery Leader:

as fighting controller, 102, 155, 172, 174
courses, *see* Central Gunnery School
need for, 14, 17
role in squadron, 153
Gurmin, Sergeant 'Taff', 105, 107, 109, 111, 113, 123
Gyro gunsight, *see* Turrets

Haig, Molly (sister's friend), 19, 20
Hal, *see* Bombing Operations
Hamburg, *see* Bombing Operations
Hanafin, Squadron Leader Pat, 35, 45, 76
Harcourt-Powell, Pilot Officer, 49
Harris, Air Marshal Arthur, 133, 137-140, 144, 162, 184
Harrison, Sergeant, 140-143 , 145
Hathaway, Flight Lieutenant, 176
Higgins, Sergeant H R, 119
Hill, Flight Sergeant, 121
Hill, Professor 'Gunner', 150, 172
Hillary, Flight Lieutenant W S, 96, 107, 112, 114
Hillebrandt, Warrant Officer R C, 160
Hitler, 34, 50, 51, 75, 97, 122
Hoare, Sergeant, 88
Hoffmann, Captain, Scharnhorst, 115
Holden, Warrant Officer G W, 119, 121
Horner, Flight Sergeant, 120
Howard-Strapp, Leonore, *see* Teddie (wife)
Humby, Pilot Officer, 76
Hutchin, Pilot Officer, 123

Inspector General reports, *see* Ludlow-Hewitt
Ismay, Sergeant, 75

James, Flying Officer P S, 119
Jarman, Wing Commander G T, 94-96, 102-105, 107-114, 117, 119, 185
Johnston, Pilot Officer, 114
Jones, Flight Sergeant, 143
Jones, Flight Sergeant V I, 160
Jones, Pilot Officer, 76

Keast, Sergeant, 47
Keith, Group Captain C H, 149-152, 154, 172
Kenworthy, Sergeant, 97
Kerr, Wing Commander, 179
Killick, Pilot Officer, 136, 143
King George VI, 98, 128, 129, 180

Lacy, Flying Officer Alan, 171, 173-175
Landale, Flying Officer, 76
La Pallice, *see* Bombing Operations
Law, Pilot Officer E J, 160
Lewin, Flight Lieutenant, 107,109, 120
Linnell, Air Marshal, 130
Linton, Sergeant, 125
Lorient, *see* Bombing Operations
Lowe, Wing Commander A E, 169, 172, 173
Ludlow-Hewitt, Sir Edgar, 18, 156-159, 167, 169
  Inspector General reports, 156-159, 168
Lumb, Pilot Officer Ray, 14-16, 18, 24, 51, 183

Maastricht, 67, 70
MacDonald, Group Captain G P, 162, 169
Machine Guns:
  American .5, 129, 159
  Browning, 11, 15, 27, 30, 36, 92, 93
  development for use in aircraft, 10-11
  Lewis, 10
  Vickers, 15, 93
  see also Turrets
Maclean, Donald (Cold War spy), 5, 6
Malan, Wing Commander 'Sailor' A G, 149, 150, 154, 155
Mannheim, *see* Bombing Operations
Marshall, Sergeant, 56
Matthews, Flight Sergeant H A, 160
McEachran, Mr (teacher), 4
McIntosh, Sergeant Angus, 62
McKenna, Pilot Officer, 107, 112, 120, 121
McLeod, Flying Officer, 120, 121
McNair, Squadron Leader, 59
Mead, Sergeant, 140-143, 145
Merseburg, *see* Bombing Operations
Millar, Pilot Officer, 121
Ministry of Aircraft Production, 130

Neau, Fernand (French rescuer), 120-122
Neau, Fernand (French rescuer's, son), 120, 121
Neau, Rose (French rescuer's, daughter), 120, 121
Nelson, Flying Officer William H, 35-37, 41-43, 45-47, 183
Newstead, Sergeant, 121
Nicholas, Flight Lieutenant W E, 160
No.1 Air Armament School, 14-17
No.1 Air Gunners' School, 161-169
No.100 Personnel Dispersal Centre, 181
Northampton, 7, 42, 46, 56, 77, 85, 123, 124, 186
  Duston, 56
Nuremberg, *see* Bombing Operations

Officers Advanced Training School, 167
Ogden, Sergeant, 111
Oise, River, bridges, *see* Bombing Operations
Oldridge, Aircraftsman Stan R, 45
Operation, code names:
  Abigail Rachel, 78
  Overlord, 162
  Sealion, 75
  Sunrise, 100, 101

Pathfinder Force, 73, 184
Patterson, Sergeant, 105, 113
Pearce, Sergeant, 125
Peers, Pilot Officer, 76, 78
Peirse, Air Marshal Sir Richard, 116, 117
Perriment, Sergeant, 121
Phillips, Flight Lieutenant, 46, 76
Phillips, Sergeant, 120
Pilbeam, Sergeant, 121
Pinkham, Flight Lieutenant R M, 147
Pointe de L'Aiguillon, France, 120

Portal, Air Chief Marshal Sir Charles, 117
Powers, Sergeant Ron, 163, 164, 167
Prince, Miss Peggy (rescuer), 56
Prinz Eugen, German heavy cruiser, 64, 65, 99, 122, 137
Prior, Flying Officer, 38, 76

RAF Stations:
  Abingdon, 18-24, 46, 104
  Angle, 161, 166
  Ansty, 37, 38
  Bassingbourn, 45
  Binbrook, 134-147
  Bircham Newton, 44, 45, 142
  Blyton, 147
  Bodney, 74, 75
  Carew Cheriton, 166
  Catfoss, 158, 169-181
  Cranwell, 167, 168
  Dale, 166
  Dishforth, 25-52, 87
  Docking, 125, 126
  Driffield, 33, 37, 51, 90, 141, 179
  Fairwood Common, 161
  Gatwick, 53
  Hemswell, 136
  Honington, 47
  Hospital, Torquay, 19-21
  Hutton Cranswick, 176
  Jurby, Isle of Man, 21, 23
  Lakenheath, 166
  Leeming, 52-90, 136
  Linton-on-Ouse, 24-25, 89-94, 185
  Manby, 14-17, 162, 176
  Manorbier, 166
  Marham, 74, 75
  Middleton St George, 92, 94-129
  Pembrey, 161-169, 176
  Pembroke Dock, 166
  South Cerney, 126
  St Eval, 17, 114
  Stannington, 165
  Stanton Harcourt, 104, 113, 114, 117
  Sutton Bridge, 147-161, 165, 170, 172
  Tangmere, 41
  Uxbridge, 181
  Valley, 167
  Warmwell, 17-18, 149
  Weston Zoyland, 114
Raphael, Flight Lieutenant, 76
Razzle, incendiary device, 65-67, 69
Reflector gunsight, *see* Turrets
Rheinfelden, *see* Bombing Operations
Rheydt, *see* Bombing Operations
Rice, Sergeant, 121
Rivaz, Flying Officer R C, 119
Robinson, Pilot Officer C N, 14-16, 18, 21, 24
Roosevelt, President, 7, 51, 88, 117
  call for bombing restraint, 26
Rowley-Blake, Sergeant, 121
Rudlin, Sergeant, 121

Ruhr marshalling yards, *see* Bombing Operations
Russell, Pilot Officer John A S, 60, 69, 71, 73, 76, 79, 82, 141, 143, 184-185

Sachs, Sergeant M A, 119
Sankey, Sergeant T N, 120
Saunders, Flight Sergeant E, 160
Saunders, Warrant Officer E J, 160
Savage, Flight Lieutenant A J, 160
Sawyer, Squadron Leader, 76
Scharnhorst, German battleship, 65, 89, 98-101, 104, 108, 109, 111, 112, 114-116, 119, 122, 133, 137
School of Administration, 165
Scott, Squadron Leader, 176
Shirley, Flight Sergeant, 121
Smith, Flying Officer, 47
Smith, Sergeant, 121
Snell, Sergeant, 75
Spreckley, Wing Commander, 129
Sprigge, Sergeant, 105, 125
Squadrons:
  10 Squadron, 25-89, 123, 136, 139, 141, 148, 183, 184
  12 Squadron, 134, 135, 141, 146
  27 Squadron, 162
  35 Squadron, 89, 91, 92, 96, 101-123, 130, 136
  51 Squadron, 29, 87
  74 Squadron, 47
  76 Squadron, 89-130, 184
  77 Squadron, 37, 51, 94
  78 Squadron, 24, 87, 95
  83 Squadron, 39
  97 Squadron, 18
  102 Squadron, 37
  103 Squadron, 146
  124 Squadron, 176
  142 Squadron, 146
  166 Squadron, 18, 21, 22
  217 Squadron, 17
  219 Squadron, 52
  466 Squadron, 176
  550 Squadron, 175
  617 Squadron, 33
  See also Flights
Staton, Wing Commander W E, 26, 30, 31, 33-36, 47, 48, 53, 183-184
Stavanger, *see* Bombing Operations
Steel, Warrant Officer, 76
Stobbs, Pilot Officer, 95
Stone, Pilot Officer, 121
Summers, Sergeant, 121
Sutton, Wing Commander J J, 149-152

Taylor, Flight Lieutenant V W C, 160
Teddie (wife), 22-24, 49, 77, 87, 91, 123, 127-129, 178, 182, 186, 187
Thomas, Sergeant, 141
Thompson, Sergeant, 125
Thousand Plan, 138-141, 143-144
Tomlinson, Flight Lieutenant, 62, 76

Tony (properly Lionel), brother-in-law, 60, 87, 123
Trier aerodrome, 66-69
Tulse Hill Hockey Club, 7, 34
Turnbull, Sergeant, 125
Turrets, 29, 30
  Bendix lower turret, 129, 131, 132
  Boulton Paul, 93, 132
  Consolidated tail turret, 129, 131, 132
  development, 11-12
  gyro gunsight, 158, 159, 172
  Martin upper turret, 129, 131, 132
  operating, 27-28, 93-94
  reflector gunsight, 12-13, 93, 159
  see also Machine Guns

USA:
  Army, 112th Regiment, 166
  Eglin Field, Florida, 130
  enters the war, 130
  Lend Lease Bill, 88, 129
  Neutrality Act, 51

Vickery, Sergeant, 120

Wakefield, Flying Officer, 76
Walker, Sergeant, 121
Walters, Sergeant W C, 111, 120
Warfield, Wing Commander J M, 149
Warren, Flying Officer, 76
Watson, Sergeant, 88
Welte, Pilot Officer H F, 14-16, 18
White, Squadron Leader P B, 171
Williams, Pilot Officer G S, 83
Williams, Squadron Leader, 107, 108, 112, 120
Wood, Flying Officer, 75, 76
Woods, Flight Sergeant 'Timber', 105, 114, 123
Woolgar, Pilot Officer R L A, 160